“营”在自贸港 “画”说新海南

Winning in the FTP: Stories of Hainan's Business Environment Construction

海南日报报业集团　海南省营商环境建设厅　主编

Co-edited by Hainan Daily Press Group and Hainan Provincial Department of Business Environment Development

海南出版社

·海口·

图书在版编目（CIP）数据

“营”在自贸港 “画”说新海南 ：汉文、英文 / 海南日报报业集团，海南省营商环境建设厅主编. 海口 ：海南出版社，2025. 3. — ISBN 978-7-5730-2392-6

Ⅰ. F752.866

中国国家版本馆CIP数据核字第20252QH135号

“营”在自贸港 “画”说新海南

“YING” ZAI ZIMAOGANG “HUA” SHUO XIN HAINAN

主　　编：海南日报报业集团　海南省营商环境建设厅
技术支持：混知团队
翻　　译：David A. Janke（杨龙贤，英国）
责任编辑：朱　奕　李佳妮　张清梅
封面设计：张少华
出版发行：海南出版社
地　　址：海口市金盘开发区建设三横路2号
邮　　编：570216
电　　话：（0898）66819831
印刷装订：海南金永利彩色印刷有限公司
版　　次：2025年3月第1版
印　　次：2025年3月第1次印刷
开　　本：787 mm × 1 092 mm　1/16
印　　张：16.5
字　　数：256千字
书　　号：ISBN 978-7-5730-2392-6
定　　价：68.00元

编委会

Editorial Board

编辑出版小组

Editing and Publishing Team

主　编： 牛晓民

Editor-in-Chief

副主编： 周　元

Deputy Editor-in-Chief

编　辑： 李梦瑶　罗清锐　陈奕霖　张成林　孙发强

Associate Editors

营商“故事汇” “画”出新未来

Illustrating the Stories of the Hainan FTP's Business Environment

一个好的故事，胜过一打道理。

A good story is worth a dozen lessons.

人们爱听故事，而一个好的故事，有张力，有吸引力，有凝聚力，充满感情和力量。在海南自由贸易港建设中，各行各业、上上下下，人们用汗水和智慧，书写了一个个精彩的故事，感人、动人、鼓舞人。尤其在营商环境方面，步步为“营”创一流的不懈努力，演绎出了许多颇具独创性、引领性的传奇故事。

People love a good story, one that is gripping, alluring, cohesive, and powerful. The construction of the Hainan Free Trade Port (FTP) has produced a wealth of moving and inspiring stories, crafted by people from all walks of life with their sweat and wisdom. This is especially true with regard to the unremitting efforts by the Hainan FTP to create a first-class business environment.

好故事源于火热实践。

A good story comes from passionate practice.

2024年12月17日，习近平总书记在听取海南省委和省政府工作汇报时的重要讲话强调：“营造市场化、法治化、国际化一流营商环境。”海南牢记嘱托，将“打造一流营商环境”放在事关自贸港建设成败的高度来谋划、推进；在“一本三基四梁八柱”战略框架中，将营商环境视为“八柱”中的重要一柱。

In his important speech on December 17, 2024, at a meeting to hear the work reports of the CPC Hainan Provincial Committee and Hainan Provincial Government, Chinese President Xi Jinping stressed the "creation of a first-class business environment that is market-oriented, law-based, and international." Keeping his instructions in mind, Hainan has planned and promoted "building a first-class business environment" at a high level as a cornerstone of the Hainan FTP's success. In the strategic framework of "one guideline, three foundations, fourfold positioning and eight pillars", the business environment is regarded as one of the most important "pillars".

成立全国首个省级营商环境建设厅、落地全国最短外商投资负面清单、把土地摆进超市橱窗、擦亮"海南自贸港请您来投诉"品牌、开展"政企面对面、服务心贴心"早餐会、丰富"信用+"应用场景……海南举全省之力开展了一系列开创性、示范性工作，推动营商环境向着一流不断迈进。

Hainan has established China's first provincial-level department dedicated to business environment development and introduced the country's shortest negative list for foreign investment. It has established a "land supermarket", refined its "Hainan FTP, Feel Free to Complain" brand, held "government-enterprise face-to-face" breakfast meetings, and expanded the application scenarios of credit scores and ratings, and streamlined business operations. By mustering the strength of the entire province, Hainan has carried out a range of pioneering and exemplary work to raise the standards of its business environment.

好故事需要生动表达。

A good story needs vivid expression.

这一个个案例，一次次创新，正是一个个动人的故事。故事里，有难解的矛盾，有你来我往的互动，有众人拾柴的合力，有攻克难题、梦想成真的喜悦。这些政策落地、创新突破背后的精彩故事，有血有肉、可感可触，成为创一流营商环境的见证，成为中国式现代化海南实践的生动注脚。

The innovation cases in this comic collection are vivid stories. Like any good story, they contain difficult-to-resolve conflicts, interactions between characters, and collective efforts to overcome difficulties and make dreams come true. Unlike fairytales, however, these incredible stories of policy implementation and innovative breakthroughs are true and tangible. They are testimony to the creation of a first-class business environment and a vivid footnote to Hainan's practice of Chinese modernization.

把故事讲好，让有意义的事情更有意思。这带来的就是凝聚力，就是生产力。

A well-told story with real meaning brings about cohesion and productivity.

基于这样的认识，《海南日报》创新表达方式，于2022年5月13日，联合海南省优化营商环境工作专班（即海南省营商环境建设厅前身），推出《“营”在自贸港 “画”说新海南——优化营商环境专刊》，首创条漫专栏，以实际案例为素材，通过漫画形式，展现各地各部门服务企业，当好“店小二”“服务员”的鲜活形象。至今，该专刊已经连续推出100余期。翻开该专刊，幽默、“接地气”的人物形象、对白设计，让营商环境“硬新闻”变得更加有趣、可感。

In line with this understanding, *Hainan Daily* has adopted a fresh, engaging approach. On May 13, 2022, in collaboration with the Hainan Provincial Business Environment Optimization Working Group (the predecessor of the Hainan Provincial Department of Business Environment Development), the paper launched its first comic column, "Winning in the FTP: Stories of Hainan's Business Environment Construction", using actual cases as material to showcase the work of various regions and departments in serving enterprises as "service specialists". To date, over 100 columns have been published. The comic takes "hard news" and transforms it into easy-to-digest, engaging content through humorous and down-to-earth characters and dialogue.

"破圈"的思维带来了"破圈"的产品。该专刊已经成为展现海南营商环境建设成效的特色品牌。直观、生动、形象的故事讲述，提升了营商环境工作的能见度，也增强了人们创一流营商环境的信心，提升了各界对海南自贸港建设的预期。

Breaking the mold in both thinking and presentation, the column has become a distinctive brand that showcases the effectiveness of Hainan's business environment construction efforts. Intuitive, vivid, and figurative storytelling has enhanced the visibility of these efforts, strengthened people's confidence in creating a first-class business environment, and increased the expectations of all sectors for the construction of the Hainan FTP.

营商环境建设，永远在路上。

Business environment construction is a never-ending journey.

我们精选2022年5月至2025年1月刊登于《海南日报》的该专刊的内容汇编成书，以期让海南的营商环境故事更加饱满、立体，让营商环境利好惠及更多经营主体，并以此作为前一阶段工作的总结以及做好下一步工作的激励，带动全省上下以更加饱满的劲头、更加务实的作风，去铺展去创作海南一流营商环境新的亮丽画卷。

We have carefully selected various comic strips published in *Hainan Daily* between May 2022 and January 2025 and compiled them into this book to offer a more complete, three-dimensional picture of Hainan's favorable business environment and enable it to benefit more business entities. The book aims to serve as a summary of work already undertaken, an incentive for future work, and a reminder for the whole province to work with greater enthusiasm and pragmatism to create a new and beautiful vision of Hainan's first-class business environment.

精彩故事仍在继续，我们期待与您共同演绎！

If work be the food of progress, march on. We look forward to your participation!

目录
Contents

第一章　简化流程，可办变好办
Section 1　Simplifying Procedures

第二章 优化服务，办事不求人
Section 2 Improving Services

第三章 破解难题，落实见真招
Section 3 Solving Problems

第四章 改革创新，擦亮"金饭碗"
Section 4 Reforming and Innovating

第五章　因地制宜，市县出实招
Section 5　Local Solutions

第一章
Section 1

简化流程，可办变好办
Simplifying Procedures

“极简”，海南是认真的！

Simplified Procedures, Hainan's Got You Covered

画外音：对企业来说，时间就是金钱，企业最怕的就是手续烦琐、材料复杂。删繁就简，牵涉的部门、环节多，本就不易，而“简”上求“简”，无疑难上加难。可海南不止步于现有的审批简化，而是力求再简化、再优化。这传递出一种态度，即尽力以最优服务促企业发展；展现出一种决心，即审批改进、环境优化永无止境。

Introduction: For enterprises, time is money. As a result, the things enterprises fear most are clunky bureaucracy and complicated paperwork. However, simplifying things is not just a matter of waving a magic wand; there are many departments and links involved. Yet, Hainan has managed not only to streamline approval processes as they currently stand but also to simplify and optimize them further. In doing so, Hainan shows both that it is committed to promoting the development of enterprises and its determination that the business environment can always be improved just a little bit more.

A05
“营”在自贸港 “画”说新海南
——优化营商环境专刊
海南日报

“极简”，海南是认真的！

海南又又又“上新”啦！7月1日起，海南将正式施行《关于深化工程建设项目领域“极简审批”制度改革优化营商环境若干措施》。这一名字超长的惠企新政策里，到底藏着哪些“干货”？

工程建设项目审批制度改革是推进政府职能转变和优化营商环境的重要内容。近年来，我省持续推进工程建设项目审批改革，取得了一定成效，但经营主体仍期待在工程建设项目审批前的材料准备、政府审批环节、系统上的审批节点、“体外循环”等方面能进一步改善提升。

企“话”自贸港

海南省安徽商会会长、华闻传媒投资集团股份有限公司董事长汪方怀：

营商环境是促进企业发展的关键

刘董，我打算在这里建一个孔明灯工厂。有了这个产业，咱们蜀汉集团定能再创辉煌！
Mr. Liu, I intend to build a Kongming lantern factory here. This industry is sure to bring prosperity to our Shuhan Group.
不错，老诸葛办事我放心！
Great idea. I'm in good hands with you, Zhuge.
①
呜呜……项目还在走审批……
Yikes...The project still hasn't been approved...
厂呢？厂呢？我连个“鬼影”都没见到！
What about the factory? What about the factory? All I see is an empty plot of land!
②
审批太慢，影响我下班耍帅！
This approval is taking forever! I've got other stuff to be getting on with.
能不能快点儿？别逼我求你！
Can't you hurry it along? Don't make me beg!
如果我有错，请让法律来惩罚我，而不是让我整天跑审批……
If I am wrong, let the law judge me. I can't spend all day working on this one thing.
③

老总们，咱来送温暖啦！
Friends! Never fear! I'm here!
店小二
好棒！
Yay!
就知道小二心里有我们！
I knew you would pull through for us!
④
这块地该做的评估评价事项，我们都给提前做完了！
Here! We've already completed the land assessment for you.
用地清单
拿地即开工！你们也太贴心了吧！
You're too kind. Now, we can get to work!
⑤
少忽悠我！哪有10个？不想娶就直说！
Stop lying! What 10 things? If you don't want to marry me, just say it!
亲爱的，等我忙完这10个审批事项就娶你。
Dear, I meant I need to get these 10 approval items out of the way, and then I'll marry you.
⑥

小赵，你去下这几个部门办下竣工备案手续。
Mr. Zhao, you go to these departments and handle the work completion registration.
小魏，去开通一下水、电、气和网络。不动产登记，你也得抓紧准备一下。
Mr. Wei, you go sort out the water, electricity, gas, and internet. You also need to get a move on with real estate registration.
⑦

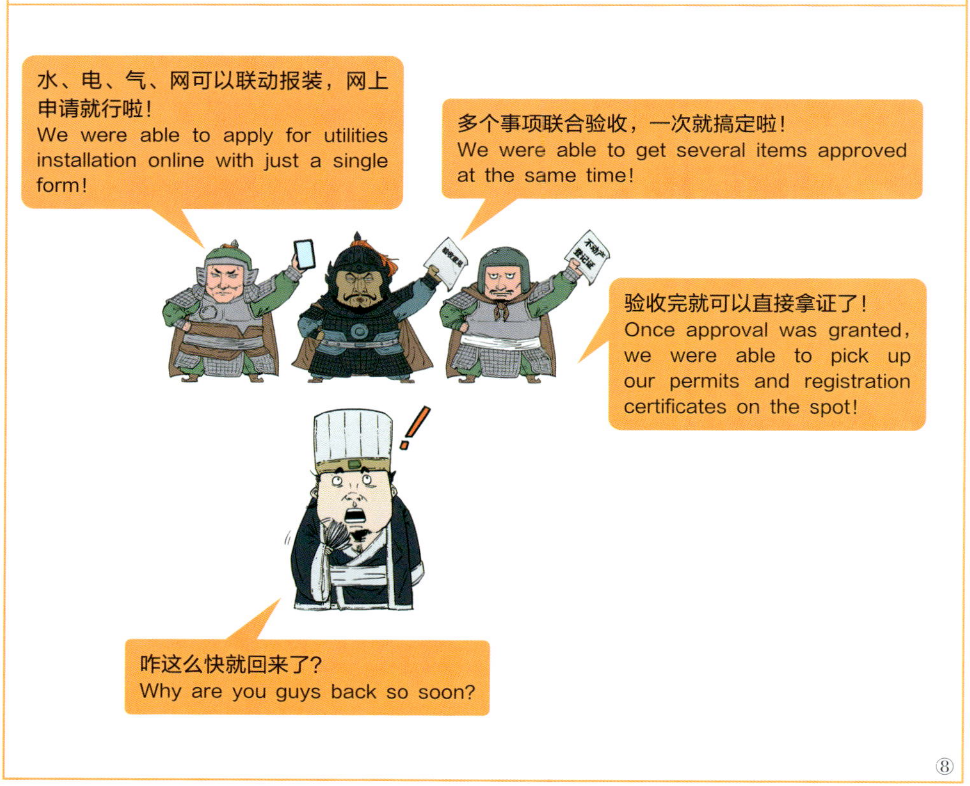
水、电、气、网可以联动报装，网上申请就行啦！
We were able to apply for utilities installation online with just a single form!
多个事项联合验收，一次就搞定啦！
We were able to get several items approved at the same time!
验收完就可以直接拿证了！
Once approval was granted, we were able to pick up our permits and registration certificates on the spot!
咋这么快就回来了？
Why are you guys back so soon?
⑧

蜀汉集团孔明灯工厂
简直不要太“丝滑”!
Things couldn't have gone more smoothly!
不愧是我三顾茅庐请来的职业经理人。
It was really worth the effort to bring this manager on board!
⑨
什么是快乐星球?
What is the meaning of happiness?
若干措施
若干措施
现在就带你研究!
Let's go and find out together!
⑩

案例注解 CASE NOTES

工程建设项目审批制度改革是推进政府职能转变和优化营商环境的重要内容。近年来，海南省持续推进工程建设项目审批改革，取得了一定成效，但经营主体仍期待在工程建设项目审批前的材料准备、政府审批环节、系统上的审批节点、"体外循环"等方面能进一步改善提升。

Reform of the approvals process for construction and engineering projects is an important part of promoting the transformation of government functions and optimizing the business environment. In recent years, a certain degree of success has been achieved in Hainan's continuous promotion of the reform of how construction and engineering projects are approved. However, business entities still expect to complete all material preparation, government approval processes, and system approvals prior to the construction project being greenlit, and aspects (such as "off-system circulation") can be further improved upon.

案例进展 CURRENT STATUS

聚焦经营主体反映和关切的堵点、痛点问题，海南省在开展企业、政府部门座谈调研的基础上，形成《关于深化工程建设项目领域"极简审批"制度改革优化营商环境若干措施》（以下简称《若干措施》），从工程建设项目的全生命周期流程出发，聚焦重点环节和关键节点改革，提出了15条改革措施，将进一步加快工程项目落地。《若干措施》于2023年7月1日起施行。

Hainan Province has conducted interviews and surveys with enterprises and government departments and—focusing on the bottlenecks and pain points reported by business entities—the *Several Measures on Deepening the Reform of a "Simplified Approval" System in Construction and Engineering Projects and Optimizing the Business Environment* was formulated. Taking a holistic approach to the life cycle process of construction and engineering projects and focusing reforms on key links and nodes, a total of 15 reform measures, which came into effect on July 1, 2023, were proposed to accelerate the approval of new construction and engineering projects.

一纸承诺　一步入市

Commit for Easy Market Access

画外音： 承诺即入，用意在“最”字，关键在“诺”字。取消许可、审批，这一突破性、标志性的举措，蕴含着海南对营商环境“四最”的目标追求；改变以往审批在前、监管前置的做法，实行承诺准入、过程监管，这一突破性改革创新，进一步理顺了政府与市场及企业的关系，不仅突出了有效市场的作用，也是对经营主体的信任、对企业自主权的尊重，背后体现出开放、包容、高效的服务理念。

Introduction: "Commitment-based access" applies to most industries and enterprises in Hainan, with "commitment" being a crucial aspect. Hainan's groundbreaking, milestone move to eliminate certain permits and approval processes embodies the province's goal of boasting the best policies, lowest costs, best service, and fastest approval times, as well as a key aspect of business environment reform: transitioning from the previous practice of upfront approval and supervision to commitment-based access and process supervision. This breakthrough reform has further clarified the relationship between the government, the market, and enterprises and not only highlights the role of an effective market but also shows trust in business entities and respect for corporate autonomy while reflecting an open, inclusive, and efficient service concept.

A10　“营”在自贸港　“画”说新海南

——优化营商环境专刊

海南日报

一纸承诺　一步入市

市场主体从事生产经营活动，往往需要各种审批手续，过多的审批就像一双双“有形之手”，束缚住企业手脚，使其失去活力。对此，做了多年生意的老王深有体会。

国家推行“先照后证”改革后，市场主体获得营业执照即可开展一般性经营活动，但对从事需要许可的生产经营活动，仍需办理许可证。海南率先探索市场准入承诺即入制改革，从减许可入手，通过地方立法的方式，在具有强制性标准的领域，取消了六项涉企经营许可事项，大幅降低市场准入门槛。

企“话”自贸港

澳大利亚资本投资有限公司董事总经理兼大中华区首席执行官何逸舟：

营商环境将成为海南自贸港突出优势

要先办好证照才给进哟，王总。
Sorry, Mr. Wang, but you need to show me your license and permits before I can let you in.
市场入口
这“章程”也是很复杂！
Now that's a lot of approvals!
不要跑来跑去啦！签个承诺书，我们就可以先给你发证。
Hold your horses! Just sign this letter of commitment and we can issue you your license and permits.
优化审批，少点“章程”。
Let's optimize and trim away the excess.
告知承诺制
啊！坏事，材料没带全！
Oh! Well, sadly, I didn't bring all the required documents.
咦？居然不设关卡了！
Eh? It's really that easy.
直通
市场入口
海南的必修课！
A must-learn skill in Hainan.
下次就去爬五指山！
Next time, I'll climb Wuzhi Mountain.
游泳
攀岩
许可证

是你对我的信任，让我的承诺可以飞越千万“章”。
Your trust keeps lifting me higher, higher than a mountain of approval stamps.
承诺书
⑤
政策创新，
Policy innovation...
特别用心！
...and a whole lot of love!
⑥
我错了……
Sorry...
黑名单
⑦
绝不食言！
I'll keep my word!
我看着你的哟！
We'll hold you to it!
⑧
符合这些条件才适用。
You have to meet these conditions to apply.
在具有强制性的领域，市场机构能够有效调节，企业能够自主管理，事中事后能够有效监管的事项。
⑨
要等审批通过才能进。
You had to wait for approval before you could enter the market.
审批单
事前
先进门，后面我监管！
Now, you can come straight in...but we'll be keeping an eye on you.
现在:
监管
事中，事后
⑩
降低门槛，
We've lowered the threshold...
提高服务！
... and improved our services!
准入门槛
⑪
监管加服务，是我的脚步，奔跑在市场经济上的路……
Supervision and services are how I help keep the market economy on the right track.
简政放权
加强监管
⑫

案例注解 CASE NOTES

国家推行"先照后证"改革后，经营主体获得营业执照即可开展一般性经营活动，但对从事需要许可的生产经营活动，仍需办理许可证。海南率先探索市场准入承诺即入制改革，从"减许可"入手，通过地方立法的方式，在具有强制性标准的领域，取消了一批涉企经营许可事项，大幅降低市场准入门槛。

After China implemented the "license before permit" reform, it became possible for business entities to immediately start carrying out general business activities once they received a business license. However, for those engaging in specific production and business activities that require additional licensure, the relevant permits were still required. Hainan has taken the lead in exploring the reform of the market access commitment-based entry system. Starting with using local legislation to reduce the number of necessary permits in areas with mandatory standards, a number of different kinds of special permits for enterprises have been canceled and the barriers to market access significantly lowered.

案例进展 CURRENT STATUS

下一步，海南将通过建立健全"审管法信"一体联动监管机制和平台，积极探索嵌入式监管、无感监管、智慧监管等多种方式，确保改革稳妥有序推进，并在总结经验的基础上逐步拓展到更多领域。

For the next step, Hainan will—via the establishment of a sound integrated supervision mechanism and platform for "examination, supervision, law, and information"—actively explore various methods (such as embedded supervision, non-intrusive supervision, and smart supervision) to ensure that the reform is carried out in a steady and orderly fashion, and gradually expanded to more areas on the basis of this experience.

打好提前量 通关快顺省

Clear Customs Faster with Advance Declaration

画外音： 以往通关有点慢，物流有点“堵”，表面看是因为程序多、手续繁，实则因为监管理念较落后、服务手段跟不上，常常让企业围着监管转，而不是监管围着企业转。海南口岸通关效率之所以得到了快速提升，是因为找准了问题的根，开出了对症的方：一方面，敢于进行制度创新，耦合各项改革；另一方面，运用科技赋能智慧监管。值得期待的是，随着创新力度加大、科技应用场景拓展，海南口岸通关速度会快上加快，而企业也能感受到更多便利。

Introduction: Previously, customs clearance took a very long time and delayed the delivery of goods. On the surface, it seemed to be down to the many procedures and complicated formalities. In fact, it was because customs supervision approaches were out-of-date. Hence, Customs could not keep up. Enterprises were typically at the mercy of customs supervision, rather than supervision working for enterprises. In Hainan, customs clearance efficiency has seen rapid improvement because the root cause has been identified, and measures have been taken to correct it. Haikou Customs has taken the initiative to carry out institutional innovation, integrated various reforms, and adopted technologies to enable smart supervision. As innovation efforts and technology application scenarios expand, we can look forward to customs clearance in Hainan becoming even more rapid and convenient.

A05 “营”在自贸港“画”说新海南
——优化营商环境专刊

打好提前量 通关快顺省

海口智慧绿洲技术有限公司总经理李晟：
营商环境持续优化让企业获得感倍增

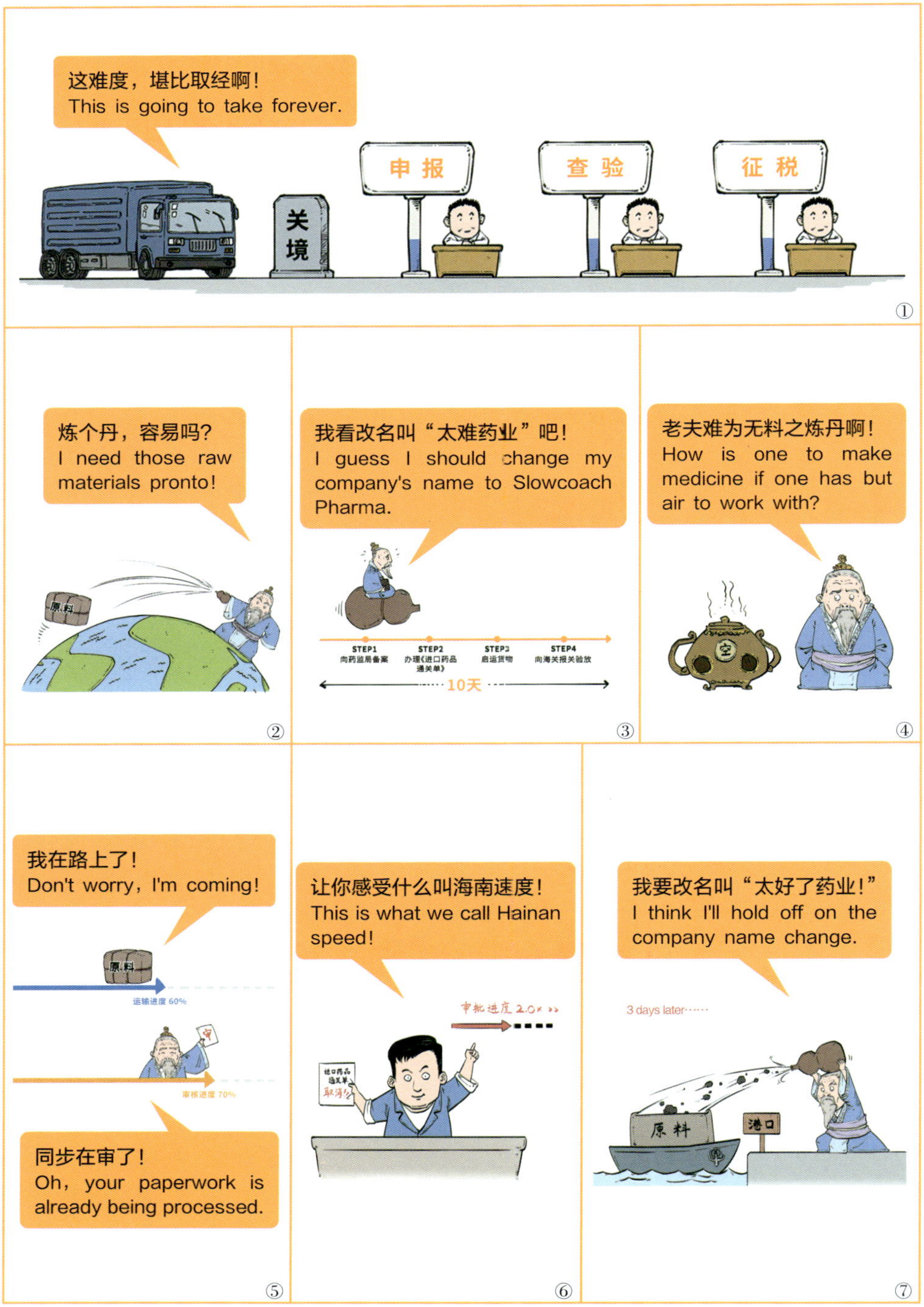
这难度，堪比取经啊！
This is going to take forever.
申 报
查 验
征 税
关境
①
炼个丹，容易吗？
I need those raw materials pronto!
原料
②
我看改名叫“太难药业”吧！
I guess I should change my company's name to Slowcoach Pharma.
STEP1 向药监局备案
STEP2 办理《进口药品通关单》
STEP3 启运货物
STEP4 向海关报关验放
10天
③
老夫难为无料之炼丹啊！
How is one to make medicine if one has but air to work with?
空
④
我在路上了！
Don't worry, I'm coming!
原料
运输进度 60%
审
审核进度 70%
同步在审了！
Oh, your paperwork is already being processed.
⑤
让你感受什么叫海南速度！
This is what we call Hainan speed!
审批进度 2.0×
进口药品通关单
取消
⑥
我要改名叫“太好了药业！”
I think I'll hold off on the company name change.
3 days later……
原料
港口
⑦

手机就能申报！
I can also submit an advance declaration on my phone.
提前申报
沙总
⑧
来晚了也不怕！
Delayed? No worries.
23:00
随到 随查 随放
港口
⑨
大师兄再也不用担心我来不及！
With this new system in place, I never need to worry about delays again.
网上办理
沙总
⑩
直接起飞！
We have liftoff!
⑪
我直接提货了啊！
Off the boat and straight onto the truck.
⑫
视频连线真方便！
I can see what's happening in real time.
海关查验
⑬
一个字，就是快！
That was fast!
绿色通道
⑭
快速通关！
Enjoy rapid customs clearance...
走你！
...pick up and take off.
⑮

案例注解 CASE NOTES

要素的自由流动，是高水平自由贸易港的基本特征。近年来，海口海关等部门不断强化政策供给，巩固压缩进出口货物整体通关时间，持续提升跨境贸易便利化水平。

The free movement of factors is one of the basic characteristics of a high-level free trade port. In recent years, Haikou Customs and other departments have continued to strengthen policy support, further reduced shorten the total customs clearance time for imported and exported goods, and improved the level of cross-border trade facilitation.

案例进展 CURRENT STATUS

2024年，海口海关研究出台并逐项落实进一步优化口岸营商环境促进跨境贸易便利化25条、支持海南省外贸高质量发展21条等系列措施，助推海南货物贸易进出口同比增长20%，增速居全国第4位。

In 2024, Haikou Customs boosted Hainan's import and export of goods by 20% year-on-year, ranking fourth in the country. This was achieved by researching, publishing, and implementing a number of new measures including 25 which further optimize the port business environment and promote cross-border trade facilitation, and 21 that support the high-quality development of Hainan's foreign trade.

买地交房　快速领证

Very Quick In-Deed

画外音：拿地、买房，企业和群众都想早点领到不动产权证。可以说，“交地即交证”“交房即交证”的推行，给投资者、购房人吃了一颗“定心丸”，是一项惠企心、暖民心的举措。这样的精简、高效，一方面源自流程再造，提前介入减短时间；另一方面，则体现在数据赋能，数据互通增加便利。为民服务，优无止境，持续推进办事流程再做“减法”、服务举措多做“加法”，定能使“零时差”成为更多事项的“标配”。

Introduction: When acquiring land or buying a house, both enterprises and the public want to pick up their deeds as soon as possible. The implementation of "issuance of deeds upon handover" for land and residential property gives investors and buyers peace of mind. Greatly increasing convenience, the streamlining of this process is a result of process reengineering, early intervention, and the empowerment and interoperability of data across different platforms. In serving the people, continuous improvements are being made by reducing paperwork and processes, enhancing services, and eliminating delays across a range of procedures for a seamless experience.

A04

“营”在自贸港“画”说新海南

——优化营商环境专刊

海南日报

买地交房 快速领证

企“话”自贸港

海南昊凡特医疗科技有限公司总经理王宇昊：

签约即拿地 拿地即开工

唐校长说得对！
How right you are, Principal Tang.
掐指一算，教育高地。
This would be the perfect place to establish a school!
①
朱老师你忙着，我去办个证。
You do that, and I'll go pick up the deeds.
俺开始施工了啊？
So, shall I get to work?
②
"猴"急啊……
Can't it be any faster?
项目拿地办证攻略
勘测定界
签订土地出让合同
(取得划拨决定书)
交齐土地出让金和相关税费
地籍调查
登记办证
秘籍就是，流程密集，时间着急！
A process longer than scripture that we need to complete faster than you can say "Journey to the West".
我人"沙"了。
Can't we axe some of this?
"戒"么办?
What can we do?
③
交地即交证
交房即交证
土地公，拿了地办个证这么难的吗?
Earth God, why is it so difficult to get the deeds?
我说老孙呐，你手里的攻略过时了，我们现在交地即交证！
Mr. Sun, you're following an outdated guide. You can now collect the deeds as soon as you take possession of the land.
④

项目拿地办证攻略
勘测定界
签订土地出让合同
(取得划拨决定书)
交齐土地出让金和相关税费
地籍调查
登记办证
勘测定界和地籍调查
土地供应
偷偷合并同类项，速度超出你想象！
We've sneakily combined two overlapping processes. It's much quicker than you could ever imagine!
⑤
这就完事儿了？
So, is that it?
不动产证
有人替你们想在前面，手续都提前办好啦！
They anticipated our needs and handled everything ahead of time.
⑥
这个楼盘好，离学校近，孙老师都不用翻筋斗，步行就能到教室。
This is a nice area close to the school. Monkey doesn't need to somersault over clouds to get to work anymore.
老师们别犹豫，交房即能拿证，嘎嘎快！
Teachers, why not buy a house nearby? You can collect the deeds as soon as you take possession of the property.
⑦
项目预售阶段
严格落实住房预售制度
确保项目已取得相关证件许可
优化合同网签备案
约定将“该房已取得不动产权证（分户证）”作为交房必备条件
对预售住宅实行预告登记
竣工验收阶段
前置测绘流程
将规划核实、土地核验、不动产测绘合并为一个验收事项
多部门联合验收
交房交证阶段
房地产开发企业在项目取得竣工验收备案手续后，即可以申请不动产首次登记手续
房地产开发企业在工程竣工验收备案后60个工作日内组织交房，交房前20个工作日完成首次登记和转移登记
⑧
数据跑，人不跑，一窗受理全办好。
We let the data do the running around, so you don't have to. Just drop by our window!
一窗受理、并行办理
不动产登记
税费征缴
房屋交易
不动产登记系统
税收征管系统
房屋交易信息管理系统
省一体化政务服务平台
⑨
曾经西天取经困难重重！
Unlike our journey to the West to retrieve Buddhist scripture...
不动产证
如今，海南办证速度嗖嗖！
...collecting our real estate deeds went without a hitch!
⑩

案例注解 CASE NOTES

2023年，海南省自然资源和规划厅、海南省住房和城乡建设厅等六部门联合下发《关于全面推进"交地即交证""交房即交证"的通知》（以下简称《通知》），全面推进"交地即交证""交房即交证"。

In 2023, six departments including the Department of Natural Resources and Planning and Department of Housing and Urban-Rural Development of Hainan Provincial jointly issued the *Notice on Comprehensively Promoting the "Issuance of Deeds at Handover of Land or Housing"* to encourage and promote the prompt and correct issuance of deeds once property ownership has been transferred.

案例进展 CURRENT STATUS

目前，海口、三亚、定安、临高等市县已有多个项目实现"交地即交证""交房即交证"。下一步，我省将加强工程建设项目审批综合服务窗口建设，深化不动产登记、税费征缴、房屋交易"一窗受理、并行办理"。对积极响应配合的开发企业进行公开表彰，鼓励企业"交地即交证""交房即交证"。

Currently, a number of cities and counties (including Haikou, Sanya, Ding'an, and Lin'gao) have already achieved "issuance of deeds upon handover" for many land and housing projects. For the next step, Hainan will strengthen the construction of a comprehensive service window for project approval, further the "one-window acceptance and parallel processing" of real estate sales, registration, and tax collection, publicly commend development companies that actively respond and cooperate, and encourage enterprises to implement "issuance of deeds upon handover" when housing or land sales are completed.

一件事一次办，服务更高效！

Life is Easier with Unified Applications

画外音：“一件事”“一次办”，两个“一”看似简单，实则不然。“一件事”的背后往往是“一堆事”，“一次办”的背后涉及的是“多部门”。海南推动“高效办成一件事”改革，真正把“一件事”办到了企业和群众心坎里，这启示我们，不仅要对企业和群众的需求“心中有数”，还要对优化政务服务流程“手头有招”，包括借助现代信息技术，推进数据共享，推进数字化政务建设，实现跨部门协同办公等。

Introduction: While streamlining multiple processes into a unified process makes sense, achieving it is not easy. Behind this unified process lies multiple sub-processes and the various government departments handling each one. Despite the challenges, Hainan has managed to roll out a "unified application" system that enables individuals and enterprises to deal with various kinds of related but different paperwork in one go. The success of this system reveals that government should not only be aware of the needs of enterprises and the public but also have "tricks up its sleeve" to optimize government service processes, including using cutting-edge IT to promote data sharing, promoting the construction of a digital government affairs platform, and realizing cross-departmental collaboration.

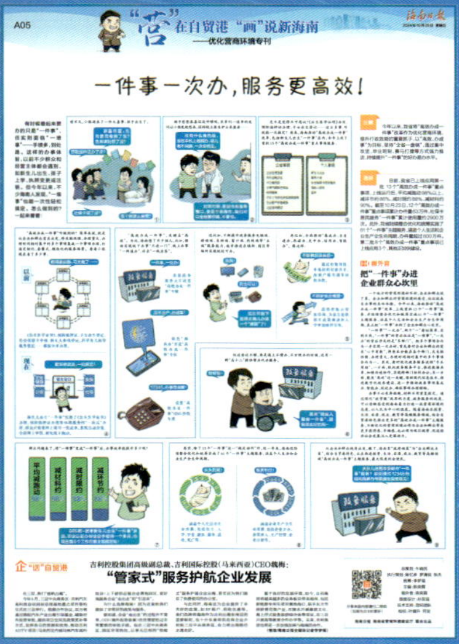
A05

“营”在自贸港 “画”说新海南

——优化营商环境专刊

海南日报

一件事一次办，服务更高效！

“话”自贸港

吉利控股集团高级副总裁、吉利国际控股（马来西亚）CEO魏梅：

“管家式”服务护航企业发展

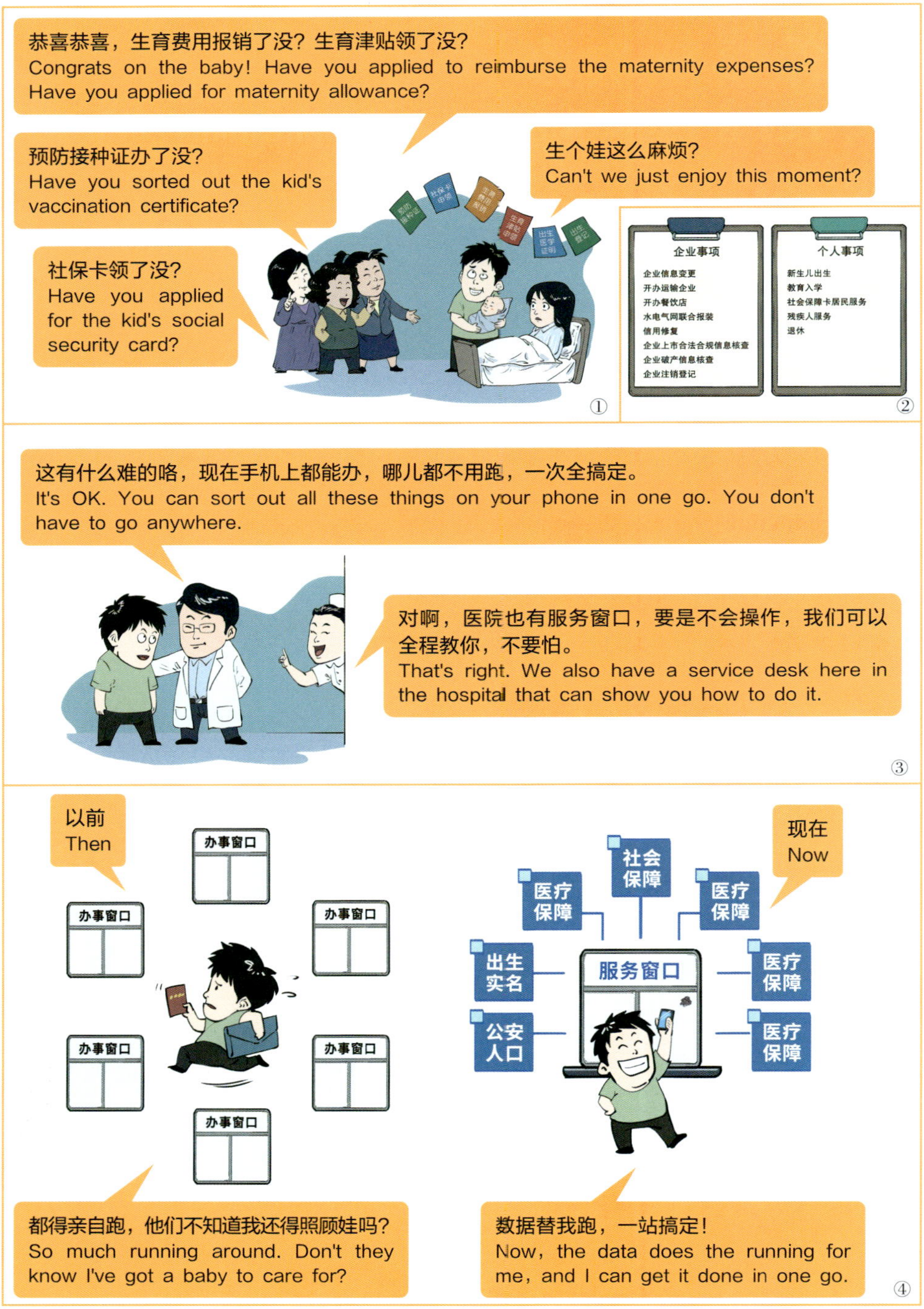
恭喜恭喜，生育费用报销了没？生育津贴领了没？
Congrats on the baby! Have you applied to reimburse the maternity expenses? Have you applied for maternity allowance?
预防接种证办了没？
Have you sorted out the kid's vaccination certificate?
社保卡领了没？
Have you applied for the kid's social security card?
生个娃这么麻烦？
Can't we just enjoy this moment?
①
企业事项
企业信息变更
开办运输企业
开办餐饮店
水电气网联合报装
信用修复
企业上市合法合规信息核查
企业破产信息核查
企业注销登记
个人事项
新生儿出生
教育入学
社会保障卡居民服务
残疾人服务
退休
②
这有什么难的咯，现在手机上都能办，哪儿都不用跑，一次全搞定。
It's OK. You can sort out all these things on your phone in one go. You don't have to go anywhere.
对啊，医院也有服务窗口，要是不会操作，我们可以全程教你，不要怕。
That's right. We also have a service desk here in the hospital that can show you how to do it.
③
以前
Then
办事窗口
都得亲自跑，他们不知道我还得照顾娃吗？
So much running around. Don't they know I've got a baby to care for?
现在
Now
社会保障
医疗保障
出生实名
公安人口
服务窗口
数据替我跑，一站搞定！
Now, the data does the running for me, and I can get it done in one go.
④

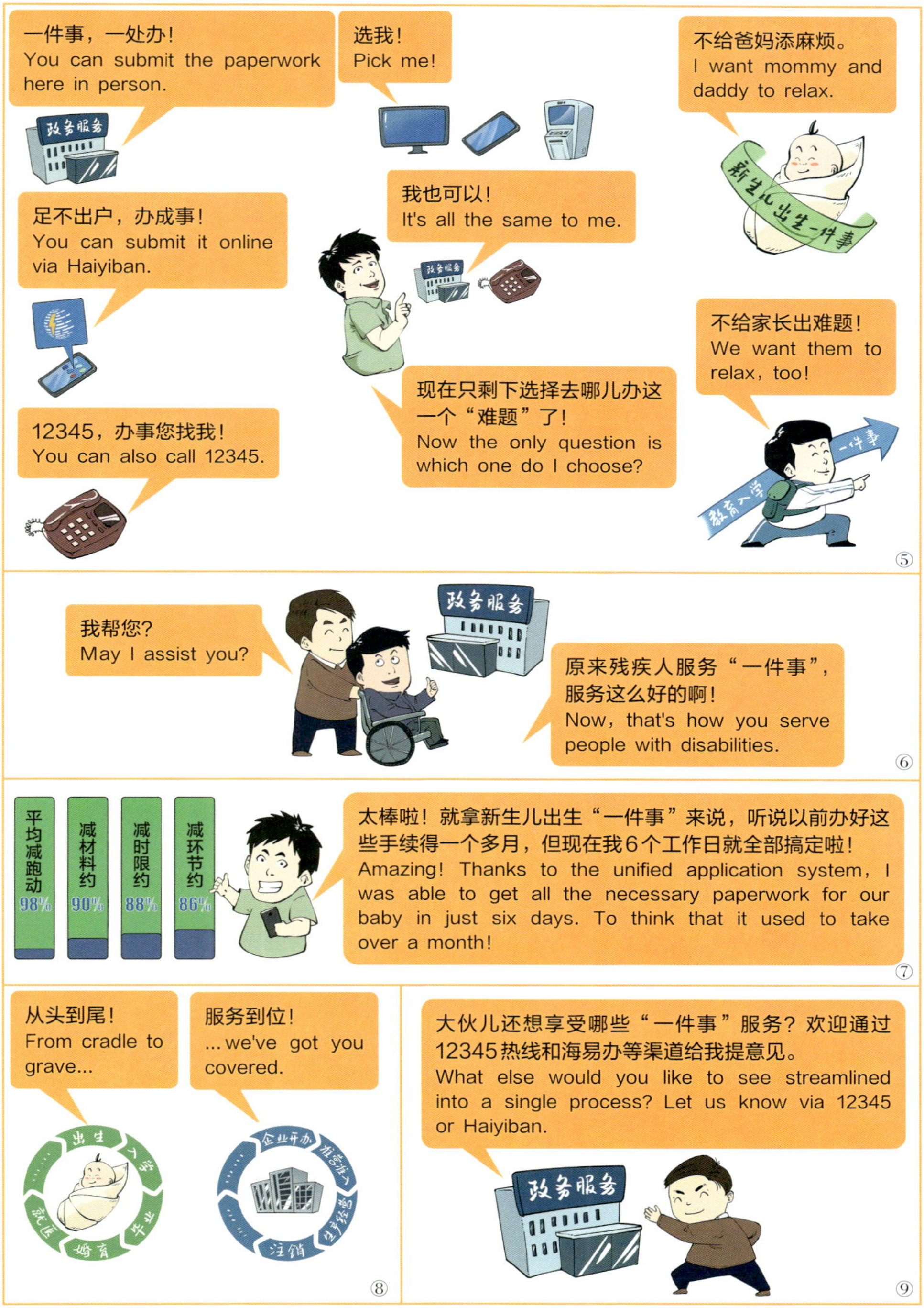
一件事，一处办！
You can submit the paperwork here in person.
政务服务
选我！
Pick me!
不给爸妈添麻烦。
I want mommy and daddy to relax.
新生儿出生一件事
足不出户，办成事！
You can submit it online via Haiyiban.
我也可以！
It's all the same to me.
不给家长出难题！
We want them to relax，too！
一件事
教育入学
现在只剩下选择去哪儿办这一个“难题”了！
Now the only question is which one do I choose?
12345，办事您找我！
You can also call 12345.
⑤
我帮您？
May I assist you?
政务服务
原来残疾人服务“一件事”，服务这么好的啊！
Now，that's how you serve people with disabilities.
⑥
平均减跑动 98%
减材料约 90%
减时限约 88%
减环节约 86%
太棒啦！就拿新生儿出生“一件事”来说，听说以前办好这些手续得一个多月，但现在我6个工作日就全部搞定啦！
Amazing! Thanks to the unified application system, I was able to get all the necessary paperwork for our baby in just six days. To think that it used to take over a month!
⑦
从头到尾！
From cradle to grave...
服务到位！
...we've got you covered.
出生
入学
毕业
婚育
就医
企业开办
注销
⑧
大伙儿还想享受哪些“一件事”服务？欢迎通过12345热线和海易办等渠道给我提意见。
What else would you like to see streamlined into a single process? Let us know via 12345 or Haiyiban.
政务服务
⑨

案例注解 CASE NOTES

2024年以来，我省将“高效办成一件事”改革作为优化营商环境、提升行政效能的重要抓手，以“高效、办成事”为目标，坚持“全省一盘棋”，通过集中攻坚、毕业班制、赛马打擂等方式强力推进，持续提升“一件事”的好办易办水平。

Starting from 2024, Hainan has taken the reform ideal of "completing things efficiently" as an important standard for optimizing the business environment and improving administrative work. Whether it is allowing applications for all government services to be completed from any location, insisting that tasks not require multiple visits, or encouraging staff to do better via competitions, concentrated efforts throughout the whole province are continuously improving the level of ease and efficiency.

案例进展 CURRENT STATUS

目前，第一批13个“高效办成一件事”重点事项已于2024年6月底全部上线，上线运行后，实现平均减跑动98%以上，减环节约86%、减时限约88%、减材料约90%，第二批8个“高效办成一件事”重点事项已于2024年12月底全部上线。

An initial batch of 13 key tasks that government staff must be capable of doing efficiently was announced at the end of June 2024. After reducing the number of steps by 86%, materials by 90%, and processing time by 88%, the average time reduction hit over 98%. This was followed by a second eight-item batch at the end of December 2024.

政务服务无界限
“全省通办”真方便

Accessing Government Services Wherever You Are

画外音：随着自贸港建设深入推进，人员流动性越来越大，服务事项“全省通办”，成为民生刚需。而今，越来越多“全省通办”事项的推出，不仅是与时俱进、顺民心之举，同时是对“全省一盘棋、全岛同城化”理念的践行，让群众不分地域，皆能享受便利服务。这彰显了海南的服务温度，有利于增加群众的归属感。乐见相关部门整合资源、统筹谋划，推出更多“全省通办”事项，给群众带去更多“马上办、就近办”的便利。

Introduction: As the construction of the Hainan FTP advances, people within the province have become more mobile, necessitating the implementation of province-wide services. The continued introduction of more province-wide services is aimed at both keeping up with the times and meeting the demands of the public and is a reflection of the concept of "whole-province coordinated development and integration". People can now enjoy a range of services with greater convenience regardless of where they are, demonstrating Hainan's warmth and increasing people's sense of belonging. Seeing government departments pool their resources and execute overarching plans to launch more province-wide services to bring added convenience to the people is a pleasing development.

A10

“营”在自贸港 “画”说新海南

——优化营商环境专刊

政务服务无界限 “全省通办”真方便

企“话”自贸港

政府服务更主动 企业更有归属感

开张日期要到了，可是我还没时间去三亚注册公司！
We're set to open soon, but I still haven't had time to go to Sanya and register the company.
1 2 3 4 5 6 7
8 9 10 11 12 13 14
15 16 17 18 19 20 21
22 23 24 25 26 27 28
①
海口办事窗口
五指山办事窗口
手续该去哪里办？海口还是五指山？这是一个问题。
Where should I handle the paperwork? Haikou or Wuzhishan? What a conundrum.
②
不必来回跑，这些手续都可以就近办哦。
You don't need to go far. Just head to the nearest government service center.
店小二
没有错，还可以自己在家上网办，很方便。
That's right. You can save even more time by submitting online!
③
线上方式
海南省政务服务网
申请人登录海南省政务服务网，进入全省通办专窗，选择可全省通办事项，填写表单，上传电子材料
属地审批部门
属地审批部门
属地审批部门
自动分发至属地审批部门进行受理和办理
办理结果
下载电子办理结果
线下方式
政务大厅
申请人选择就近政务大厅窗口填写表单
工作人员上传电子材料，自动分发至属地审批部门进行受理和办理
办理结果
窗口打印发放办理结果
④

我来派活儿了！
I've got some paperwork for you!
海口
三亚
文昌
⑤

哪里需要寄哪里，办事情so easy!
The paperwork is sent to wherever it is needed. It's as simple as that!
寄件地址
收件地址
申请人或窗口人员填写寄件地址和收件地址窗口打印发放办理结果
属地审批部门
邮政部门上门取件，邮寄到属地审批部门
纸质办理结果邮寄到家
⑥

这事儿上次我在其他市县办过，半小时就搞定了，超快的。
Last time, I managed to get this done somewhere else in just half an hour. How's that for fast?
全省通办
哪里办都一样！
It's the same wherever you go!
⑦

有政务地图，办事不迷路！
We also have a map showing the locations of government service centers, so you won't get lost.
全省通办政务地图
叮！根据您要办理的业务，
已为您找到最近的政务服务大厅！
⑧

拥有好信用，通办加速办！
You've got good credit. We'll get that done for you straight away.
全省通办
我还得努力提升！
I've still got some way to go.
⑨

省时省力！
Saving time and energy!
全省通办
一通百通！
Everything you need at your fingertips!
⑩

案例注解 CASE NOTES

近年来，海南持续加强政务服务跨区域协作联动，提升"全省通办"服务能力，推进实现政务服务更优、办事效率更高、营商环境更好。

In recent years, Hainan has continued to strengthen cross-regional collaboration in government services, improve province-wide service capabilities, promote better government services, higher efficiency, and a better business environment.

案例进展 CURRENT STATUS

2024年，海南全面推行政务服务"全省通办"改革，印发了《海南省推进政务服务"全省通办"改革工作实施方案》《海南省政务服务"全省通办"工作任务清单》，并在全省各级政务服务大厅设置113个"全省通办"窗口，配备"全省通办"窗口人员273人。目前共实现两批次2134个事项"全省通办"，累计产生703.55万办件量。

In 2024, the idea that all government services should be equally capable of being handled from anywhere in the province was promoted throughout Hainan. The *Implementation Plan for Hainan to Promote Province-Wide Government Services and the Task List for Implementing Province-Wide Government Services in Hainan* were promulgated, and 113 province-wide service windows with 273 staff were set up in government service halls across the province. As of now, the province-wide service windows can handle a total of 2,134 items and have processed over seven million cases.

异地办事不用愁
“跨省通办”很轻松

Accessing Government Services and Benefits Anywhere

画外音：异地申领身份证、异地就医结算、异地提取住房公积金……“跨省通办”体现的是一种理念，是坚持以群众需求为先，民有所呼，我有所应；是一种革新，是以创新思维整合资源力量，打破地域限制和信息壁垒，形成高效协同的服务机制；是一种思维，是以更宽广的视野，推进横向协同、网上网下联动，做到系统谋划、协同推进。群众“就近办”的背后，正是各地各部门着眼“一盘棋”、服务“加速跑”的努力。

Introduction: Be it applying for ID cards, settling medical bills, or withdrawing housing provident funds, "inter-provincial processing" enables the public to handle almost anything anywhere in China, reflecting the government's insistence on putting people's needs first and responding to their demands. It is an innovation that integrates resources with innovative thinking while breaking down geographical and information barriers to form an efficient and coordinated service mechanism. It is an approach that promotes horizontal coordination and the merging of online and in-person processes to achieve systematic planning and coordinated follow-through. Propelling this system is the focus of various localities and departments on "integration" and "acceleration."

A05
“营”在自贸港 “画”说新海南
——优化营商环境专刊
异地办事不用愁 “跨省通办”很轻松
入籍“中国洋浦港” 领到海南“户口本”

异地就医直接结算
身体抱恙不用等，异地也能用医保！
Don't wait till you get home to seek medical treatment. Use inter-provincial settlement for your medical bills.
①
终于在老家置业了！
Finally, a home of my own...back in my hometown!
异地也能用公积金，在"海易办"APP上就能办！
You can withdraw your housing provident fund here, too. Just apply through the Haiyiban APP.
②
距离不是问题！
Just log on to the Haiyiban APP.
婚姻登记
生育登记
户口迁移
不动产抵押
在线解决就行！
Distance isn't an issue.
③
这刚落地，岛服才换上，身份证就丢了，咋整啊？
I've just arrived and changed into the mandatory shorts and Hawaiian shirt, but I lost my ID card in the process. What am I going to do now?
④
老王，别慌，都是老乡！
Relax, Mr. Wang, we're still in China!
HAINAN
海南政务服务网
全国一体化在线政务服务平台
跨省通办
事项名称
城镇企业职工基本养老保险关系跨省转出
操作
在线办理
⑤

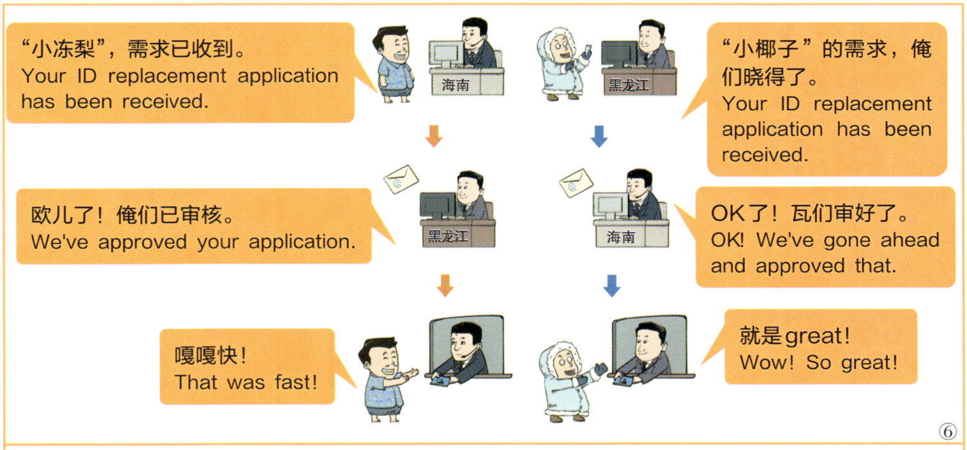
“小冻梨”，需求已收到。
Your ID replacement application has been received.
海南
黑龙江
“小椰子”的需求，俺们晓得了。
Your ID replacement application has been received.
欧儿了！俺们已审核。
We've approved your application.
黑龙江
海南
OK了！瓦们审好了。
OK! We've gone ahead and approved that.
嘎嘎快！
That was fast!
就是great！
Wow! So great!
⑥

跨省通办！
Inter-provincial government services...
通通好办！
...easily accessible wherever you are!
“跨省通办”合作
⑦

省与省的距离！
You may be far from home...
跨省通办自助机
政务服务大厅
社保中心
部分社区
药店
银行营业网点
公安办证中心
超市
药店
有了我都不是问题！
...but I'm here to bridge the distance!
⑧

新年快乐
过年放心出行！
We're even on duty...
跨省办事能行！
...during the Spring Festival holiday!
福
福
⑨

案例注解 CASE NOTES

2021年9月，海南与福建、江西、湖南、广东、广西、四川、贵州、云南正式建立泛珠三角区域内地九省区"跨省通办"合作。2024年1月，海南省和黑龙江省签订政务服务"跨省通办"框架合作协议，两省实现首批300项高频政务服务事项"跨省通办"。

In September 2021, Hainan formally entered into a nine-province pan-Pearl River Delta regional inter-provincial government services cooperation agreement with Fujian, Guangdong, Guangxi, Guizhou, Hunan, Jiangxi, Sichuan, and Yunnan. After signing a framework cooperation agreement on inter-provincial government services in January 2024, Hainan and Heilongjiang provinces have implemented "inter-provincial handling" for an initial batch of 300 common government service items.

案例进展 CURRENT STATUS

下一步，海南还将进一步扩展"跨省通办"区域范围、事项范围，推动更多通办事项能够"就近办""多点办""自助办"，尽最大可能为群众异地工作生活提供便利。

To provide the greatest level of convenience for people working and living in other places, Hainan will continue to further expand the number of regions and matters for inter-provincial government services. It will promote the ability for services to be handled anywhere, as well as the self-service handling of more common matters.

组团服务，让企业“进退自如”

A One-stop Shop for Company Incorporation, Amendment, and Closing

画外音： 海南多部门延伸“证照联办”服务，形成贯穿经营主体准入、经营、退出的三条部门协同服务链，反映出政府部门从“办事员”到“店小二”的角色转变、从“完成工作”到“做好服务”的理念更新、从“单点突破”到“系统集成”的制度创新以及从要办“一堆事”到只办“一件事”。这样的变化不是轻易能够实现的，其离不开相关部门完善服务手段、创新服务方式、精简审批程序、打通数据壁垒、优化流程机制、提升服务质效。

Introduction: Various government agencies in Hainan have consolidated their procedures under the "joint license and permit application" service, forming a three-link collaborative service chain that covers the incorporation, amendment, and closing of operating entities. This service represents a shift in role from mere "processing officers" to "service specialists", an update in concept from "completing work" to "providing good services", and an institutional innovation from "single-point breakthrough" to "system integration". Achieving the consolidation of "multiple applications and processes" into a "single application, joint processing" model was challenging, and required relevant departments to innovate their service approach, streamline approval procedures, overcome data barriers, optimize process mechanisms, and improve service quality and efficiency.

A07
“营”在自贸港“画”说新海南
——优化营商环境专刊
组团服务，让企业“进退自如”
企“话”自贸港
来得越多，留下来的念头越强烈

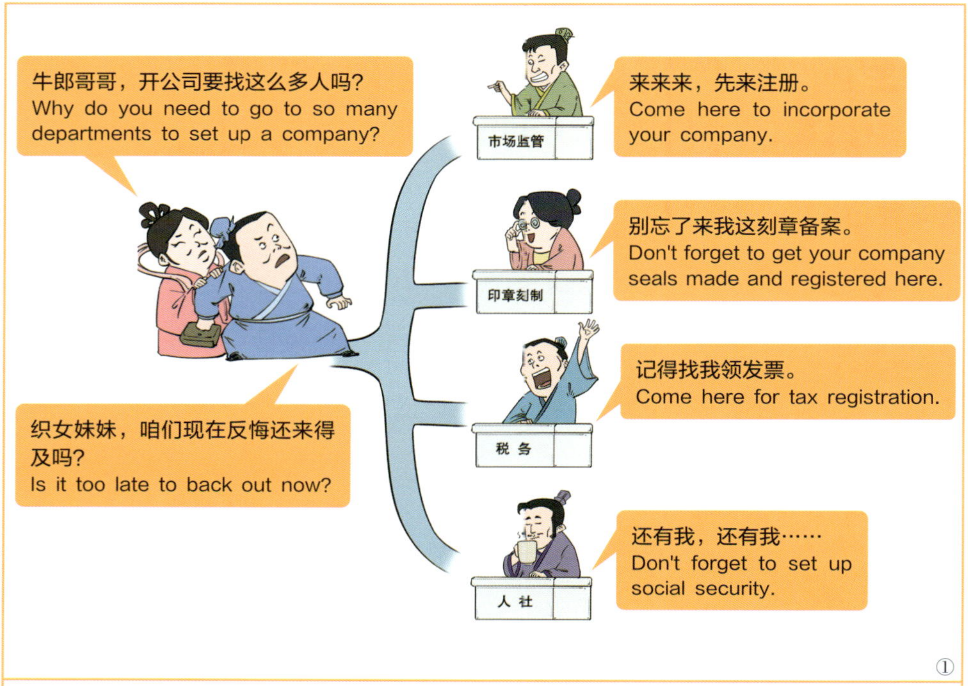
牛郎哥哥，开公司要找这么多人吗?
Why do you need to go to so many departments to set up a company?
织女妹妹，咱们现在反悔还来得及吗?
Is it too late to back out now?
市场监管
来来来，先来注册。
Come here to incorporate your company.
印章刻制
别忘了来我这刻章备案。
Don't forget to get your company seals made and registered here.
税 务
记得找我领发票。
Come here for tax registration.
人 社
还有我，还有我……
Don't forget to set up social security.
①

家人们，谁懂啊，开公司门槛这么高!
Well, folks, who knew that opening a company would be so difficult?
门槛高? 这是在打我们脸啊!
Difficult? Don't get me started.
看来得合作一下，动点真格的了!
It looks like we'll have to divide and conquer.
②

海南 e登记
原来这就是传说中的“一言为定”！
So, this is the one-stop platform spoken of in legends!
③
拿了照，还得办证，哎，还得再跑一趟。
So, that's the business license done. Now I need to get the permits sorted.
证照联办
办事窗口
不用，你去喝杯下午茶，我顺手就给你搞定了！
Chill out, my friend. You go relax and I'll handle the permits.
④
想改公司名，结果这么多东西要改，想想都头大。
All I want to do is change the company name, but there's so much that needs amending. What a headache!
放着我来！
Just leave it with me!
证照联办
办事窗口
⑤

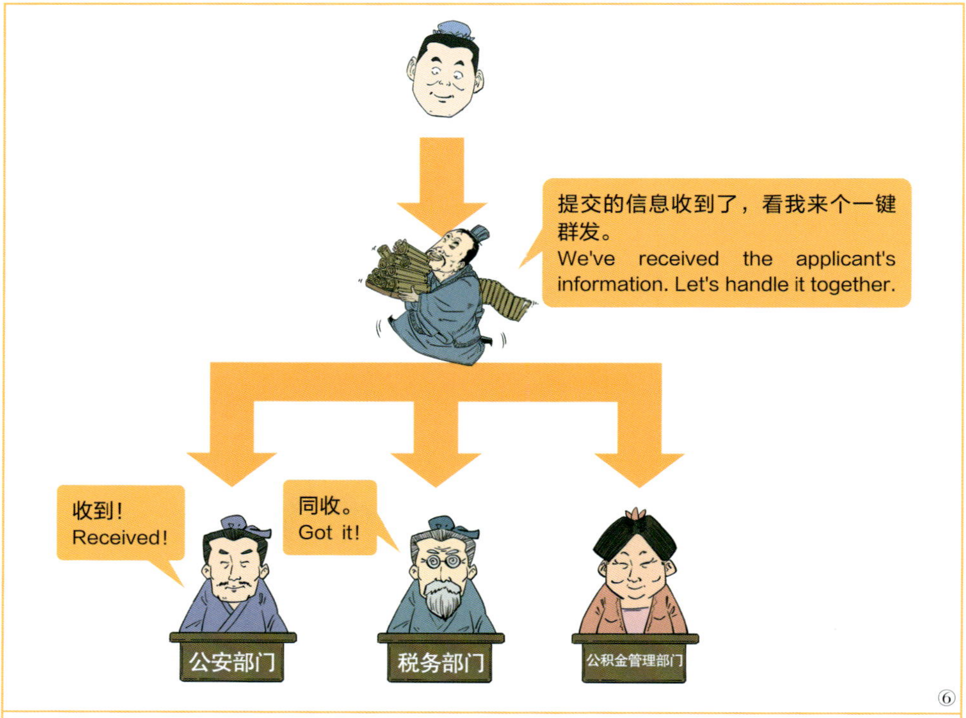
提交的信息收到了，看我来个一键群发。
We've received the applicant's information. Let's handle it together.
收到！
Received!
同收。
Got it!
公安部门
税务部门
公积金管理部门
⑥

刚办完营业执照，许可证变更还没提，这就自动审批完了？
So, the business license has been processed, but there's no mention of the permits. Were they approved automatically?
免申请、免提交、免审批，零跑动、零材料，主打"免申即享"！
That's what we mean by "automatic approval". There's no need to submit separate applications or materials, and no additional review is required!
⑦

鹊桥相会在即，关门追妻去！
Well, it's time to pack it in. I have to focus on my love life.
真是太感动了！
Giving it all up for love? So sweet!
⑧

人事关系都处理完了吧?
没啥债务了吧?
税清得咋样了?
社 保
海 关
公积金
市场监管
税务
海南e登记
申请注销
⑨

我们还会再回来的！
We'll meet again, don't know where, don't know when...
⑩

案例注解 CASE NOTES

2023年，海南省市场监管局联合省营商环境建设厅、省税务局、省社保服务中心、省住房公积金管理局、省公安厅等部门延伸"证照联办"服务链，上线变更、注销证照联办功能，在全省铺开"变更一件事""注销一件事"改革。此举意味着我省服务经营主体准入、经营、退出全生命周期的三条部门协同服务链正式形成。

In 2023, working together with Hainan Provincial Department of Business Environment Development, Hainan Provincial Tax Service, Social Insurance Service Center, Housing Provident Fund Management Bureau, and Public Security Department—the joint application service chain for licenses and permits was extended by the Hainan Provincial Market Supervision and Administration Bureau. With "one-stop amendment" and "one-stop cancellation" reforms being rolled out across the province, more and more licenses and permits can now be amended or canceled online, and a multi-department collaborative service chain encompassing the market entry, operation, and exit life cycle has been formally created.

案例进展 CURRENT STATUS

下一步，海南省市场监管局还将会同相关部门，把更多事项纳入"变更一件事"和"注销一件事"，并持续优化企业开办流程，让服务经营主体准入、经营、退出的三条服务链更加优化，为经营主体"自由出生"、规范健康成长、有序退出营造便捷、规范、可预期的市场环境。

For the next step, the Hainan Provincial Market Supervision and Administration Bureau will work with the relevant departments to include more items in the scope of "one-stop amendment" and "one-stop cancellation"; the process of starting a business will continue to be optimized; and the processes of entry into the market, market operation, and exit from the market will also be ootimized to create a convenient, standardized and predictable market environment where business entities can be "born freely", grow in a standardized and healthy manner, and exit in an orderly manner.

第二章

Section 2

优化服务，办事不求人

Improving Services

“政企约见”等您来约

Face-to-face Access to Government Officials? Just Make an Appointment

画外音： 政府服务更加精准贴心，企业发展才会更加稳健有力。“政企约见”充分体现了我省服务企业“有求必应、有诺必践”的诚意和决心，是我省不断完善企业服务体系的又一生动实践。这一机制给企业带来的便利，最直接的体现就是“找得到人”。政企直接对话，为企业开辟了表达诉求的“绿色通道”，有效促进了政府服务与经营主体需求“靶向对接”，不仅大大减少企业的时间成本和沟通成本，也大大提高了解决问题的效率。

Introduction: Government services that are more precise and considerate enable businesses to develop more steadily and robustly. The "government-enterprise engagement" platform initiative fully demonstrates Hainan's sincerity and determination to serve businesses with the principle of "responding to every request and fulfilling every promise". It represents another step forward in the continuous improvement of the province's business service system. The most immediate benefit this mechanism brings to businesses is the assurance that "they can reach the right people". Facilitating direct dialogue between the government and businesses opens a "green channel" for enterprises to voice their needs, effectively promoting a "targeted alignment" between government services and the demands of market entities. This not only significantly reduces the time and communication costs for businesses but also dramatically enhances the efficiency of problem-solving.

A05

“营”在自贸港 “画”说新海南

——优化营商环境专刊

“政企约见”等您来约

找得到人，更办得成事

18

52

757

海南冠锐科技有限公司负责人刘丹：

“店小二”贴心服务推动难题解决

想要扩建厂房，可这周边都是山林，用地问题踩到“红线”就麻烦了，咋办啊？
I'd like to expand my factory, but it's boxed in by the surrounding geography. How do I do this without breaking the law?
洪
①
点击“政企约见”，解决问题来碰面！
Just book an appointment to meet with government officials face-to-face and resolve your issues on the "Government-Enterprise Engagement" platform on Haiyiban.
政企约见
②
已发送一条约见邀请。
I've already submitted an appointment request.
登陆“海易办”
点击“企业码”
进入“政企约见
点击“我要约见”
填写约见信息
提交确认
企业点名 有约必见
企业名称
统一信用代码
联系方式
约见单位
拟约见时间
诉求内容
③
来活儿了伙伴们！
We've got a new appointment request, lads!
约见信息
这个时间我OK，速速接单！
I can take that slot.
④

和所有的烦恼说“白白”～
It's time to say goodbye to all my troubles.
还有什么尽管提！
Is there anything else at all?
这么快就被解决了！
Well, that's us discarded with!
麻烦
⑤

我想咨询政策！
I'd like to ask about policies!
我要投诉！
I'd like to complain!
我要请求帮助！
I'd like some help!
大家别急，只要诉求合理，企业点名，有约必见！
Hold your horses! We're happy to arrange appointments for any enterprise with reasonable requests or concerns.
⑥

哇！这么快就回复了?! 比我的车速还快！
Wow! That was quicker than I can say the word "scooter!"
单位回复
约见部门：XX县资规局
安排时间：12月4日
约见地点：XX县资规局会议室
负责人姓名：店小二
负责人职务：局长
⑦

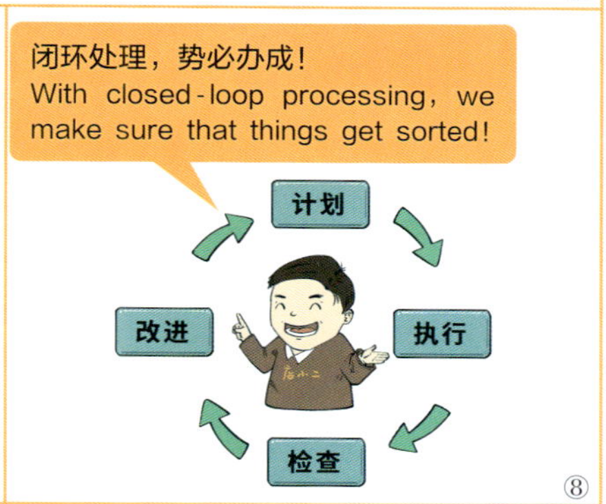
闭环处理，势必办成！
With closed-loop processing, we make sure that things get sorted!
计划
执行
检查
改进
⑧

有事约见！
Something on your mind? Make an appointment!
必来赴约！
Don't worry, we'll be there!
企业
“政企约见”系统
单位部门
单位部门
单位部门
单位部门
⑨

“营”在海南！
Do business in Hainan...
事事不难！
...where we do the running for you!
“政企约见”系统
12345政务服务热线平台
营商环境投诉平台
⑩

案例注解 CASE NOTES

2024年6月，海南省营商环境建设厅在总结三亚、陵水等地经验做法的基础上，基于“海易办”平台开发“政企约见”系统，并制定约见规则向全省推广实施，进一步畅通政企沟通渠道。

In June 2024, the Hainan Provincial Department of Business Environment Development created a "Government-Enterprise Engagement" system on the Haiyiban service platform based on the summary of the experience and practices of Sanya, Lingshui and other places, formulating appointment rules for promotion and implementation throughout the province and further unblocking communication channels between government and enterprises.

案例进展 CURRENT STATUS

目前，我省“政企约见”系统已上线52个省直部门机构，覆盖全省18个市县共计757个单位。2024年7月至年底，全省共收到约见问题工单862单，已全部完成约见。

At present, Hainan's "Government-Enterprise Engagement" system has been launched in 52 provincial departments and institutions, covering 757 units in 18 cities and counties acrcss the province. From July 2024 to the end of the year, the province received a total of 862 appointment requests, all of which were fulfilled.

12345，有事您找我！

Call 12345 and Help Will Arrive

画外音： 热线，一头连着群众诉求，一头连着政府职能。其能否精准高效运转，直接关乎“急难愁盼”问题的解决质效。海南以“12345+”多重服务场景，架起了一座沟通的桥梁，也疏通了发展中的堵点难点，这背后是治理能力的提升，也是治理理念的转化。实践表明，以绣花般的细心，以春风般的暖心，精准满足不同群体多样化、差异化的需求，才能不断提升企业和群众的获得感。

Introduction: The 12345 government service hotline links the queries and complaints of the general public to the functions of the government. Its accurate and efficient operation depends directly on the quality and effectiveness of solving "urgent, difficult, and pressing" problems. Hainan's "12345+" platform offers a variety of functions, building a bridge of communication by addressing bottlenecks and challenges during its development. Behind this is the improvement of governance capabilities and the transformation of governance concepts. Experience has shown that only by accurately meeting the diverse and differentiated needs of different groups with empathy and warmth can enterprises and the public perceive the hotline's benefit.

A06
“营”在自贸港 “画”说新海南
——优化营商环境专刊
海南日报
12345，有事您找我！
海南金海浆纸业有限公司关务部课长潘荣贵：
无感监管 有感服务

让我们的学生仔摸黑走路多危险！我打12345反映一下！
It's much too dangerous to be letting students walk home in the dark. Let me call 12345 and report it.
小黑我隐身了。
How can you even see us?
①
照亮我的美！
Thanks for shining a light on the issue!
②
海南12345
虽然路面可以通行，但是路灯不通电，影响市民和师生出行，存在安全隐患。
海南12345
有啥解决办法不?
儋州12345
能不能提前进行电力接驳?
@儋州市项目管理中心
儋州市项目管理中心
好的，我们马上安排！
③
去年受理诉求
805.4万件
按时办结率达
98.59%
12345
④
您反映的问题，我们正在核实中，下午给您回复。
We are currently verifying the issue you have reported to us. We will respond to you this afternoon.
不会是在“踢皮球”吧?
You promise you won't pass the buck?
放心咯，一定负责到底！
Rest assured, we'll get to the bottom of this.
⑤
晕头“转”向！
You get an issue, you get an issue, and you get an issue.
工单
社区
一线部门
工单
一线部门
一步到位！
Received! We're on it.
⑥

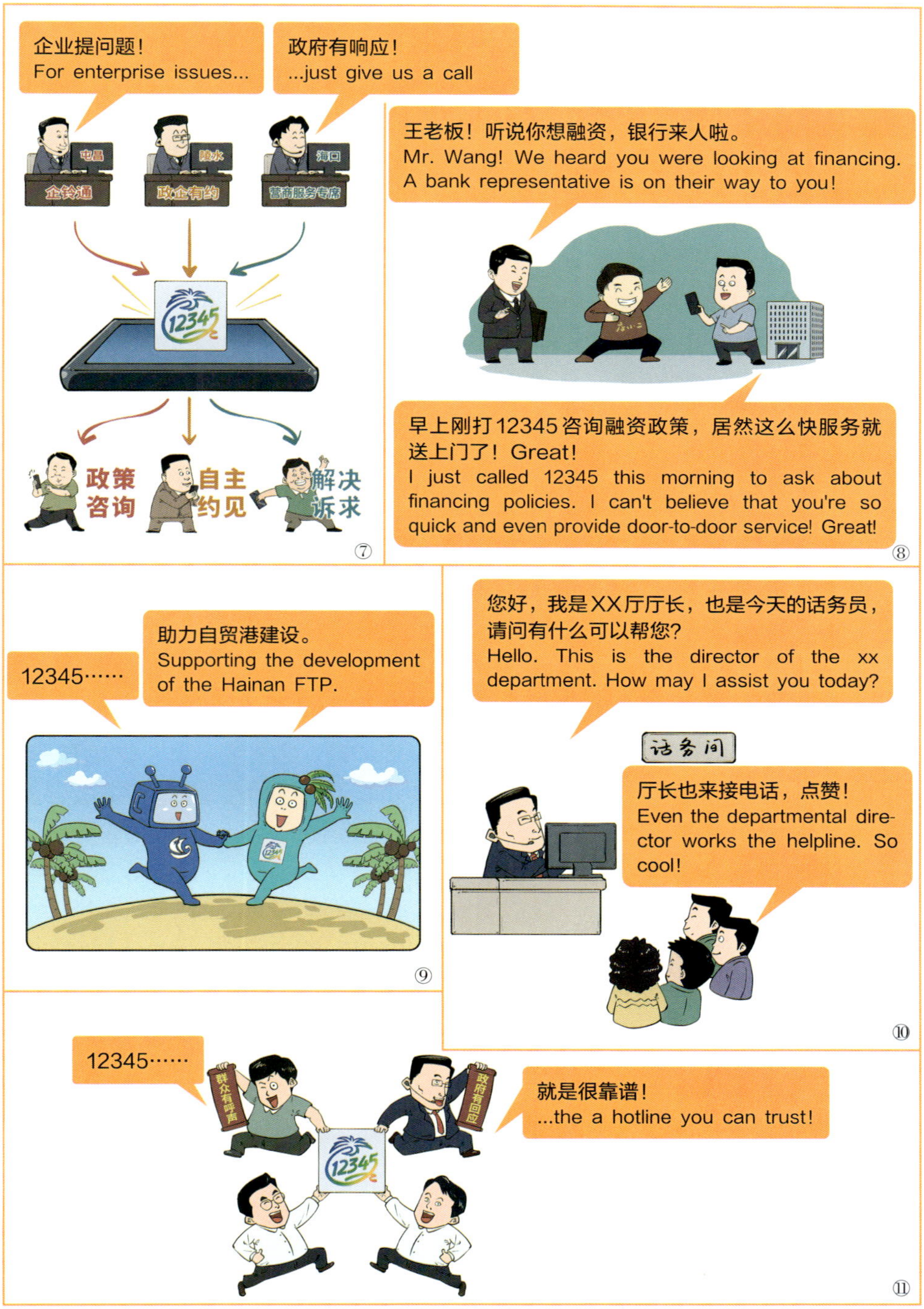
企业提问题！
For enterprise issues...
政府有响应！
...just give us a call
屯昌
陵水
海口
企铃通
政企有约
营商服务专席
12345
政策咨询
自主约见
解决诉求
⑦
王老板！听说你想融资，银行来人啦。
Mr. Wang! We heard you were looking at financing. A bank representative is on their way to you!
早上刚打12345咨询融资政策，居然这么快服务就送上门了！Great!
I just called 12345 this morning to ask about financing policies. I can't believe that you're so quick and even provide door-to-door service! Great!
⑧
12345……
助力自贸港建设。
Supporting the development of the Hainan FTP.
⑨
您好，我是XX厅厅长，也是今天的话务员，请问有什么可以帮您?
Hello. This is the director of the xx department. How may I assist you today?
话务间
厅长也来接电话，点赞！
Even the departmental director works the helpline. So cool!
⑩
12345……
群众有呼声
政府有回应
12345
就是很靠谱！
...the a hotline you can trust!
⑪

案例注解 CASE NOTES

2024年，海南12345热线平台创新"12345+网格化+直通联办"工作机制，建立热线紧急救援机制应对"摩羯"大考，拓展"12345+"协同工作模式，强化与"监督一张网"贯通机制，加强热线标准化建设，为两项国家标准、两项团体标准的编制贡献海南经验。2024年，海南12345热线受理诉求816.06万件，按时办结率98.89%，实际参评满意率94.98%。

In 2024, faced with the severe test of Super Typhoon Yagi, the 12345 government services hotline cooperated with the power company and emergency services to establish a grid-based emergency rescue mechanism, expand the "12345+" collaborative working model, strengthen the integration mechanism and standardization of hotlines, and contributed Hainan's experience to the formulation of two new national standards and two project standards. In 2024, Hainan's 12345 hotline received over eight million complaints and requests, with a 98.89% on-time completion rate and a 94.98% reported satisfaction rate.

案例进展 CURRENT STATUS

海南省12345管理中心和三亚市热线办顺利通过国家级标准化试点建设中期评估和终期验收。海南12345热线在各类质量评估评价中均名列前茅，如在第六次全国政务热线服务质量研究中获评A+等级省份，在2024年全国热线运行质量监测中获得省级热线第五名，标准化建设成果入选"全国政务服务便民热线创新发展典型案例（2023—2024）"和"2024年全国数字政府标准案例50强"。

The Hainan Provincial 12345 Management Center and Sanya Municipal Hotline Office successfully passed evaluation and acceptance to be included in the national standardization pilot program. In various quality assessments, Hainan's 12345 government services hotline ranks among the best in China. Among provinces that were rated A+ in the sixth national government hotline service quality study in 2024, Hainan ranked fifth in terms of hotline operation quality monitoring. The results of the standardization of Hainan's 12345 services were selected as a 2023–2024 "Model National Government Service Hotline Innovation and Development Case" and a 2024 "Top 50 National Digital Government Model Case".

步步为“营” 端稳“金饭碗”

Hainan’s Service Specialist Superheroes

画外音：营商环境建设是一个系统工程，不可能一气呵成、一蹴而就。解答营商环境建设“多元方程式”，关键在于扭住制度集成创新这个“牛鼻子”。把分散在不同部门的职能聚合在一起，成立全国首个省级营商环境建设厅，正是海南敢为人先、大胆探索制度集成创新取得的一项重要成果。这意味着海南将营商环境建设上升到自由贸易港体制机制改革的全局和高度来谋划部署、推进落实，展示出海南矢志不渝打造一流营商环境的坚定决心、信心。

Introduction: Building a business environment is a systematic project and cannot be accomplished overnight. The key to resolving the multiple variables of business environment construction lies in grasping the bull of “institutional integration and innovation” by the horns. Bringing together the functions of different departments and established China's first provincial-level department dedicated to business environment development. It is one of Hainan's important achievements in pioneering institutional integration and innovation. This also means that Hainan sees business environment construction as a key component in the planning, deployment, and implementation of the free trade port system and demonstrates its firm determination and confidence in creating a first-class business environment.

A05

“营”在自贸港 “画”说新海南

——优化营商环境专刊

步步为“营” 端稳“金饭碗”

用制度集成创新 涵养“生命之氧”

海南营商环境有温度

良好营商环境 提升自贸港软实力

企业在琼发展添信心

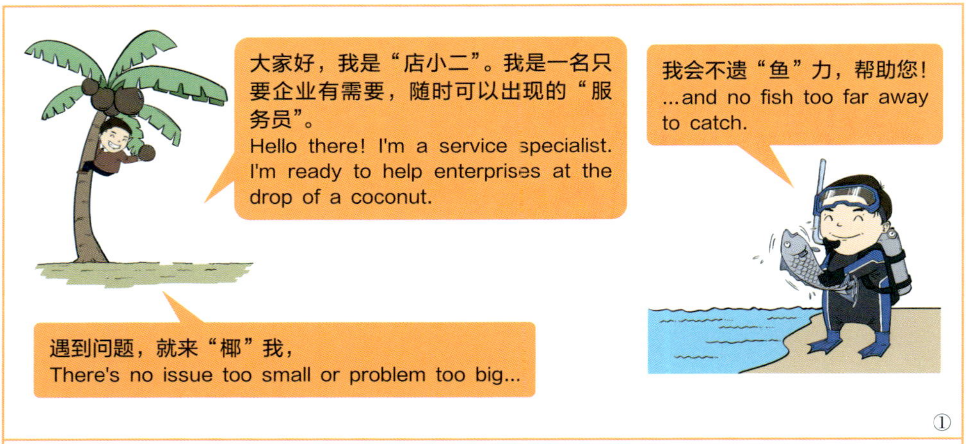
大家好，我是“店小二”。我是一名只要企业有需要，随时可以出现的“服务员”。
Hello there! I'm a service specialist. I'm ready to help enterprises at the drop of a coconut.
遇到问题，就来“椰”我，
There's no issue too small or problem too big...
我会不遗“鱼”力，帮助您！
...and no fish too far away to catch.
①

让我来跑腿！你们不用亲自跑来跑去啦！
I'll run your errands for you. You just put your feet up and relax!
化繁为简！
I simplify complex issues.
谢谢拉我一把，帮我渡过难关！
Thanks for the leg up! I don't know how I could have managed.
别担心，有我呢！
No worries. I'm here for you!
收到！马上办！
Understood. I'll get right to it!
②

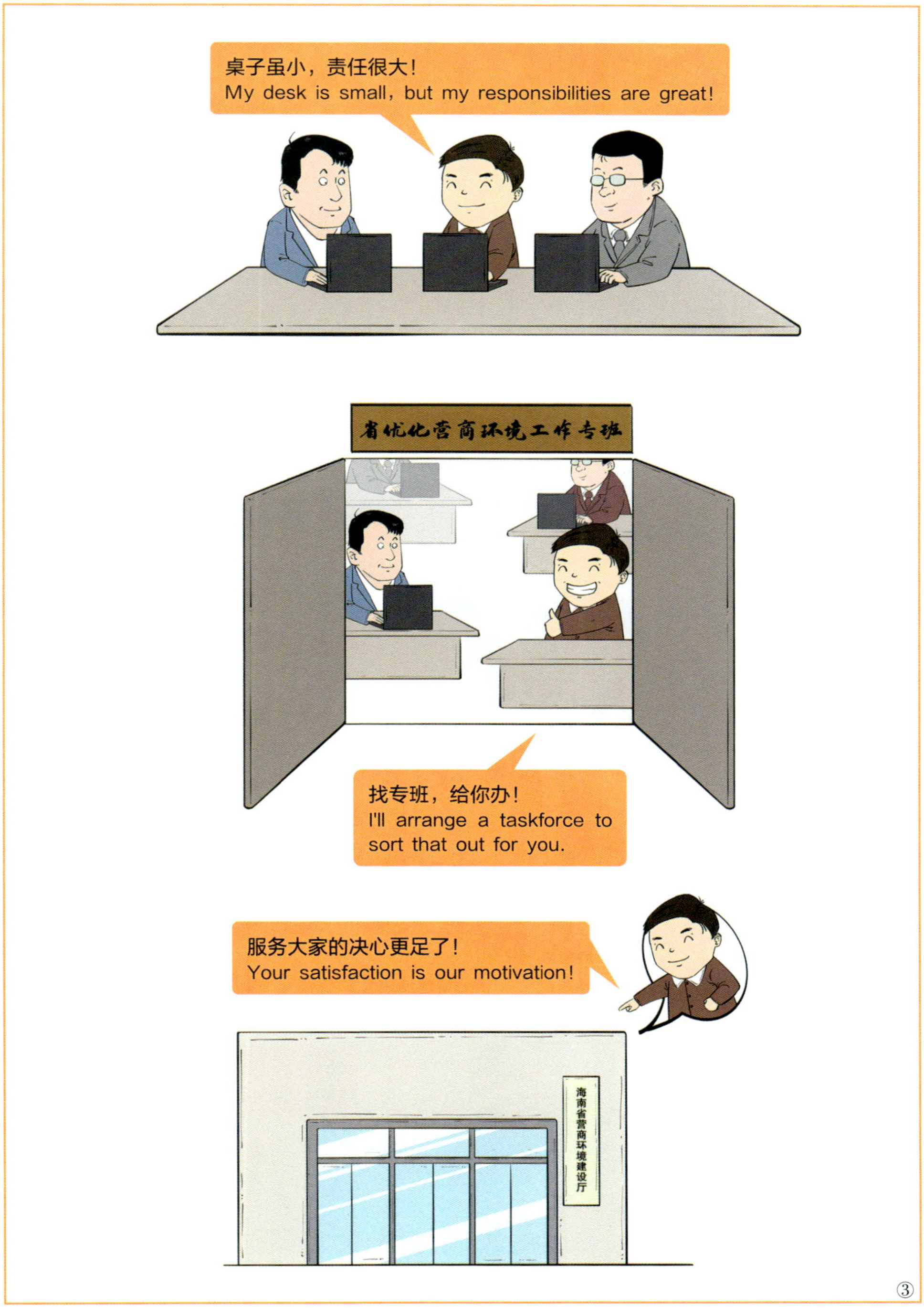
桌子虽小，责任很大！
My desk is small, but my responsibilities are great!
省优化营商环境工作专班
找专班，给你办！
I'll arrange a taskforce to sort that out for you.
服务大家的决心更足了！
Your satisfaction is our motivation!
海南省营商环境建设厅
③

在海南做生意，把心放肚子里！
I feel at ease running a business in Hainan.
海南省营商环境建设厅
有人罩了！
You've got us covered.
遇到问题，就来找我！
If you have any issues, come to me!
拧成一股绳！
I take all these functions and roll them into one.
部分职责
省政府电子政务办
省发展改革委
省政务服务中心
省大数据管理局
海南省营商环境建设厅
数据共享
政务服务
营商环境
社会信用
齐心协力共创一流营商环境！
Work together to create a first-class business environment!
④

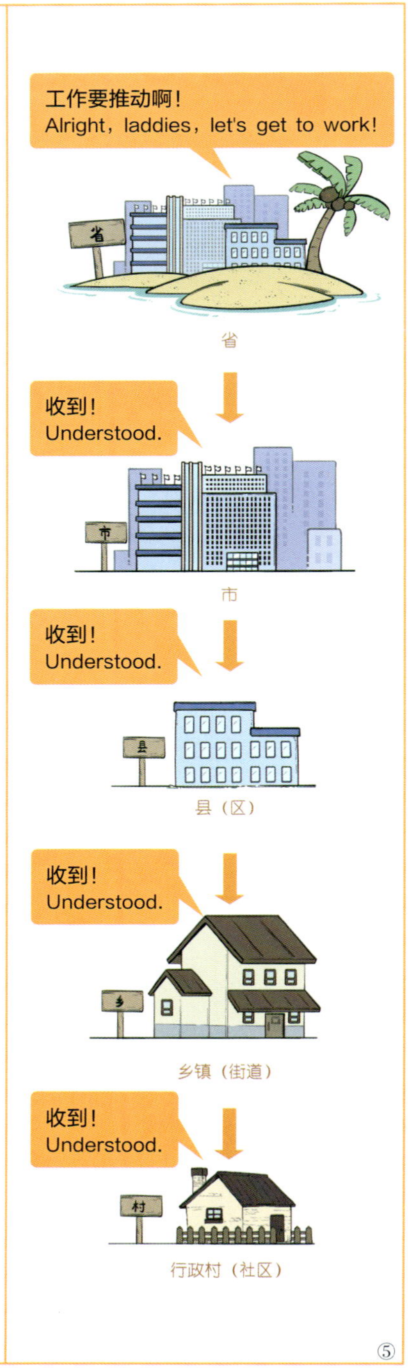
工作要推动啊！
Alright, laddies, let's get to work!
省
省
收到！
Understood.
市
市
收到！
Understood.
县
县（区）
收到！
Understood.
乡
乡镇（街道）
收到！
Understood.
村
行政村（社区）
⑤

去其糟粕，高效便捷！
I cut through red tape to provide you with more efficient and convenient services.
准入不准营
乱执法
往返跑
统筹全局，
I look at the big picture...
发现问题，
...find the issues...
解决问题！
...and solve them.
尖刀班
你们放心冲，我来守护！
You guys focus on winning while I focus on supporting you!
经商环境好，我们变更强！
This beefed-up business environment is really good for business.
⑥

“海南自贸港请您来投诉”
问题受理平台
登录“海南省人民政府网”-营商环境问题受理平台;
微信公众号“海南省政府网”—政民互动—营商问题线索;
微信小程序“海南营商环境”；
“海易办”APP—营商环境投诉;
热线电话：65865012、65865015。
“店小二”们一定有求必应，无事不扰！
Hainan FTP service specialists： any issue，any time!
⑦

案例注解 CASE NOTES

经中央批准，2022年12月13日，海南省营商环境建设厅挂牌成立。作为正厅级省政府组成部门，该厅负责统筹推进营商环境、政务服务、数据共享、社会信用等工作。

The Hainan Provincial Department of Business Environment Development was established with the approval of the central government on December 13, 2022. As a provincial-level government department, they are responsible for the unified advancement of the work such as improving the business environment, better government services, data sharing, and social credit.

案例进展 CURRENT STATUS

目前，海南省营商环境建设厅以全省优化营商环境的“指挥部”、营商环境建设工程的“施工队”、经营主体和群众的“店小二”、营商环境制度创新的“排头兵”为定位，全力服务全省近400万经营主体和1000万海南百姓，努力营造市场化、法治化、国际化一流营商环境。

Fully serving nearly four million business entities and 10 million Hainan residents, and striving to create a first-class business environment that is market-oriented, law-based, and international, the Hainan Provincial Department Business Environment Development is positioned as the provincial "headquarters" for optimizing Hainan's business environment, the "laborers" on the project of constructing the business environment, the "servers" for business entities and the public, and the "vanguard force" for systematic innovation of the business environment.

企业吹哨　服务报到

You Call, We Deliver

画外音：企业办事，最怕的是折腾，对政策的不熟悉、对流程的不了解，都会造成“来回跑”。海南推行企业首席服务专员制度，其突出亮点是充分发挥了服务专员懂政策、知流程、善沟通的专业优势，架起了直达企业的“直通车”。效率的提升、服务的改善，固然离不开服务专员的专业、高效。但往更深一层看，是由于其有着以企业心为心、以企业事为事的“店小二”精神，将服务前置，变“被动”为“主动”，把企业放在了“C位”，把项目放在了心上。

Introduction: Enterprises hate hassle, but unfamiliarity with policies and processes often results in a lot of back and forth. In light of this, Hainan has deployed chief service specialists who understand policies, know the procedures, and excel at communication, helping enterprises navigate their way through administrative processes. While the professionalism and efficiency of these service specialists have led to massive improvements in service levels, at a deeper level, these improvements are down to the service specialists standing in the shoes of the enterprises they serve, prioritizing service above all else, taking a proactive approach, and making enterprises and projects the heart of their mission.

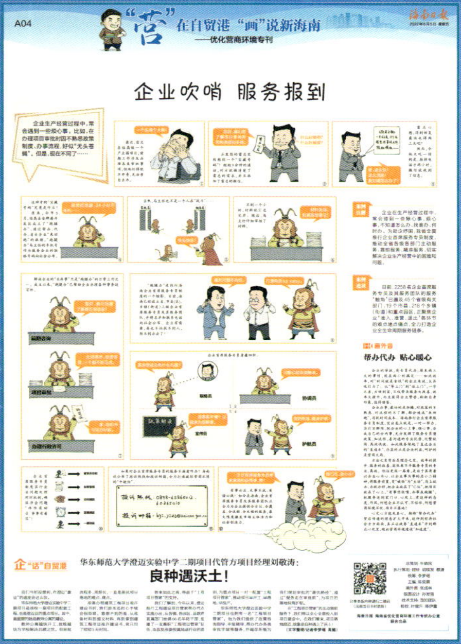

一个头两个大啊!
Grrr! So much to get done!
①
您好，我们想了解项目拿地所需的流程和手续。
Hello. I want to inquire about the process and application materials for acquiring land for a development project.
有求必应
什么时候用? 什么时候要?
When will the land be used? When do you need it?
②
哇，这么快! 这么清晰! 我知道怎么办了!
Wow, so quick! So clear! I know exactly what to do!
《投资手册》
一共62页、17个流程整理事项文件、报批模板……
③
做您的跑腿，24小时不关机。
We're here for you around the clock.
④
资规局
税务局
快去快回!
Go, go, go!
⑤

材料无误，赶紧发给雷总！
Everything is in order. I better let Mr. Lei know!
⑥

您好，请问您想了解哪方面的信息？
Hello. What's your query regarding?
前期咨询
立项用地、投资审批，一个都不能马虎。
Land approval and investment approval: We take care of the "lots".
项目审批
许可证
亲，您的许可证办好啦！
Hello. Your permit is ready!
办理行政许可
⑦

遇到问题不用慌。
Don't let yourself get flustered.
打我电话so easy。
Just give us a call!
⑧
雷总您这边有什么问题?
Mr. Lei, how can I help?
问题已经协调解决。
We have already coordinated a solution.
政策看不懂? 让我来为您解读。
Don't understand a policy? Let me spell it out for you.
政策解读
您的权益，我来护航!
We help protect your legitimate rights and interests!
⑨

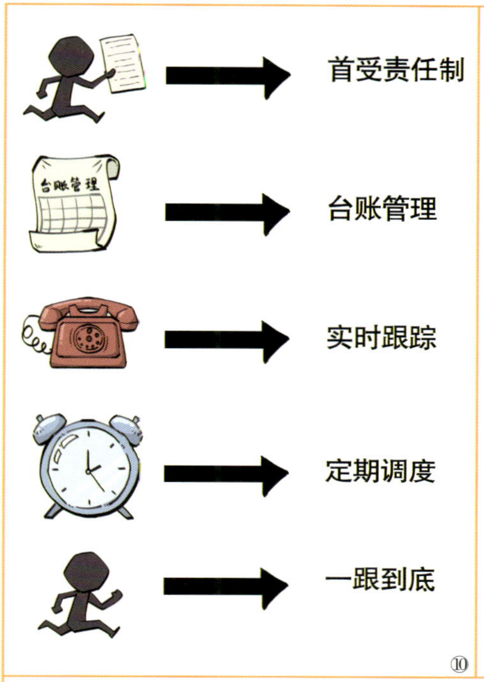
首受责任制
台账管理
台账管理
实时跟踪
定期调度
一跟到底
⑩

投诉热线：0898-65865012、
0898-66865015
投诉邮箱：bgs_yszb@hainan.gov.cn
⑪

我们在，放心冲！
With us by your side, just chase the tide!
企业首席服务专员带来满满的获得感，赞！
I really feel taken care of, thanks to the enterprise chief service specialist!
⑫

案例注解 CASE NOTES

企业在生产经营过程中，常会碰到一些揪心事、烦心事，不知道怎么办、找谁办、何时办。为助企纾困，我省全面推行企业首席服务专员制度，推动全省各级各部门主动服务、靠前服务、精准服务，切实解决企业生产经营中的困难和问题。

In the process of production and operation, when encountering annoying or worrying things, it is often the case that people or enterprises don't know what to do, who to ask or when to do it. In order to help alleviate these difficulties, Hainan has fully implemented a system of chief service specialists for enterprises, and encouraged all levels and departments in the province to provide proactive, front-line and precise services that effectively solve the production and operation difficulties and problems encountered by enterprises.

案例进展 CURRENT STATUS

目前，2258名企业首席服务专员及其服务团队的服务"触角"已遍及44个省级有关部门、19个市县、218个乡镇（街道）和13个重点园区，正聚焦企业"准入、准营、退出"各环节的难点堵点痛点，全力打造企业全生命周期服务链条。

To date, the service capability of 2,258 chief specialists and their teams has spread to 44 relevant provincial-level departments, 19 cities and counties, 218 towns (sub-districts), and 13 key industrial parks. They are focusing on the difficulties, bottlenecks and pain points which enterprises face during entry to the market, market operations, and exit from the market and are striving to build a full-life-cycle service chain for enterprises.

外国友人在琼生活SO EASY!

Hainan Brings Foreign Friends More Convenience

画外音：随着自贸港建设的深入推进，海南的对外开放程度不断提高，来海南的外籍人员越来越多，他们在琼工作、生活、学习、旅游中可能会遇到各种各样的卡点堵点问题。以问题为导向，海南依托“海易办”平台，推出“国际服务专区”，为外籍人员提供在琼办事、生活、工作、旅游、投资、购物等一站式指南服务。这是海南提升国际化服务水平的重要举措，也是打造国际化营商环境的具体实践。

Introduction: As the construction of the Hainan FTP continues to advance, Hainan has grown increasingly open to the outside world. Increasing numbers of foreign nationals are coming to Hainan, sometimes encountering issues when it comes to working, living, studying, and traveling in the province. Faced with these issues, Hainan has launched the "International Services" portal on the Haiyiban APP to provide expats and visitors with one-stop guides and services for doing business, living, working, traveling, investing, shopping, etc. in Hainan. This measure is crucial for Hainan to improve its international services and create a global business environment.

A06

“营”在自贸港“画”说新海南

——优化营商环境专刊

外国友人在琼生活SO EASY!

Hainan Brings “Foreign Friends” More Convenience

JACK: "我是Jack，征向导一名，要求英语流利，还得是个'海南百事通'"（I am Jack, I am looking for a guide who is fluent in English and has intimate knowl-edge of Hainan"）
市民："这要求可有点难了"（You're asking for a lot.)
海易办："Don't worry, let me do it"（别担心，让我来）
①
这个怎么用？
How do I use this?
我来教你。
Let me show you.
②
海易办，在海南的事情都好办！
With the Haiyiban (Hainan Government Service Platform) APP, things in Hainan are easier to manage.
主题服务场景
政务服务
Government Services
自贸港特色服务
Free Trade Port Services
投资
Do Business
旅游
Travel in Hainan
生活
Live in Hainan
工作
Work in Hainan
留学
Study in Hainan
购物
Shop in Hainan
8大主题场景
③
欢迎来吃长桌宴！
Welcome to our long-table banquet!
哇，从来没有跟这么多人一起吃过饭！想去想去！
Wow, I've never had dinner with so many people before. I wanna go!
④
想买个椰壳工艺品，去哪儿才能买到呢？
I want to buy coconut shell handicrafts. Where can I pick some up?
Jack，来这里！
Over here, Jack!
⑤

So easy!
现金
扫码
⑥
开始喜欢上海南了，我要赶紧查一查怎么留下来工作。
I'm really falling in love with Hainan. Let's find out how I can stay and work here.
国际服务专区
来华工作许可申请
96项
涉外事项办事指南
⑦
我是不是还要去公安机关办理登记报备?
Do I need to go to the police station to register my accommodation?
不用麻烦，打开海易办“国际服务专区”就可以线上登记啦!
There's no need. Just register via the "Accommodation Online" mini-program on the Haiyiban APP International Services portal.
民宿
⑧
新增境外直接投资所得免征企业所得税
Tax exemption on new foreign-source direct Income
感觉我也要成为“海南百事通”了!
I think I'll become an expert on Hainan pretty soon.
⑨
A GUIDE TO HAINAN FOR EXPATS
海南概览About Hainan
来到海南Staying in Hainan
探索海南Explore Hainan
本地服务Local Services
⑩
对了，海南政务服务网（wssp.hainan.gov.cn）也上线“国际服务办事专窗”了哦!
There's also the "Hainan International Services" on the Hainan Government Services Portal (wssp.hainan.gov.cn).
⑪

案例注解 CASE NOTES

为提升外籍人员在琼工作生活的便利化水平，2024年4月，海南省营商环境建设厅和海南省大数据管理局（2024年10月正式更名为海南省大数据发展中心）依托“海易办”平台，推出国际服务专区，为外籍人员提供在琼办事、生活、工作、旅游、投资、购物等一站式指南服务。

To make things more convenient for foreigners working and living in Hainan, in April 2024, the Hainan Provincial Department of Business Environment Development and Big Data Administration of Hainan Province (officially renamed as Big Data Development Center of Hainan Province in October 2024) used the local government's Haiyiban service platform to launch an International Services portal that provides one-stop guide services for foreign nationals on handling government services, living, working, traveling, investing, and shopping in Hainan.

案例进展 CURRENT STATUS

目前，国际服务专区主要为外籍人员提供三方面的便利：一是推出主题服务指引。二是提供英文导办服务。三是实现高频事项网上办。

Currently, Haiyiban's International Services portal primarily provides three kinds of conveniences for foreigners: thematic service guidelines, English guidance services, and the ability to handle common matters online.

来海南，创新更放心！

No False Starts for Start-ups in Hainan

画外音： 知识产权凝结了人们的创新热情、创新实践、创新精神，重视、保护知识产权，体现的正是对创新创造的肯定，由此这也正是打造一流营商环境的必然要求。换言之，越是强化创新驱动，越要在知识产权保护利用上下功夫。海南多措并举强化知识产权保护，法律为约束，服务有温度，对侵权行为不手软，推动形成全社会共同保护知识产权的良好氛围，必能让创新主体在海南更有安全感、更添信心动力，也必能激发海南创新发展的澎湃动力。

Introduction： Intellectual property rights are the embodiment of people's enthusiasm and labor in innovation. Respecting and protecting these rights are the government's way of affirming that innovation and creation are a core requirement for creating a first-class business environment. In other words, the more we strengthen innovation-driven efforts, the more we need to focus on protecting and utilizing intellectual property rights. Hainan has adopted various measures to strengthen intellectual property protection, putting legal safeguards in place, offering great services, and showing no mercy toward infringements. It has promoted an atmosphere where society as a whole jointly protects intellectual property rights, reassuring innovation entities in Hainan and stimulating the power of innovation and development.

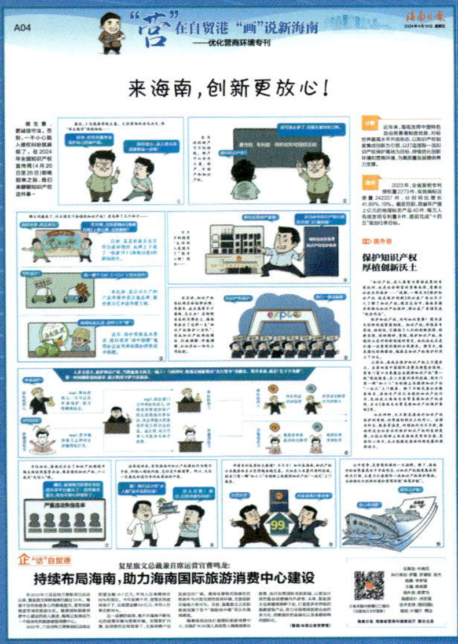
A04 "营"在自贸港 "画"说新海南 ——优化营商环境专刊

来海南，创新更放心！

持续布局海南，助力海南国际旅游消费中心建设

阿侬，你首先要学会保护自己的财产哦。
Anong, you need to learn how to protect your assets.
那你放心，没人能从我这里偷走一分钱！
Don't worry. No one can steal even a single penny from me.
①

啥叫知识产权？
What are intellectual property rights?
著作权 专利权 商标权和地理标志权
那可就太多了，但最主要的有三种。
Well, there are many different kinds, but these are the three main types.
②

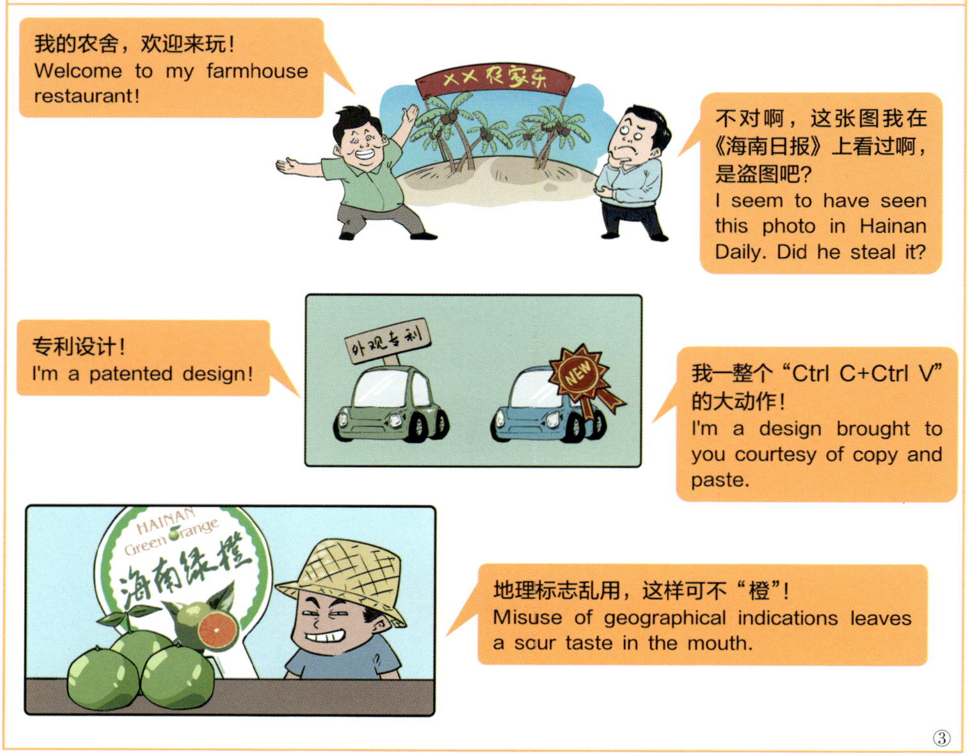
我的农舍，欢迎来玩！
Welcome to my farmhouse restaurant!
××农家乐
不对啊，这张图我在《海南日报》上看过啊，是盗图吧？
I seem to have seen this photo in Hainan Daily. Did he steal it?
专利设计！
I'm a patented design!
外观专利
NEW
我一整个"Ctrl C+Ctrl V"的大动作！
I'm a design brought to you courtesy of copy and paste.
HAINAN Green Orange
海南绿橙
地理标志乱用，这样可不"橙"！
Misuse of geographical indications leaves a scur taste in the mouth.
③

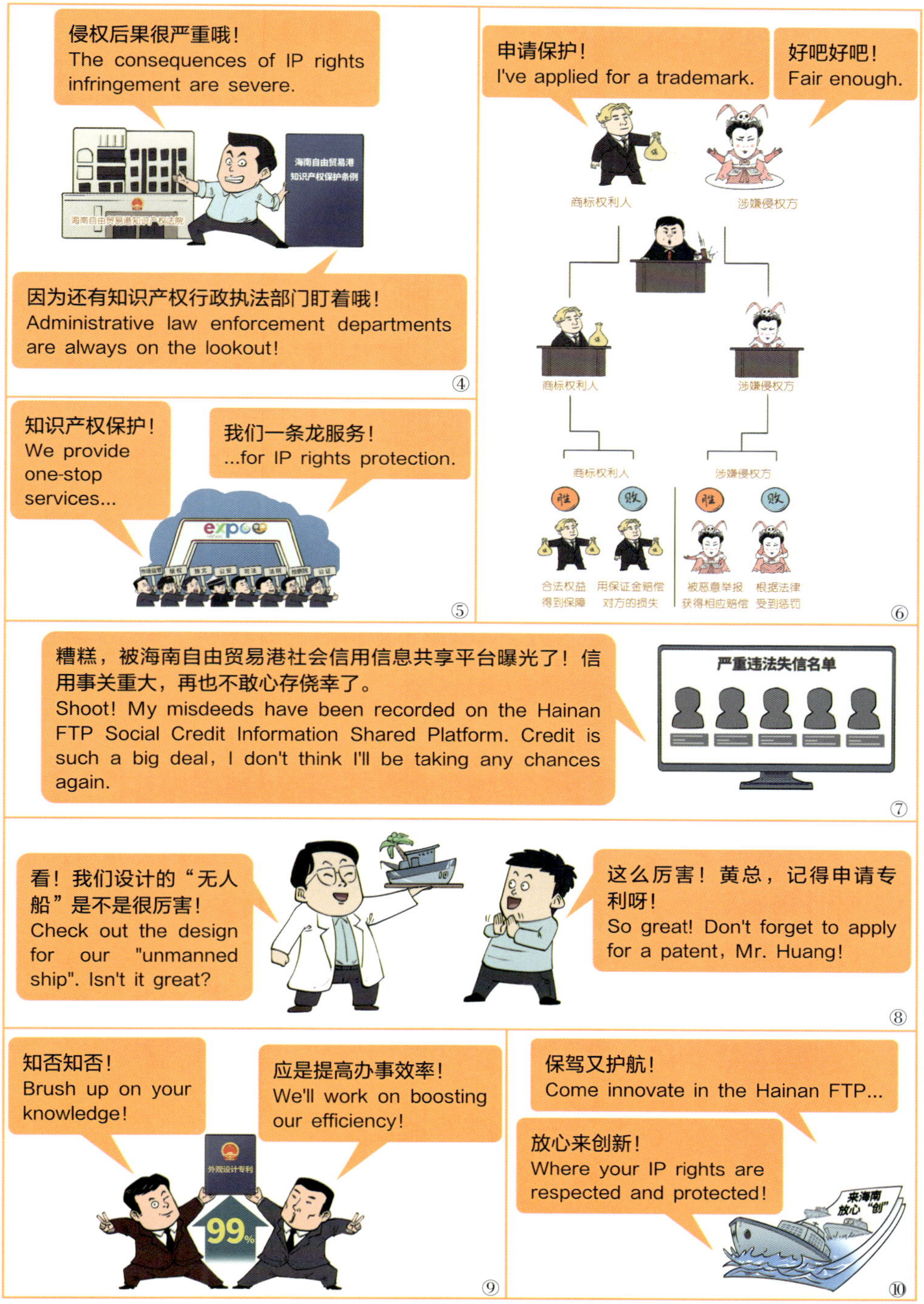
侵权后果很严重哦！
The consequences of IP rights infringement are severe.
海南自由贸易港知识产权保护条例
海南自由贸易港知识产权法院
因为还有知识产权行政执法部门盯着哦！
Administrative law enforcement departments are always on the lookout!
④
申请保护！
I've applied for a trademark.
好吧好吧！
Fair enough.
商标权利人
涉嫌侵权方
商标权利人
涉嫌侵权方
商标权利人
涉嫌侵权方
胜
败
胜
败
合法权益得到保障
用保证金赔偿对方的损失
被恶意举报获得相应赔偿
根据法律受到惩罚
⑥
知识产权保护！
We provide one-stop services...
我们一条龙服务！
...for IP rights protection.
⑤
糟糕，被海南自由贸易港社会信用信息共享平台曝光了！信用事关重大，再也不敢心存侥幸了。
Shoot! My misdeeds have been recorded on the Hainan FTP Social Credit Information Shared Platform. Credit is such a big deal, I don't think I'll be taking any chances again.
严重违法失信名单
⑦
看！我们设计的“无人船”是不是很厉害！
Check out the design for our "unmanned ship". Isn't it great?
这么厉害！黄总，记得申请专利呀！
So great! Don't forget to apply for a patent, Mr. Huang!
⑧
知否知否！
Brush up on your knowledge!
应是提高办事效率！
We'll work on boosting our efficiency!
外观设计专利
99%
⑨
保驾又护航！
Come innovate in the Hainan FTP...
放心来创新！
Where your IP rights are respected and protected!
来海南 放心“创”
⑩

案例注解 CASE NOTES

近年来，海南发挥中国特色自由贸易港的制度优势，对标世界最高水平开放形态，以知识产权制度集成创新为引领，以打造国际一流知识产权保护高地为目标，持续优化创新环境和营商环境，为高质量发展提供有力支撑。

Guided by integrated innovation of the intellectual property system, Hainan has recently been leveraging the institutional advantages of being a free trade port with Chinese characteristics, continued to move towards the benchmark of having the world's highest level of openness, and—with the goal of building itself into a world-class intellectual property protection highland—has both continued to optimize the innovation and business environments, and provided strong support for high-quality development.

案例进展 CURRENT STATUS

2024年，全省发明专利授权量2595件、有效商标注册量292315件，分别同比增长14.17%、20.62%。截至目前，全省共有13个地理标志保护产品，112件地理标志商标，年产值上亿元的地理标志产品达40件。

In 2024, the province registered 2,595 patents (up 14.17% year-on-year) and 292,315 valid trademarks (up 20.62% year-on-year). To date, the province has 13 geographical indication-protected products, 112 geographical indication trademarks, and 40 geographical indication products with an annual output value of over 100 million yuan.

活力园区　创业沃土

Getting Ahead in the Hainan FTP's Industrial Parks

画外音： 2023年，海南自贸港重点产业园区交出了亮眼的高质量发展答卷。从更深层次看这张“成绩单”，足见园区企业发展的蓬勃面貌、产业壮大的强劲势头。一方面，各重点园区用足用好国家、省级层面出台的各项政策，在用地、资金、税收等层面做好要素保障；另一方面，各重点园区以“多领域、全方位”的创新服务为企业生产经营支持助力。可以预见，在园区与企业的“双向奔赴”当中，定会铺陈海南自贸港高质量发展的满“园”春色。

Introduction: In 2023, the Hainan FTP's key industrial parks delivered a brilliant "report card" of high-quality development. Delving deeper into this "report card," the vigorous development of enterprises in the parks and the strong momentum of industrial growth are clear to see. At the policy level, the key industrial parks make full use of the various national and provincial policies to support and secure preferential treatment in aspects like land use, funding, and taxation. In terms of services, they support the production and operation of enterprises through innovative, comprehensive, cross-sector services. With the synergy between enterprises and industrial parks in full flow, the high-quality development of the Hainan FTP is assured.

A05

“营”在自贸港“画”说新海南

——优化营商环境专刊

海南日报

活力园区　创业沃土

2023年，海南自贸港重点产业园区营业收入突破2万亿元大关！作为海南高质量发展的主阵地，这些园区究竟亮出了哪些“赢商”秘籍？

通关顺畅　企业无忧

海南自贸港来为您服务!
The Hainan FTP is here to serve you!
①
石化新材料
洋浦经济开发区
数字经济
海口复兴城
现代金融
三亚中央商务区
②
我想下个月火速开工，可以吗?
We should be able to hit the ground running next month, right?
要素保障
店小二
全力解决，妥妥的!
We'll make sure of it!
③
跨境通关，"1"步到位!
Cross-border customs clearance: one (hour) and done!
海口江东新区
海关
1小时
通关效率提升98%
④
办结速度快到飞起，大半个月变1天搞定!
It takes just a day to sort out what used to take almost a month. That's efficiency!
海口综保区
审批
1日
⑤
Don't worry!
Thanks for your help!
⑥

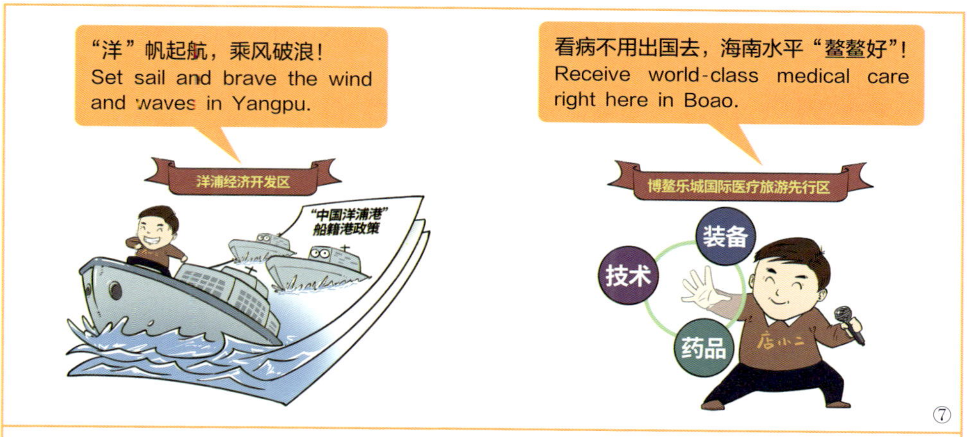
"洋"帆起航，乘风破浪！
Set sail and brave the wind and waves in Yangpu.
洋浦经济开发区
"中国洋浦港"船籍港政策
看病不用出国去，海南水平"鳌鳌好"！
Receive world-class medical care right here in Boao.
博鳌乐城国际医疗旅游先行区
装备
技术
药品
⑦

陵水黎安国际教育创新试验区
I like Lao Ba tea very much!
你这个外教很local哟！
I see you're becoming a local already!
⑧

你就放心干！
Just go ahead and get to it...
便捷有保障！
...we'll take care of the rest!
⑨

创业来园区，跨上新台阶！
Start on your new start-up adventure here in the Hainan FTP's key industrial parks.
补短板
强基础
优服务
⑩

案例注解 CASE NOTES

全国首个商业航天发射场顺利建设，洋浦百万吨乙烯项目建成投产，园区平台公司首单境外债券发行破题……近年来，海南重点产业园区在应对多重挑战中，实现经营主体加速聚集、有效投资和对外开放水平迈上新台阶，产业导入加速落地，重点产业集群初具规模。

Hainan has successfully built China's first commercial space launch site, put a million-ton ethylene project into production, and had an industrial park platform company successfully issue its first round of overseas bonds. In recent years, although Hainan's key industrial parks have faced multiple challenges, they have—as key industrial clusters have begun to take shape—achieved the accelerated gathering of business entities, have taken effective investment and opening-up to a new level, and are seeing a greater number of industries settle at a faster rate.

案例进展 CURRENT STATUS

2024年，海南自贸港13个重点园区累计实现营业收入25590.54亿元，增长7.9%。11个园区营业收入实现增长，其中6个园区实现两位数增长。

In 2024, the Hainan FTP's 13 key industrial parks achieved close to 2.56 trillion yuan in total operating income, representing a year-on-year increase of 7.9%. 11 of the 13 parks' operating income increased, and six of the 13 achieved double-digit growth.

厅局长走流程，“走新”更“走心”

Never Fear, the Director is Here!

画外音：走流程，发力在厅局长，落脚在群众，重点是解决企业和群众的“急难愁盼”。如何更好地做到这一点，实践已经给出答案：领导干部必须走在一线，走进现场。走好流程，不仅在一时之变，还要看长久之态。只有久久为功，走到深处，走到实处，将走流程活动更深入推进，才能将工作方式上的创新转化为制度革新的有力推手，真正构建起服务群众、助力发展的桥梁。

Introduction: Putting department and bureau directors on the front line and face-to-face with members of the public enables them to rapidly uncover pressing issues and bottlenecks within their department's workflow. This way, solutions can be achieved more easily. And it's not just for show. These department and bureau directors can be regularly found working on the front line, enabling them to discover more issues, propose changes, and monitor progress in optimizing and reforming workflows and processes in service of the public good.

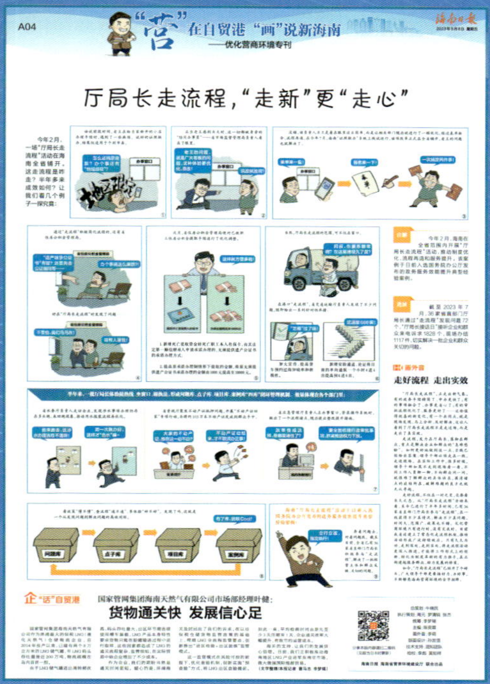
A04 “营”在自贸港 “画”说新海南 ——优化营商环境专刊 海南日报

厅局长走流程，“走新”更“走心”

今年2月，一场“厅局长走流程”活动在海南全省铺开。这走流程是咋走？半年多来成效如何？让我们看几个例子一探究竟：

走好流程 走出实效

企“话”自贸港

国家管网集团海南天然气有限公司市场部经理叶健：

货物通关快 发展信心足

海南日报 海南省营商环境建设厅 联合出品

怎么还搞限定款？办个事还有“地域歧视”？
Is this province running a "limited edition"? Why should location even matter for this application?
办事窗口
①
老王的问题，就是广大老板的问题，这种体验要优化，得改！
Your issue is one faced by many business owners. It's time for a change! We're going to optimize the process.
办事窗口
说改就改啊？
As simple as that?
②
表单来一套！
Fill in the form...
办事窗口
签名来一下！
...sign it...
表单
一次搞定两件事！
...and there we go!
许可证
③

“遗产继承公证书”有不？要先去公证哦，阿哥……
Do you have the notarized certificate of inheritance? You have to go get it notarized first...
省住房公积金管理局
办个事搞这么麻烦！
Such a hassle!
省住房公积金管理局
哇，有人罩我！
It's nice to have someone in my corner.
不要怕，我们马上改！
It's all good, sir. We'll optimize the process.
④
这样就方便多啦！
This is way more convenient!
提取死亡资金转入社保卡
办理金额提高至10000元
⑤
阿叔，你要去哪里啊？在这里堵很久了吧？
Where are you heading to, sir? Have you been stuck here long?
“预约”过了哦！
Booking confirmed!
预约
这速度太快了啊！
Now THIS is fast!
⑥

跑来跑去，这涉水办理流程不通啊！
This running around like a headless chicken just won't do!
跑一次就办好，这样才“色水”嘛。
One trip should be all you need!
大家的不动产证，放在这儿一动不动？
Should we really just be keeping everyone's real estate deeds here?
难
难
难
省自然资源和规划厅
不动产证动起来，才不耽误办正事！
Come grab your deeds. Don't wait until when you need them!
效率低成这样，是哪里堵住了？
This is taking forever. What's the issue?
堵
省应急管理厅
要全面梳理行政审批事项，抓紧推进权力下放。
It's time to review approval processes and see where we can delegate authority.
堵
⑦

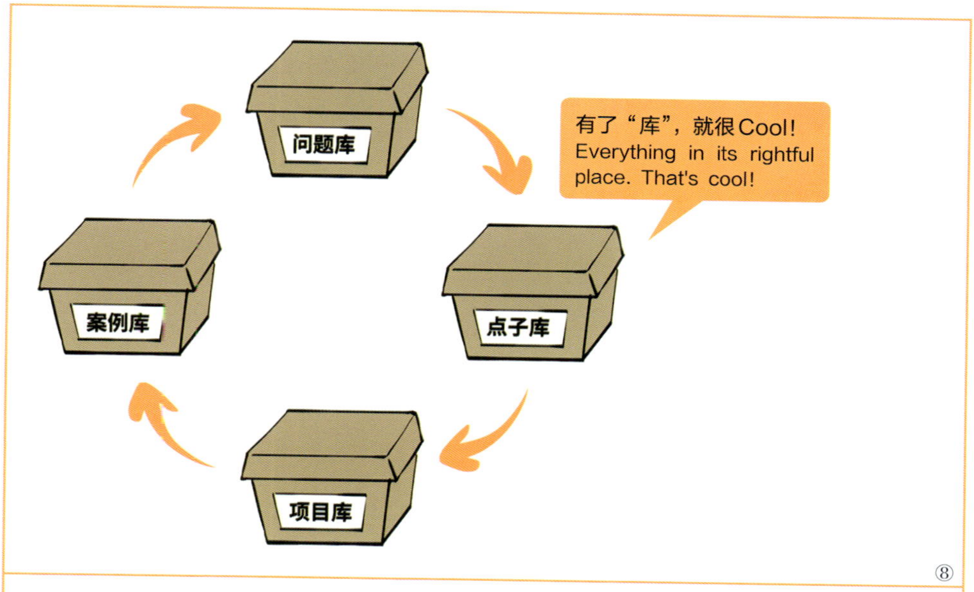
问题库
点子库
项目库
案例库
有了“库”，就很Cool! Everything in its rightful place. That's cool!
⑧

立行立改，指定能行! Review, revise, reform. We can do it!
⑨

案例注解 CASE NOTES

2023年2月，海南在全省范围内开展"厅局长走流程"活动，推动制度优化、流程再造和服务提升。该案例已入选国务院办公厅发布的政务服务效能提升典型经验案例。

In February 2023, Hainan launched a province-wide campaign to get department and bureau directors to go through application and approval procedures, promote institutional optimization, process reengineering, and service improvement. This case was selected by the General Office of the State Council as one of the model experience cases on improving the efficiency of government services.

案例进展 CURRENT STATUS

2024年，全省48个省直成员单位和18个市县共开展走流程1313次，发现并解决问题962个。"厅局长接话日"接听企业和群众来电诉求1222件，现场办结713件，转办办结509件，满意度达91.84%，切实解决一批企业和群众关切的问题。

In 2024, all 48 of Hainan's provincial-level work units, and all 18 cities and counties conducted a total of 1,313 process inspections, and identified and addressed 962 problems. Effectively solving a number of issues that concern enterprises and the general public, "Director is In" activities received 1, 222 calls from businesses and members of the public, with 713 cases handled on site, 509 cases transferred and completed, and a satisfaction rate reaching 91.84%.

纳税“信”时代，诚信赢未来！

Tax Integrity: Trust Wins the Future

画外音：海南建设自由贸易港，营造稳定、公平、透明、可预期的营商环境，深入推进社会信用体系建设是题中应有之义。随着信息技术的不断发展，信用体系建设包含的内容、适用的范畴也进一步扩大，影响力与日俱增。加快社会信用体系建设，需要政府部门和全社会一起努力，积极倡导和培育全社会诚信意识，推动形成崇尚诚信、践行诚信的良好风尚，让信用成为最好的通行证，让守信者畅通无阻，让失信者寸步难行。

Introduction: In the process of building a free trade port, Hainan is striving to create a stable, fair, transparent, and predictable business environment, which involves deepening the construction of a social credit system. With the continuous development of information technology, the content and scope of the credit system construction have been further expanded, and its impact continues to grow. To accelerate the construction of a social credit system, it is necessary for government departments and society as a whole to work together to actively advocate and cultivate honest behavior and make personal credit a key factor in determining trustworthiness, so that those who are trustworthy can enjoy added convenience and those who are not are restricted in their business activities.

A06

“营”在自贸港 “画”说新海南

——优化营商环境专刊

纳税“信”时代，诚信赢未来！

不久前，2023年度全国信用承诺案例评选结果公布，海南省税务局报送的一项经验做法获优秀案例奖，怎么个优秀法？赶紧来瞧一瞧……

企“话”自贸港

中国铁建投资集团副总经理、总会计师刘宇栋：

在海南，办事省心、投资放心、兴业顺心

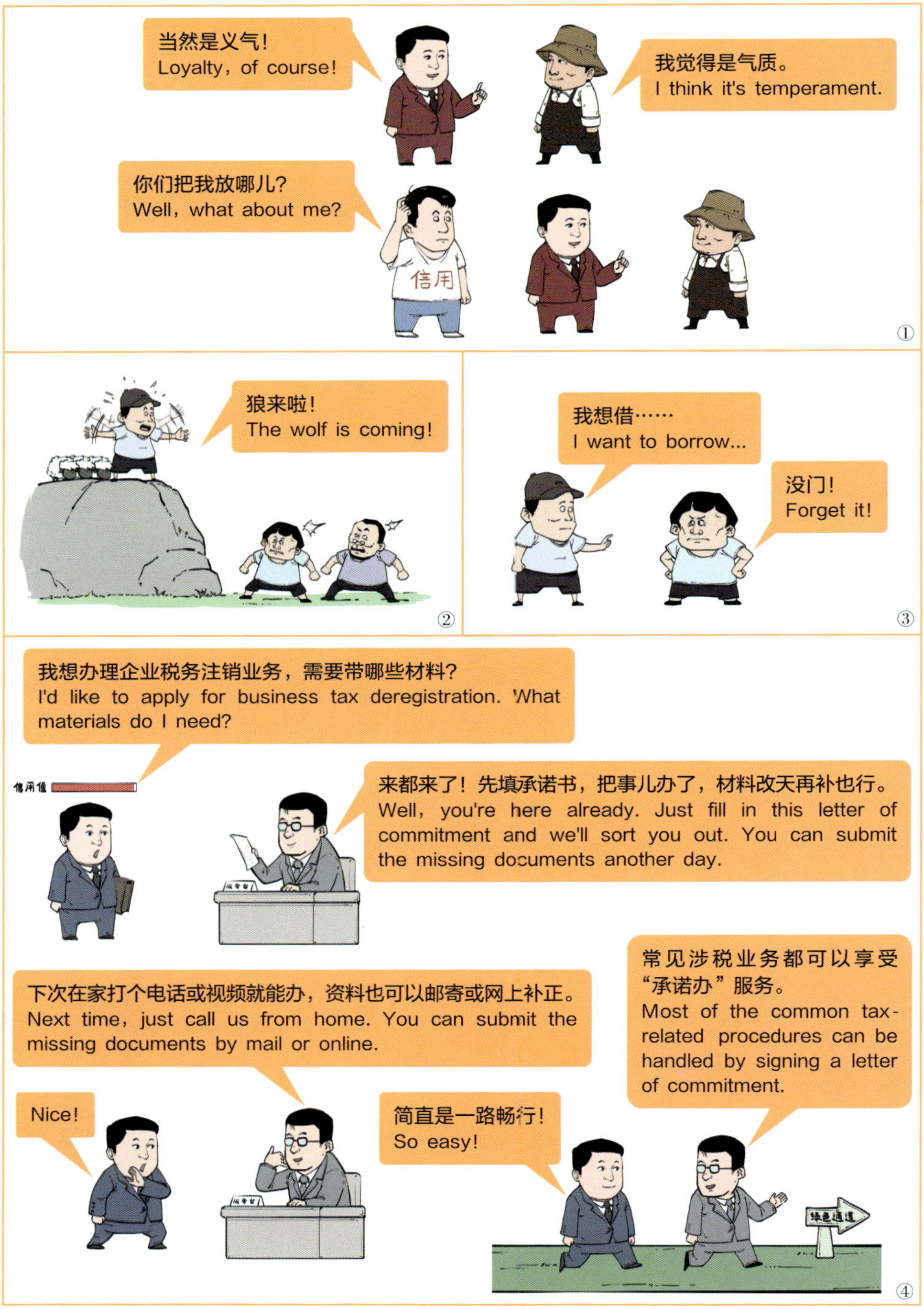
当然是义气！
Loyalty, of course!
我觉得是气质。
I think it's temperament.
你们把我放哪儿？
Well, what about me?
信用
①
狼来啦！
The wolf is coming!
②
我想借……
I want to borrow...
没门！
Forget it!
③
我想办理企业税务注销业务，需要带哪些材料？
I'd like to apply for business tax deregistration. What materials do I need?
信用值
来都来了！先填承诺书，把事儿办了，材料改天再补也行。
Well, you're here already. Just fill in this letter of commitment and we'll sort you out. You can submit the missing documents another day.
下次在家打个电话或视频就能办，资料也可以邮寄或网上补正。
Next time, just call us from home. You can submit the missing documents by mail or online.
Nice!
简直是一路畅行！
So easy!
常见涉税业务都可以享受"承诺办"服务。
Most of the common tax-related procedures can be handled by signing a letter of commitment.
④

是我给你自由过了火……
As for you, well...perhaps my confidence in you was overestimated.
虚假承诺书
失信惩戒名单
⑤
我们的目标是：让守信者处处受益，失信者寸步难行！
Our goal is to reward the trustworthy with convenience and impose restrictions on the dishonest.
⑥
实力不允许我低调。
And that's how the cookie crumbles!
另一个是万宁的“信用+免审”政务服务新模式，去年咱就介绍过了。
There's also the new "credit+exemption" model for government services in Wanning that was introduced last year.
等等，不是说这一次海南拿到了两个优秀奖吗?
Wait. Didn't Hainan win two Excellence Awards this time?
一看就是没认真听讲，赶紧扫码复习复习。
It seems that someone wasn't listening. Scan the QR code and read it over again.
⑦

案例注解 CASE NOTES

海南税务系统在信用办税“承诺办”“容缺办”基础上，从服务广度和服务深度两个维度进一步探索创新，强化守信激励和失信惩戒价值导向，不断提升纳税信用应用的经济效益和社会效益。

Based on the tax credit system, which includes "commitment-based processing" and "conditional approval", the Hainan's tax system will further explore innovation in terms of both service breadth and depth, strengthen the value orientation of rewarding trustworthiness and punishing dishonesty, and continuously improve the economic and social benefits of tax credit utilization.

案例进展 CURRENT STATUS

海南省税务局依托纳税信用管理系统，以多个层面多种方式建立信用激励惩戒机制，并不断完善纳税信用管理制度，为诚信纳税人提供便捷服务，对失信纳税人采取惩戒措施，“宽办”与“严管”并行，有效倡导诚信涉税理念、激发经营主体活力，有效促进诚信体系建设。

Relying on the tax credit management system, the Hainan Provincial Tax Service has established multiple kinds of credit incentive and punishment mechanisms at various levels, improved the tax credit management system, provided convenient services for honest taxpayers, and taken disciplinary measures against dishonest taxpayers. "Leniency" and "strict management" go hand in hand, effectively advocating the concept of honesty in tax-related matters. This not only stimulates the vitality of business entities, but also serves to advance the construction of an integrity system.

法治护航，让企业经营更安心

A Law-based FTP: Better for Business

画外音：法治是最好的营商环境。海南要打造的一流营商环境，是市场化、法治化、国际化的营商环境，从法治化的“排名”也不难看出其地位。设立涉企执法工作联系点、推进行政机关负责人出庭应诉改革……只要花心思、动脑筋，下功夫、出实招，从影响企业和群众法治获得感的痛点堵点着手，主动作为、攻坚克难，充分保障经营主体合法权益，海南打造的法治化营商环境，既有“法”的刚性约束力，又能有接地气的人情味。

Introduction: A law-based business environment is the best kind of environment. The first-class business environment that Hainan wants to create is market-oriented, law-based, and international, and convenient, and its status can be easily seen by how it ranks in terms of the legal environment. Hainan is establishing contact points for enterprise-related law enforcement and is ensuring that heads of administrative agencies appear in court to respond to lawsuits. By investing time and effort, taking practical measures, and tackling issues and bottlenecks that affect the sense of gain of enterprises and the public under the rule of law, Hainan aims to take proactive steps, overcome difficulties, and fully protect the legitimate rights and interests of business entities. In doing so, the province is building a law-based business environment that combines the rigid binding force of the law with a down-to-earth human touch.

A05

“营”在自贸港 “画”说新海南

——优化营商环境专刊

法治护航，让企业经营更安心

法治既是市场经济的内在要求，也是其良性运行的根本保障。为了优化法治营商环境，近年来，海南各部门及市县想出了不少新招——

企“话”自贸港

中国石化海南炼油化工有限公司安全消防保卫岗主管赫荣杰：

贴心服务让消防验收省时省心

赵老板，检查一下。
Mr. Zhao, I'm here to perform an inspection.
里面请。
Come in, please.
xx酒店
xx部门
赵老板，我们要检查哦。
Mr. Zhao, I'm here to perform an inspection.
又来???
Again?!
xx酒店
①
不查，怕漏掉风险隐患。
If we don't inspect, we might end up missing risks or hidden dangers.
查嘛，又影响人家做生意。
But if we do inspect, we might end up impacting business.
②
赵老板，这次检查时间、要求、事项都在表里，辛苦你看一看。
Mr. Zhao, the inspection time, requirements, and items are shown here on this form. Please take a look.
好的，我提前准备一下，就可以不影响营业。
OK. I'll make the necessary arrangements so that it doesn't impact my business.
检查时间:
检查内容:
检查要求:
问题清单收好哦，这些改好就行啦。
Here's a list of issues we found. Please make the necessary changes.
xx部门
xx部门
收到，马上改!
Received! I'll get right on it!
③

涉企执法工作联系点
有意见，尽管提。
Don't hesitate to share your suggestions or complaints with us.
④
不利于促进公平竞争、损害营商环境的制度规定，通通都丢掉！
We're chucking away all institutional regulations that are not conducive to promoting fair competition or are damaging the business environment.
垃圾桶
⑤
加快办案速度，不给游客添堵，帮助企业恢复营业。
We're speeding up procedures so that tourists aren't impacted, and businesses can get back in business quickly.
⑥
你有困难，我有办法！
We won't overburden you with fines if you can't pay.
减免执行费
23400元
⑦
法治政府建设，我看行！
This law-based approach really is the bee's knees!
原告
被告
我们要直面问题，才能真正解决问题！
We can only properly solve problems if we face them head-on!
⑧
放心来经营！
Running a business in Hainan?
海南有办“法”！
Let the law look after you!
⑨

案例注解 CASE NOTES

法治是最好的营商环境。近年来，海南各部门、各市县加快推动政府职能转变，不断提高依法行政水平，依法平等保护各类经营主体产权和合法权益，并持续打造公平、透明、可预期的法治化营商环境。

The best business environment is one that is law-based. In recent years, Hainan's provincial-level departments, cities, and counties have been accelerating the transformation of government functions. They have continuously worked to improve the level of administration according to the law, have equally protected the property rights and legitimate rights and interests of all types of business entities in accordance with the law, and continued to create a fair, transparent, and predictable business environment based on the rule of law.

案例进展 CURRENT STATUS

2024年，海南开展了为期4个月的优化法治化营商环境专项普法活动，通过送法进企业进园区、法治赋能企业发展集中宣传、民营企业"法治体检"、防范非法集资普法宣传等系列举措，更好地回应经营主体法治需求，并引导经营主体增强诚信守法经营意识。

In 2024, Hainan launched a four-month-long special legal education campaign to optimize the law-based business environment. Through a series of measures (such as bringing legal education to enterprises and industrial parks, concentrated publicity on how the rule of law empowers enterprise development, "legal health checks" of private enterprises, and popularization of legal knowledge on topics such as illegal fundraising), Hainan has been able to better respond to the legal needs of business entities, and guide business entities towards enhancing their awareness of abiding by the law and operating with integrity.

经营主体有了“全景画像”

What's in a Name?

画外音：归集、更新涉企信息，并将各类涉企信息纳入经营主体社会信用记录，海南相关部门给近百万经营主体“画像”，为企业经营活动及政府监管工作提供数据支持和重要依据。从中，我们能看到数据资源的价值和作用。相关部门需要推动多层级数据联通、多领域数据融合，打破部门、区域之间的数据壁垒，提供更多满足各方需求的数据服务，以数据资源的整合共享和开发利用，为自贸港建设提供更加坚实有力的数据支撑。

Introduction: By collecting and updating enterprise-related information and including all types of enterprise-related information in the social credit records of business entities, the relevant departments of the Hainan Provincial Government have "portraits" of nearly one million business entities, providing data support and an important foundation for business operations and government supervision. From this, we can see the value and role of data resources. Relevant departments should strive to promote multi-level data connectivity and multi-field data integration, break down data barriers between different departments and administrative regions, provide more data services that meet the needs of all parties, and provide more solid and powerful data support for the construction of the Hainan FTP through the integration, sharing, development and utilization of data resources.

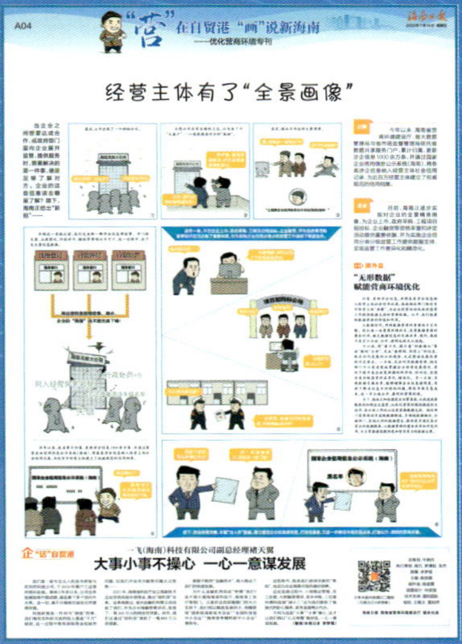
A04

“营”在自贸港 “画”说新海南

——优化营商环境专刊

经营主体有了“全景画像”

当企业之间想要达成合作，或政府部门要向企业展开监管、提供服务时，需要解决的第一件事，便是要了解对方。企业的这些信息该去哪里了解？眼下，海南正给出“新招”——

目前，海南正逐步实现对企业的全景精准画像，为企业上市、政府采购、工程项目招投标、企业融资等资格审查和评定活动提供重要依据，并为实施企业信用分类分级监管工作提供数据支持，实现监管工作差异化和精准化。

画外音

“无形数据”赋能营商环境优化

企“话”自贸港

一飞（海南）科技有限公司副总经理褚天翼

大事小事不操心 一心一意谋发展

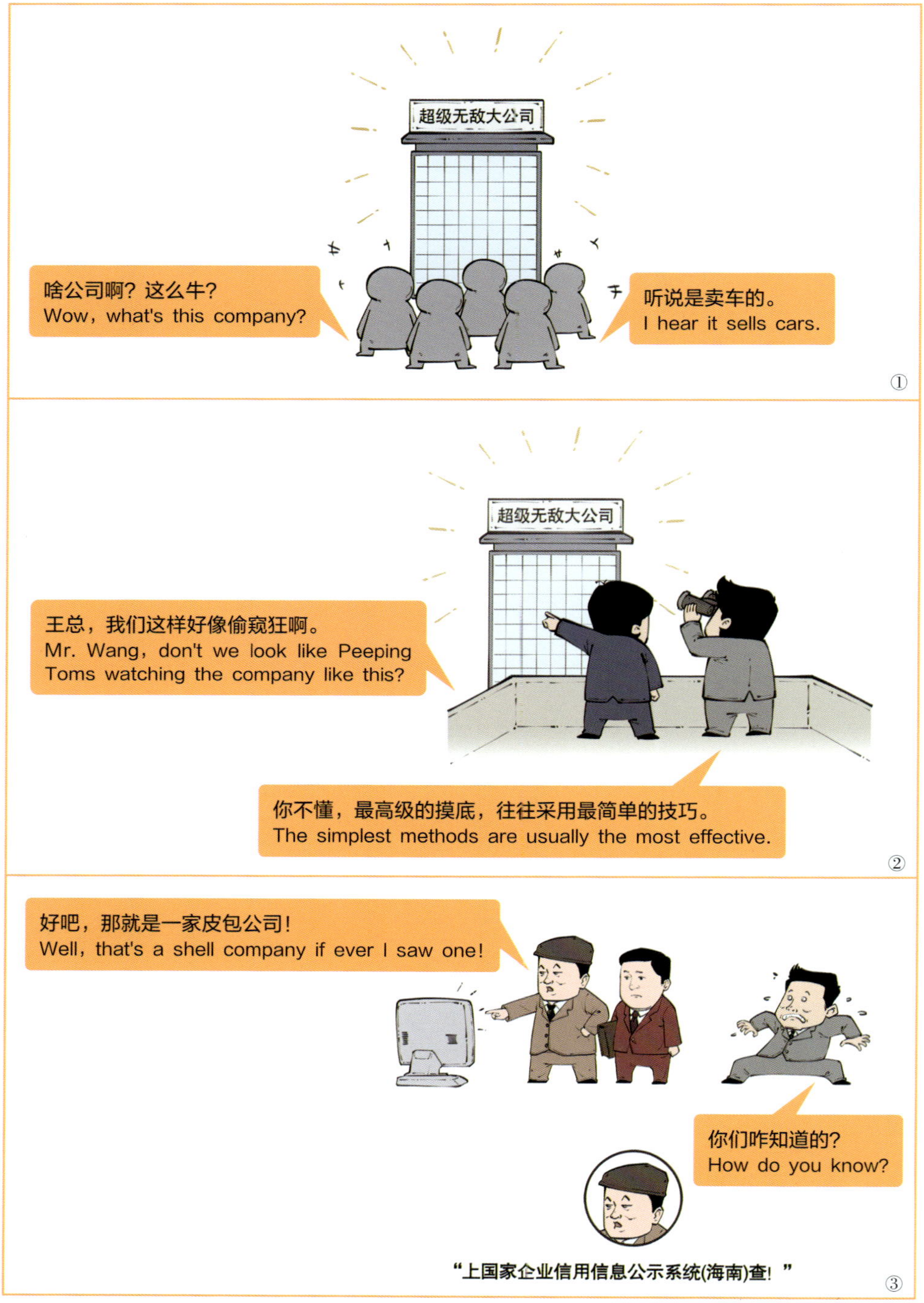
超级无敌大公司
啥公司啊？这么牛？
Wow, what's this company?
听说是卖车的。
I hear it sells cars.
①
超级无敌大公司
王总，我们这样好像偷窥狂啊。
Mr. Wang, don't we look like Peeping Toms watching the company like this?
你不懂，最高级的摸底，往往采用最简单的技巧。
The simplest methods are usually the most effective.
②
好吧，那就是一家皮包公司！
Well, that's a shell company if ever I saw one!
你们咋知道的？
How do you know?
“上国家企业信用信息公示系统(海南)查！”
③

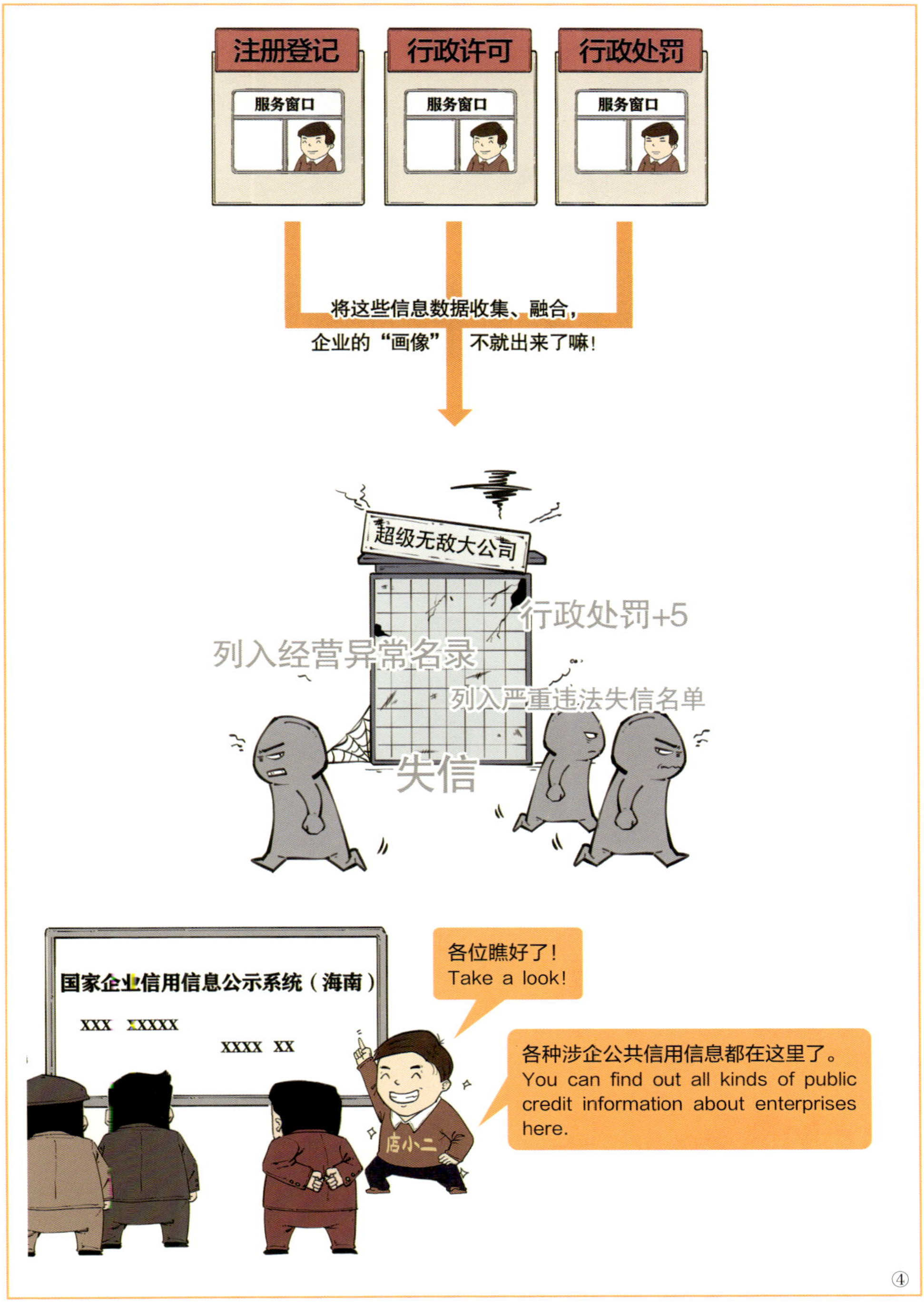
注册登记
服务窗口
行政许可
服务窗口
行政处罚
服务窗口
将这些信息数据收集、融合，
企业的“画像”不就出来了嘛！
超级无敌大公司
行政处罚+5
列入经营异常名录
列入严重违法失信名单
失信
国家企业信用信息公示系统（海南）
XXX XXXXX
XXXX XX
各位瞧好了！
Take a look!
各种涉企公共信用信息都在这里了。
You can find out all kinds of public credit information about enterprises here.
店小二
④

借点钱花花……
Please, I...need...money...
不能借哦，你们公司上了失信黑名单。
I'm sorry, we can't extend a loan to you today. Your company has been blacklisted.
我资金厚！
I've got lots of cash.
项目招投标会场
我实力强！
I've got lots of skills.
我名声好！
I've got a reputation.
你名声好臭，OUT！
Yes, a stinking reputation. OUT!
你为啥总查这家？
Why are you always checking on this company?
风险高
你看看，他家信用风险多高，不检查勤点能行吗？
Look here! This company has a high credit risk. Isn't it better to keep an eye on it?
⑤

投这个项目，每月多赚“亿”点点！
Invest in this project. I guarantee a handsome return!
你的真面目，我早就一清二楚了！
I've already clocked you.
国家企业信用信息公示系统（海南）
黑名单
还想有两副面孔？你问问公示平台答不答应！
Who do you think you're fooling? Certainly not the National Enterprise Credit Information Publicity System!
⑥

案例注解 CASE NOTES

2023年以来，海南省营商环境建设厅、海南省大数据管理局（2024年10月正式更名为海南省大数据发展中心）与海南省市场监督管理局依托海南省数据共享服务门户，累计归集、更新涉企信息1000余万条，并通过国家企业信用信息公示系统（海南），将各类涉企信息纳入经营主体社会信用记录，为约百万经营主体建立了权威规范的信用档案。

Starting from 2023, the Hainan Provincial Department of Business Environment Development, Big Data Administration of Hainan Province (officially renamed as Big Data Development Center of Hainan Province in October 2024) and Hainan Provincial Market Regulation Bureau have relied on the Hainan Provincial Data Sharing Service Portal to collect and update over ten million pieces of enterprise-related information, and—through the National Enterprise Credit Information Publicity System (Hainan)—included all types of enterprise-related information in business entities' social credit records, and established authoritative and standardized credit files for approximately one million business entities.

案例进展 CURRENT STATUS

目前，海南正逐步实现对企业的全景精准画像，为企业上市、政府采购、工程项目招投标、企业融资等资格审查和评定活动提供重要依据，并为实施企业信用分类分级监管工作提供数据支持，实现监管工作差异化和精准化。

Currently, Hainan's gradual realization of a comprehensive and accurate portrait of its enterprises is providing an essential reference for qualification review and assessment activities such as being listed on the stock market, government procurement, project bidding, and corporate financing, and it also provides data support for the implementation of enterprise credit classification and grading supervision to achieve differentiated and precise supervision.

第三章
Section 3

破解难题，落实见真招
Solving Problems

鹦鹉出岛记

The Parrot's Departure

画外音：人工繁育的鹦鹉无法检验检疫，也就无法入市交易。面对企业的燃眉之急，督办人员对问题紧盯不放，反复沟通、协调，相关单位担当作为，遇事不后退，深入研究规章制度，在政策范围内大胆创新、协同攻关，最终寻得破题之策。这启示我们，解决问题，要去掉一个“怕”字，抓好一个“实”字，不畏难、不惧责，方能赢得企业好口碑。

Introduction: Under current regulations, parrots bred in captivity cannot usually be inspected and quarantined and, therefore, cannot be traded. However, a parrot-breeding enterprise urgently needed to export parrots, so quarantine and inspection supervisors sprang into action, communicating and coordinating with relevant agencies. These agencies studied the current rules and regulations in depth, innovating within the regulatory framework, working together to tackle key problems and eventually came up with a solution. When faced with such challenges, all government departments and agencies should be similarly bold and proactive to achieve results and win the admiration of the individuals and enterprises they serve.

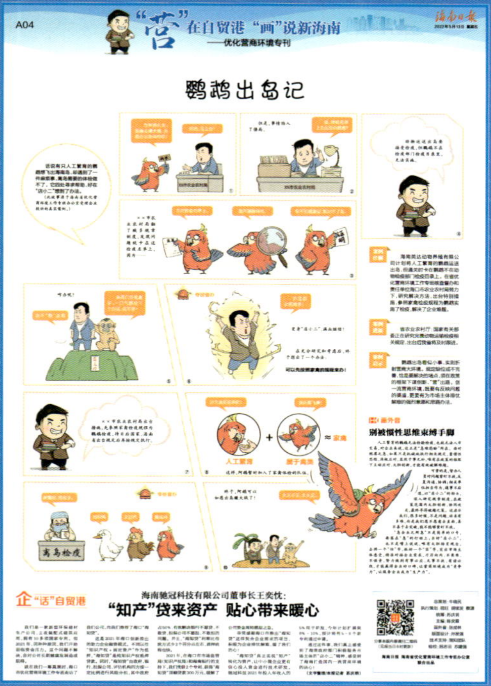
A04 “官”在自贸港 “画”说新海南

——优化营商环境专刊

鹦鹉出岛记

别被惯性思维束缚手脚

企“话”自贸港

海南驰冠科技有限公司董事长王奕忱：

“知产”贷来资产 贴心带来暖心

世界那么大，我要去赚大钱，为我办出岛体检吧！
It's a big world out there with lots of opportunities. Sir, I'm here for my physical!
诉求
好的，马上办！
Let's get you sorted, then!
XX市农业农村局
①
咦，检验检疫名单上怎么没有“鹦鹉”？
Huh? Why don't I see "parrot" on the quarantine inspection list?
XX市农业农村局
②
不在名单上，
Because I'm not on the list...
名单
就不能做体检。
...I can't get my physical.
拿不到健康证，就出不了岛。
Without a health certificate, I'm stuck here in Hainan.
证明
③

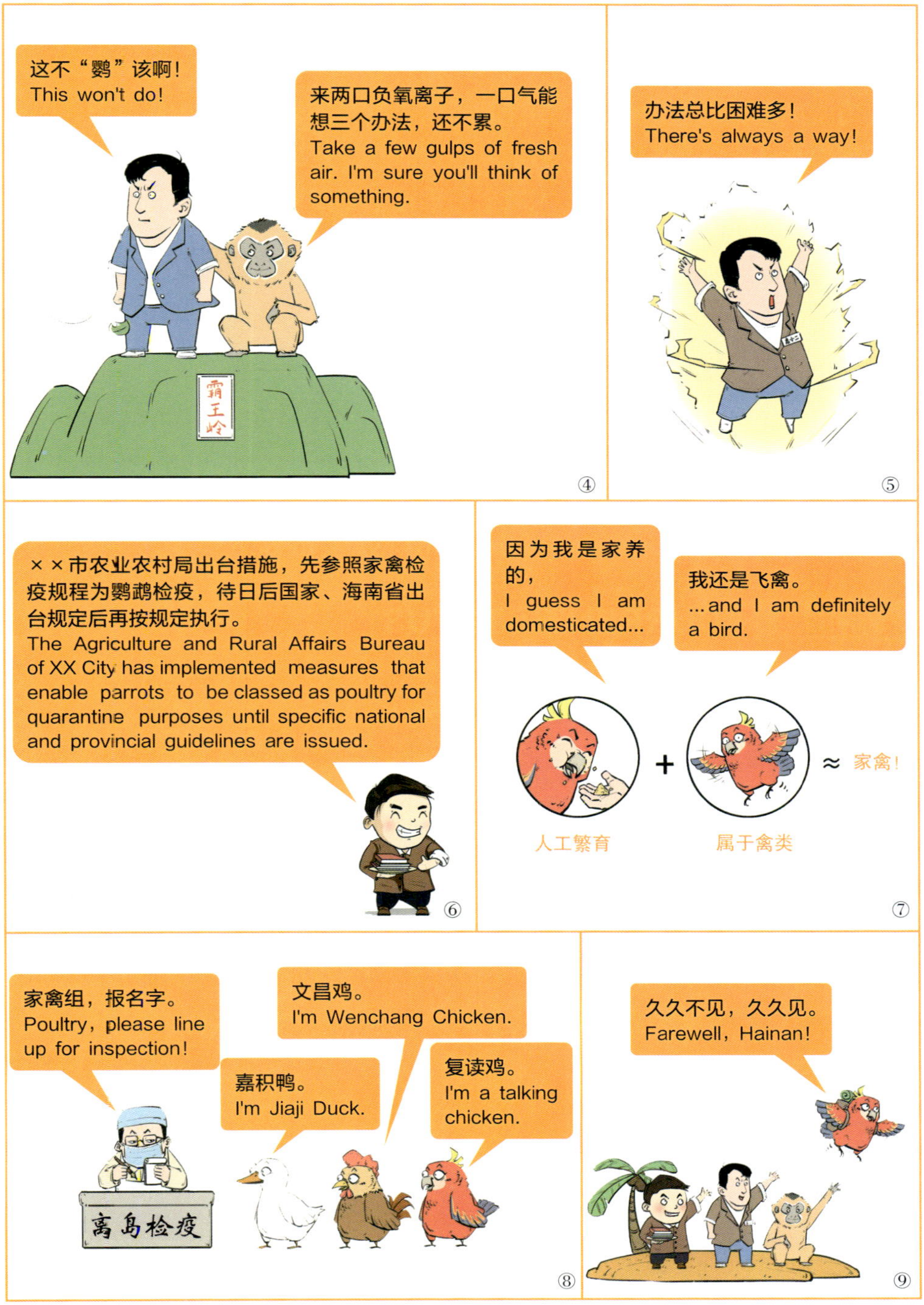
这不“鹦”该啊！
This won't do!
来两口负氧离子，一口气能想三个办法，还不累。
Take a few gulps of fresh air. I'm sure you'll think of something.
霸王岭
④
办法总比困难多！
There's always a way!
⑤
× × 市农业农村局出台措施，先参照家禽检疫规程为鹦鹉检疫，待日后国家、海南省出台规定后再按规定执行。
The Agriculture and Rural Affairs Bureau of XX City has implemented measures that enable parrots to be classed as poultry for quarantine purposes until specific national and provincial guidelines are issued.
⑥
因为我是家养的，
I guess I am domesticated...
我还是飞禽。
...and I am definitely a bird.
人工繁育
+
属于禽类
≈ 家禽！
⑦
家禽组，报名字。
Poultry, please line up for inspection!
离岛检疫
嘉积鸭。
I'm Jiaji Duck.
文昌鸡。
I'm Wenchang Chicken.
复读鸡。
I'm a talking chicken.
⑧
久久不见，久久见。
Farewell, Hainan!
⑨

案例注解 CASE NOTES

海南英达动物养殖有限公司计划将人工繁育的鹦鹉运送出岛，但通关时卡在鹦鹉不在动物检疫部门检疫目录上。在海口市农业农村局努力下，研究解决方法，出台特别措施，参照家禽检疫规程为鹦鹉实施了检疫，解决了企业难题。

Hainan Yingda Animal Breeding Co., Ltd. planned to transport artificially bred parrots off the island, but the parrots got held up during customs clearance procedures. However, after much hard work and effort on the part of the Haikou Municipal Bureau of Agriculture and Rural Affairs, special measures were introduced to implement quarantine for the parrots in accordance with poultry inspection and quarantine procedures, and the company's problems were resolved.

最新进展 CURRENT STATUS

海南省农业农村厅：国家有关部委正在研究完善动物运输检疫相关规定，出台后我省将及时跟进。

According to the Hainan Provincial Department of Agriculture and Rural Affairs, "relevant state ministries and commissions are now looking into how to improve relevant regulations on animal transportation and quarantine. Once these come out, Hainan will make a timely follow-up".

受理“吐槽”，“店小二”是认真的！

Service Specialists Take Complaints Seriously

画外音：以往，企业遇到难题，要到多个部门反馈，甚至会遭遇“踢皮球”的无奈。如此一来，政企沟通不畅，堵点难以解决，营商环境优化无从谈起。海南上线营商环境问题受理平台，架起直达企业的桥梁，成为发现问题的“眼睛”，倾听企业意见的“耳朵”，排忧解难的“出气筒”，传递出一种态度，展现出一种决心。直面“吐槽声”，在动真碰硬中努力做到事事有答复、件件有回应，必能持续释放平台效应，稳稳托起海南发展“金饭碗”。

Introduction: In the past, when enterprises encountered problems, they had to give feedback to multiple departments that may have ended up playing hot potato with their responsibilities. As a result, communication between the government and enterprises was clunky, bottlenecks were numerous and challenging to resolve, and there was no way to optimize the business environment. Hainan has launched a provincial business environment complaint-handling platform, linking enterprises directly with government departments and becoming the eyes, ears, and hands of the government in listening to, responding to, and handling complaints. By tackling challenges head-on and ensuring that every issue gets a response and every concern is addressed, the platform will continue to amplify its impact, providing solid support for Hainan's development.

A04

“营”在自贸港“画”说新海南

——优化营商环境专刊

受理“吐槽”，“店小二”是认真的！

企“话”自贸港

陆安置业集团有限公司副总经理王丰伟：

情系企业办实事 高效服务暖人心

说好的“渔翁得利”呢?
Eh? I was here first!
政府用地
哎呀！怎么选到同一块地了?
How did we end up with the same plot of land?
100
100
100
说好的扶我一把呢?
I thought you said you would help me!
建设方案
使用权，我有啊!
I have the right to use the land.
这是新事物，不敢随便批。
I'm sorry, sir. This project is something new to us. We can't just give you the green light.
①

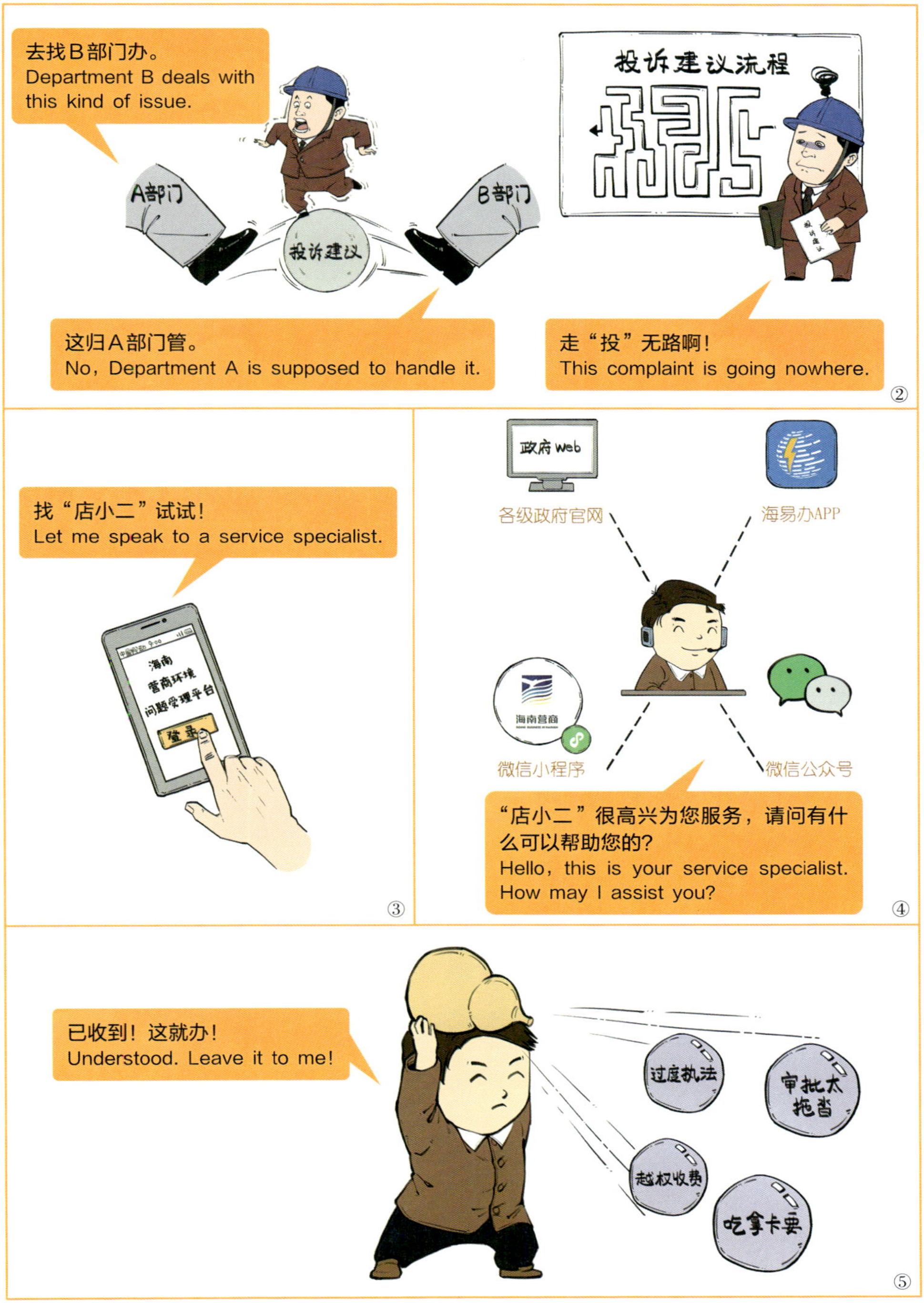
去找B部门办。
Department B deals with this kind of issue.
A部门
B部门
投诉建议
这归A部门管。
No, Department A is supposed to handle it.
投诉建议流程
投诉建议
走“投”无路啊！
This complaint is going nowhere.
②
找“店小二”试试！
Let me speak to a service specialist.
海南
营商环境
问题受理平台
登录
③
政府web
各级政府官网
海易办APP
海南营商
微信小程序
微信公众号
“店小二”很高兴为您服务，请问有什么可以帮助您的？
Hello, this is your service specialist. How may I assist you?
④
已收到！这就办！
Understood. Leave it to me!
过度执法
审批太拖沓
越权收费
吃拿卡要
⑤

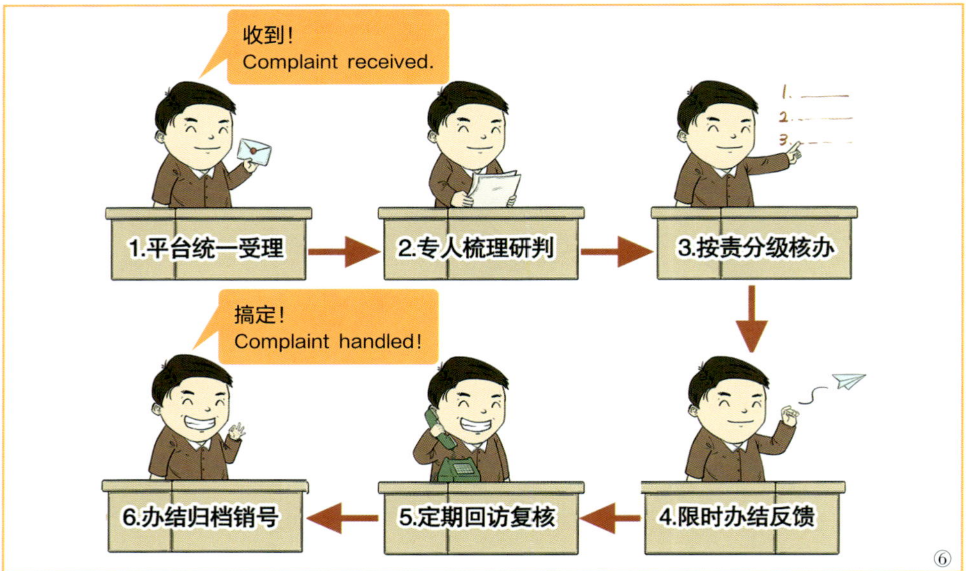
收到！
Complaint received.
1.平台统一受理
2.专人梳理研判
3.按责分级核办
搞定！
Complaint handled!
4.限时办结反馈
5.定期回访复核
6.办结归档销号

⑥

这地总算能用起来了。
Finally! I can use the land.
政府规划打了架，可不能让企业背锅。
Sorry, this issue was caused by government planning. The enterprise is not to blame.

⑦

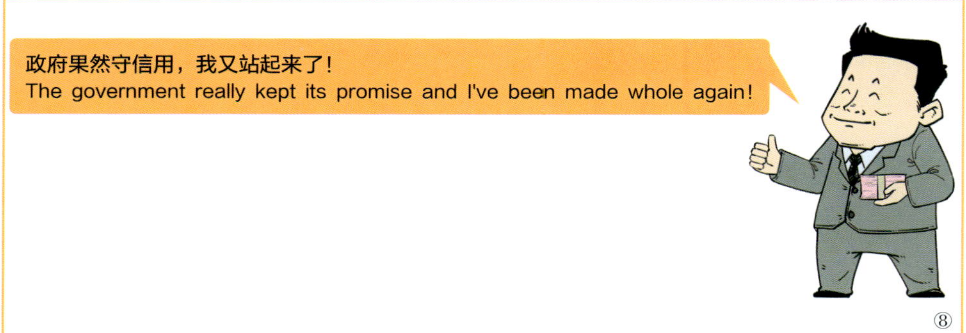
政府果然守信用，我又站起来了！
The government really kept its promise and I've been made whole again!

⑧

建设方案
总算通过了！
Finally! The project has been approved!
合理的新鲜事物，咱得鼓励！
We must encourage new kinds of projects, within reason of course.
⑨
有了这个，问题批量解决，直接“消消乐”！
Thanks to these official opinions, we can handle relevant issues in one go and satisfy all parties.
不动产登记
历史遗留问题
处理意见
海南营商环境问题受理平台
⑩
我有个建议……
I have a suggestion...
诸葛总但说无妨。
Let's hear it, Mr. Zhuge.
海南营商环境问题受理平台
⑪
绝不回避，接诉即办！
We face complaints head-on. Just let us know!
⑫

案例注解 CASE NOTES

为构建一个畅通、高效的政企沟通渠道，海南于2021年6月上线“海南营商环境问题受理平台”，充分当好发现问题的“眼睛”，倾听企业意见的“耳朵”，排忧解难的“出气筒”，及时收集解决经营主体遇到的各类问题，从而更好地服务于各类经营主体，更精准、更高效优化营商环境。

In order to build a smooth and efficient communication channel between government and enterprises, Hainan launched its Hainan Business Environment Issues Acceptance Platform in June 2021. To better serve various business entities and accurately and efficiently optimize the business environment, this platform not only collects and solves various problems in a timely fashion, but also serves as the "eyes" that see problems encountered by business entities, the "ears" that listen to their opinions, and the "punching bag" for venting their frustrations. By addressing these issues effectively, the platform better serves market entities, ensures a more precise and efficient response to their needs, and continuously improves the business environment.

案例进展 CURRENT STATUS

截至2025年2月，海南营商环境问题受理平台共收到营商环境问题8776件，办结8248件，办结率93.98%，扎实推进存量问题的逐步清零，新增问题得到有效遏制，正不断提升经营主体的满意度和获得感。

Constantly improving business entities' satisfaction and sense of gain and solidly promoting both the gradual elimination of existing problems and the effective containment of new problems, 8,248 of the 8,776 business environment-related complaints received by the Hainan Business Environment Issues Acceptance Platform in February 2025 were solved, a rate of 93.98%.

大话“信”游

A Case of Broken Credit

画外音：信用是最好的通行证，守信者一路畅行，失信者寸步难行。一旦被认定为失信者，是不是意味着终身要顶着“失信”的帽子？海南推行的信用修复制度可帮助失信主体修复信用，不仅有利于激发已有失信记录的商事主体自我纠错的动力，还可以促进守信激励和失信惩戒机制全面发挥作用，体现了监管的包容审慎和容错纠错的温度。

Introduction: Having good credit opens doors. Trustworthy enterprises will be welcomed in, but untrustworthy ones will have those same doors slammed in their faces. Should this mean that enterprises that have been labeled untrustworthy need to bear this label for life? The credit repair system implemented by Hainan helps discredited entities restore their creditworthiness. This arrangement is not only conducive to motivating commercial entities with negative records to correct their own mistakes, but it also promotes the thorough application of incentive and punishment mechanisms, all while reflecting the inclusiveness and prudence of supervision and the warmth of tolerance and correction.

A04

“营”在自贸港 “画”说新海南

——优化营商环境专刊

海南日报

大话“信”游

企“话”自贸港

三亚用友软件科技有限公司基建工程部负责人朱兆志：

政府“买单”为企业减负增效

孙总，你有个手续没报批，有笔费用也没及时交！
Mr. Sun, you've failed to submit paperwork for approval and haven't paid your bills on time.
哎呀！大意了，给忙忘了！
Oops! I was just so caught up with other things that I forgot.
花果山公司
①
老二钱庄
老二，我……
My friend, would you...
别套近乎，跟你不熟。
Don't "friend" me. I barely know you.
②
这地块不错，给我来块！
I like this plot. I'll take it!
国有土地出让
孙总，我突然想起家里煤气没关，先走一步。
About that... erm... sorry, I left the gas on at home. I'll be going now.
③

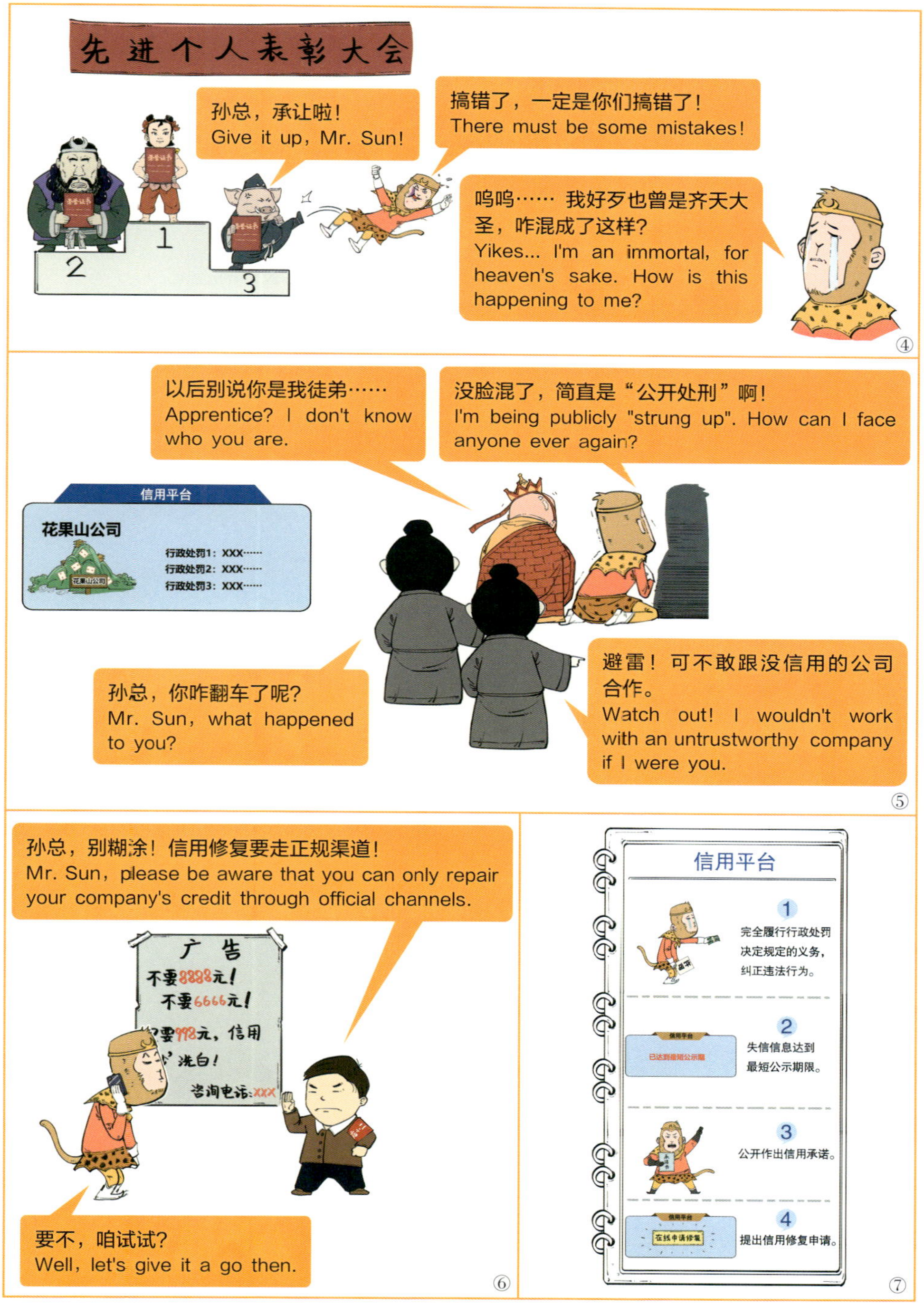
先进个人表彰大会
孙总，承让啦！
Give it up, Mr. Sun!
搞错了，一定是你们搞错了！
There must be some mistakes!
呜呜…… 我好歹也曾是齐天大圣，咋混成了这样？
Yikes... I'm an immortal, for heaven's sake. How is this happening to me?
1
2
3
④
以后别说你是我徒弟……
Apprentice? I don't know who you are.
没脸混了，简直是“公开处刑”啊！
I'm being publicly "strung up". How can I face anyone ever again?
信用平台
花果山公司
行政处罚1：XXX……
行政处罚2：XXX……
行政处罚3：XXX……
孙总，你咋翻车了呢？
Mr. Sun, what happened to you?
避雷！可不敢跟没信用的公司合作。
Watch out! I wouldn't work with an untrustworthy company if I were you.
⑤
孙总，别糊涂！信用修复要走正规渠道！
Mr. Sun, please be aware that you can only repair your company's credit through official channels.
广 告
不要8888元！
不要6666元！
要998元，信用
洗白！
咨询电话：XXX
要不，咱试试？
Well, let's give it a go then.
⑥
信用平台
1 完全履行行政处罚决定规定的义务，纠正违法行为。
2 失信信息达到最短公示期限。
3 公开作出信用承诺。
4 提出信用修复申请。
⑦

信用查询
花果山公司:
无行政处罚记录
这算不算是信用"洗白"了?
Is my company in the all-clear then?
想啥呢?只是不公示了而已,信息都在数据后台存着呢。
Not exactly. The public can't see your negative record, but we still have the information in our system.
⑧

知错就改,还是我的乖徒儿。
You righted your wrongs. That's my good apprentice!
孙总,"宝地"都给你留着呢。
Mr. Sun, I've kept that plot of land for you.
老孙,钱我带来了,要借多少你尽管说。
Mr. Sun, I've brought the money. Just tell me how much you want to borrow.
⑨

给俺老牛个机会?
Does this old ox have a chance at redemption?
给!
Yup!
⑩

企业不讲信用，为啥还要给他们修复？
Why allow companies to repair their credit if they can't be trusted?
那种性质特别恶劣的“老赖”，也能申请信息修复吗？
What about companies that have done something really bad? Can they apply to repair their credit?
个人征信也能修复吗？
Can personal credit be repaired, too?
创业不易，总要给一个知错就改的机会嘛！
Starting a business is not easy. It's better to give enterprises a chance to fix their mistakes.
不是所有的“信用污点”都能修复，咱也是有标准的！
Besides, not all "stains" can be "washed" away. We still have standards to maintain!
信用修复主要针对企业，而且根本没有征信修复这一说！
Credit repair is primarily for enterprises. It doesn't apply to individuals.
⑪
边改正边修复，完美！
I've been working on fixing our issues, and our credit is being repaired!
信用修复提醒书
行政处罚决定书
⑫
诚信海南
如果上天可以给我再来一次的机会，我一定准时报批，按时缴费！
I promise that if I have another chance, I will regularly submit the required paperwork and pay all my bills on time.
⑬

案例注解 CASE NOTES

海南实施信用修复"一件事"，推行事前"柔性执法、审慎处罚"，事中全省"一口受理、一网通办"，事后"同步下架、整体修复"，帮助愿意纠正失信行为、履行相关义务、消除不良影响的主体恢复信用。

The implementation of Hainan's credit repair process emphasizes "a light touch in enforcement and a cautious approach to penalties" pre-process, "convenient single-window and online access" during the process, and "simultaneous removal and thorough repair" post-process. This process helps restore credit to business entities that are willing to rectify their credit-damaging behavior, execute their relevant obligations, and eliminate their negative impact.

案例进展 CURRENT STATUS

2024年，海南共完成企业行政处罚信用修复2378件。

In 2024, Hainan processed 2, 378 applications for credit repair resulting from administrative penalties.

动动手指　融资“so easy”

Financing at Your Fingertips

画外音：经营主体面临的问题，既有共性，也有个性。这意味着政府部门发现问题、解决问题都务必精准。锁定问题的共性，大胆进行制度集成创新，推出管用的制度机制，才能找到解决问题的“总钥匙”。针对问题的个性，善用大数据等技术手段，对具体情况进行具体分析，才能号准脉、开对方，真正把服务送到心坎上。这正是构建、运营线上智慧金融综合服务平台带给人们的启发。

Introduction: The problems faced by business entities are both common to all market entities and highly personalized. This means that government departments must be precise in identifying and solving them. It is only by focusing on the common characteristics, boldly carrying out system integration and innovation, and launching effective system mechanisms that a "master key" to solve problems can be found. For specific issues, we can make good use of diagnostic tools, such as big data, and conduct specific analyses of particular situations to accurately diagnose issues, prescribe the right advice, and deliver targeted services. This is precisely how the construction and operation of an online smart financial comprehensive service platform inspires people.

A05　“营”在自贸港“画”说新海南
——优化营商环境专刊
海南日报

动动手指　融资“so easy”

中小企业融资过程中，常常会遇到各种各样的问题，比如“难”“慢”“贵”，好在如今在海南，有了新办法……

为解决中小微企业融资“难、贵、慢”问题，海南省地方金融监督管理局牵头建设了海南省智慧金融综合服务平台，初步建成金融产品超市，打通银行金融产品和市场主体需求通道，建立供需机制，让市场主体自主选择适合自己的产品。

截至 2022 年 12 月中旬，海南省智慧金融综合服务平台……

精准服务见智慧显温度

企“话”自贸港
琼海中正管桩有限公司财务总监黄玉永：
我们“有米下锅”了

年底搏一搏，单车变摩托。
It's time to take this pedal bike and turn it into a hypercar.
搞清楚选哪家银行，年都过完了！
But by the time I figure out which bank to use, the fiscal year will have already ended.
¥
啥时候才能通关给币呀？
When exactly will I be able to get the money?
快速配对，手动钱来！
Try out the quick-match function and watch the money come in!
还有这种好东西？我试试！
Oh really? I'd better give it a shot.
为您找到"天选"之款！
Check out these "perfect" matches I've found.
B银行 贷款 产品
A银行 贷款 产品
与老王 匹配度 100%
C银行 贷款 产品
D银行 贷款 产品

这么精准的画像，是写实派的吧？
Such a perfect match-this must be a hyper-realistic portrait!
营业利润
员工数量
企业资产
⑥
线上购物好选多了！
It's much easier online.
金融产品超市
⑦
王老板，您申请的贷款已到账，请注意查收。
The loan you applied for has been deposited into your account.
果然是动动手指资金就来了！
It really is financing at my fingertips!
⑧
"叮"！你收到一个合适的金融产品推荐!
都不用自己跑银行，智慧金融的推荐很懂我的心啊！完美！
No more running to banks. Smart financial matching really understands my needs! Nice!
⑨
"五心"守护。
Friendly, functional, fair, fast, and fiscally sound.
五星好评！
That's a five-"F" review from me!
产品贴心
体验舒心
服务公心
隐私安心
监管放心
⑩

案例注解 CASE NOTES

为解决中小微企业融资"难、贵、慢"问题，海南省地方金融监督管理局牵头建设了海南省智慧金融综合服务平台，初步建成金融产品超市，打通银行金融产品和经营主体需求通道，建立供需机制，让经营主体自主选择适合自己的产品。

To solve small-and medium-sized enterprises' problems with financing being "difficult", "expensive", and "slow", the Hainan Provincial Local Financial Supervision and Administration Bureau took the lead in establishing the Hainan Smart Financial Comprehensive Service Platform. Initially starting with the creation of a supermarket for financial products, the service platform opens up a channel between the financial products provided by banks and the needs of business entities. By establishing mechanisms for supply and demand, business entities can independently choose the products that suit them.

案例进展 CURRENT STATUS

截至2025年2月11日，海南省智慧金融综合服务平台已累计入驻各类金融机构486家，注册企业超57.28万家，累计申请金额653.64亿元，促进放款约172.61亿元，为5801家企业（含个人及个体工商户）解决了融资问题。

As of February 11, 2025, the Hainan Smart Financial Comprehensive Service Platform has attracted 486 financial institutions of various types, has registered over 572,800 enterprises, processed applications totaling around CNY 65.4 billion, successfully loaned out roughly CNY 17.26 billion, and resolved financing problems for 5,801 enterprises (including both individuals and sole proprietorships).

“宝地”留给好项目

Learning to Share Land and Prosperity

画外音：常言道，好钢要用在刀刃上。随着自贸港建设蓬勃兴起，项目用地需求大增，与供给趋紧的矛盾日益加剧。矛盾如何缓解？节约集约是必经之路。海南土地节约集约利用措施，突出了高质量、系统性、可操作性，可提升企业、项目的层级，推动实现土地效益最大化，倒逼高质量发展。坚持“以亩产论英雄”，变粗放管理为精细治理，对每一块土地都精打细算、用足用好，定能节地挖潜，让有效的土地资源发挥出无限的效用。

Introduction: As the saying goes, good steel should be used to make quality blades. With the booming construction of the Hainan FTP, the demand for land has significantly increased, but supply has tightened dramatically. What's the best way to solve this? Maximizing and intensifying land use. Measures to maximize and intensify land use emphasize high quality, a systematic approach, and operability, making sure that only the right enterprises and projects are appropriately paired to land, promoting the maximization of land benefits, and inducing high-quality development. Hainan adheres to the principle of maximizing land use, transitioning from extensive management to precision governance, and carefully tabulating and deploying every plot of available land. In doing so, land can be used more sparingly while tapping maximum benefits and allowing effective land resources to realize unlimited potential.

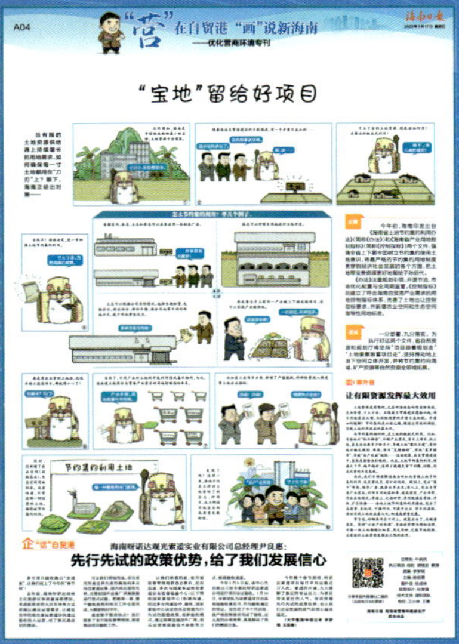
A04
海南日报
“营”在自贸港 “画”说新海南
——优化营商环境专刊
“宝地”留给好项目
当有限的土地资源供给遇上持续增长的用地需求，如何确保每一寸土地都用在“刀刃”上？眼下，海南正给出对策——

让有限资源发挥最大效用
企“话”自贸港
海南呀诺达观光索道实业有限公司总经理尹良惠：
先行先试的政策优势，给了我们发展信心

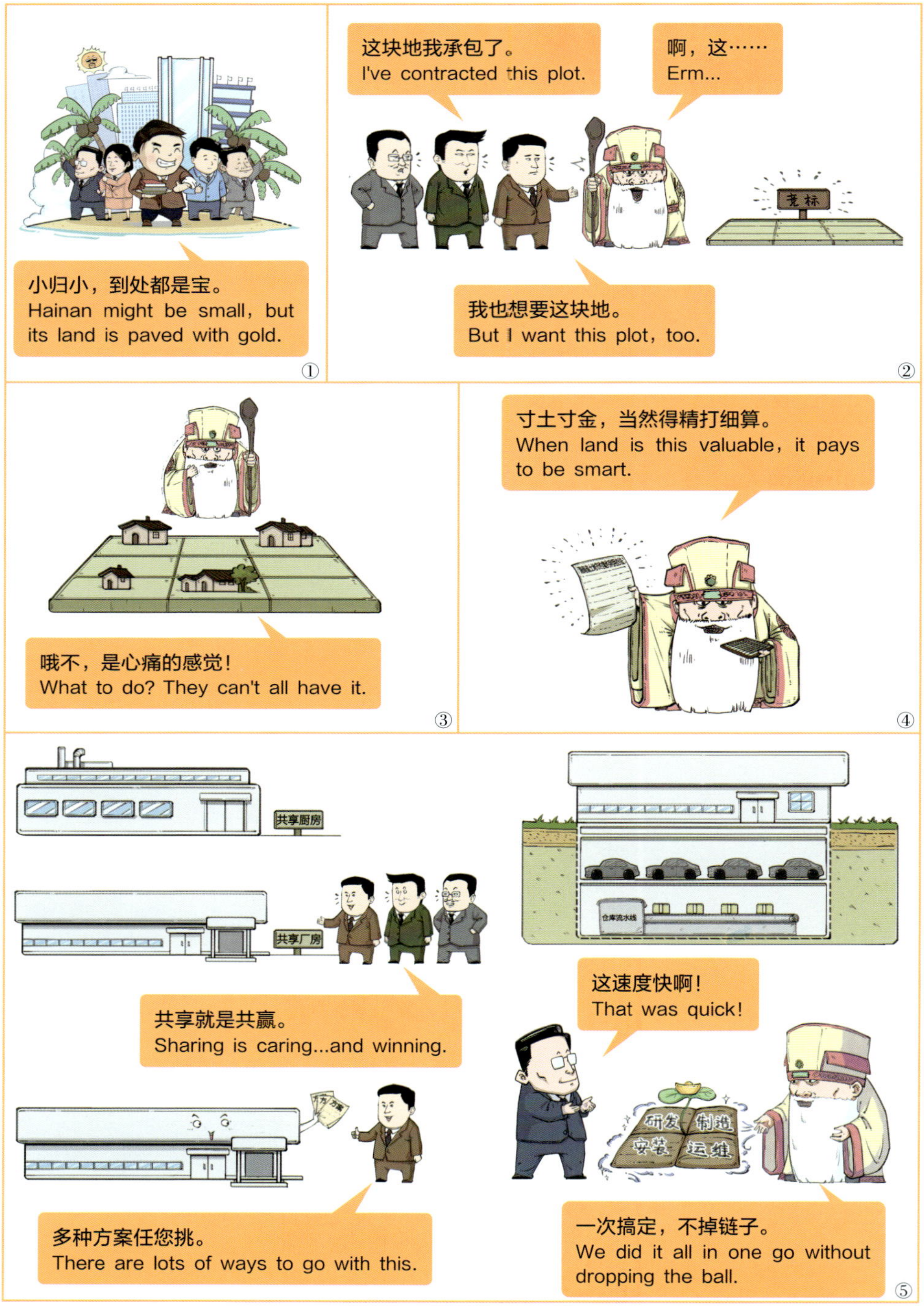
小归小，到处都是宝。
Hainan might be small, but its land is paved with gold.
①
这块地我承包了。
I've contracted this plot.
啊，这……
Erm...
竞标
我也想要这块地。
But I want this plot, too.
②
哦不，是心痛的感觉！
What to do? They can't all have it.
③
寸土寸金，当然得精打细算。
When land is this valuable, it pays to be smart.
④
共享厨房
共享厂房
共享就是共赢。
Sharing is caring...and winning.
多种方案任您挑。
There are lots of ways to go with this.
仓库流水线
这速度快啊！
That was quick!
研发 制造 安装 运维
一次搞定，不掉链子。
We did it all in one go without dropping the ball.
⑤

想圈地？没门！
Planning to hog big plots of land? You're out of luck!
收回
⑥

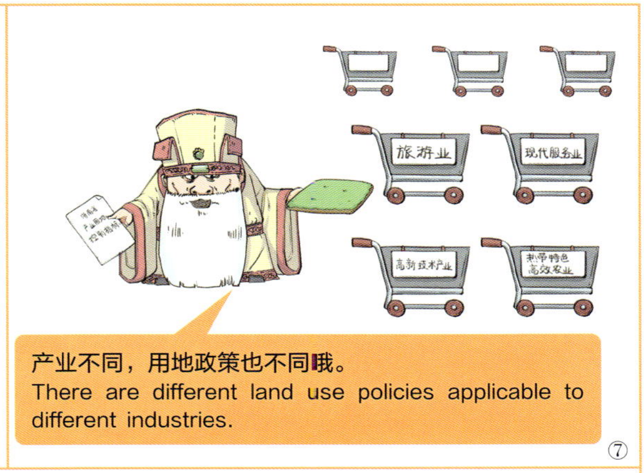
旅游业
现代服务业
高新技术产业
热带特色高效农业
产业不同，用地政策也不同哦。
There are different land use policies applicable to different industries.
⑦

选我！选我！
Pick me! Pick me! Pick me! Pick me!
计划书
计划书
猜猜我会选谁？
So, who will I pick?
⑧

节约集约利用土地
每一种都有用地门槛哦。
Every type of land has different requirements.
⑨

“亩产”论英雄！
Maximizing land use is the way to go!
寸土生寸金！
The ground is indeed paved with gold!
⑩

案例注解 CASE NOTES

2023年初，海南印发出台《海南省土地节约集约利用办法》（简称《办法》）和《海南省产业用地控制指标》（简称《控制指标》）两个文件，强调全省上下要牢固树立节约集约使用土地意识，将最严格的节约集约用地制度贯穿到经济社会发展的各个方面，把土地等宝贵资源更好地留给子孙后代。《办法》注重规划引领、开源节流、市场优化配置与全周期监管。《控制指标》则建立了符合海南自贸港产业需求的用地控制指标体系，完善了土地出让控制指标要求，并新增农业空间和生态空间指导性用地标准。

Early in 2023, Hainan promulgated both the *Measures for the Conservation and Intensive Utilization of Land in Hainan Province* and the *Hainan Province Industrial Land Use Control Standards*. In order to better leave precious resources to future generations, these documents emphasize that the whole province should firmly establish the awareness of intensive use of land and of saving land, and integrate the most stringent land conservation and intensive use systems into all aspects of economic and social development. The *Measures* specifically focus on planning guidance, increasing revenue and reducing expenditure, market optimization and allocation, and full-cycle supervision, whereas the *Control Indicators* establish a land use control indicator system that meets the industrial needs of Hainan FTP, improves the land transfer control index requirements, and adds new land use standards for agricultural and ecological spaces.

案例进展 CURRENT STATUS

一分部署，九分落实。为执行好这两个文件，海南省自然资源和规划厅将坚持“项目跟着规划走”“土地要素跟着项目走”，坚持推动地上地下空间立体开发，并将节约集约向海域、矿产资源等自然资源全领域拓展。

One part planning, nine parts implementation. To execute these two documents, the Department of Natural Resources and Planning of Hainan Province will adhere to the principle of "projects following planning" and "land resources following projects"; will continue to promote the three-dimensional development of abovegroud and underground space; and will expand the conservation and intensive use to all areas of natural resources, including both marine areas and mineral resources.

异乡看病有"医"靠

Out-of-Province Medical Treatment? We've Got You Covered!

画外音： 海南从结算覆盖面、备案流程、备案手续等方面，不断优化异地就医结算工作，提升医疗领域信息技术能力和公共服务水平，既保障了广大群众切身利益，也进一步解决了企业落地海南共享机遇、外来人才干事创业的后顾之忧。在持续深化异地就医结算"放管服"改革中，凸显的是海南一以贯之坚持以人民为中心，将群众的关心和期盼想在前头、放在心头、做到实处，从无到有，从有到优，让更多改革发展成果由百姓共享。

Introduction: Hainan has continued to optimize the inter-provincial settlement of medical treatment costs in terms of settlement coverage, application process, and application materials, as well as improve information technology capabilities and public services. In doing so, it is able to protect the vital interests of the general public and alleviate the worries of enterprises and talents looking to settle in Hainan and share in its development. As the "delegation, regulation, and service" reforms of inter-provincial settlement continue to be intensified, we can see that Hainan has consistently adhered to a people-centered approach, anticipating the concerns and expectations of the public as it transitions from nothing to something and then to excellence, enabling the people to share in the fruits of the province's reform and development.

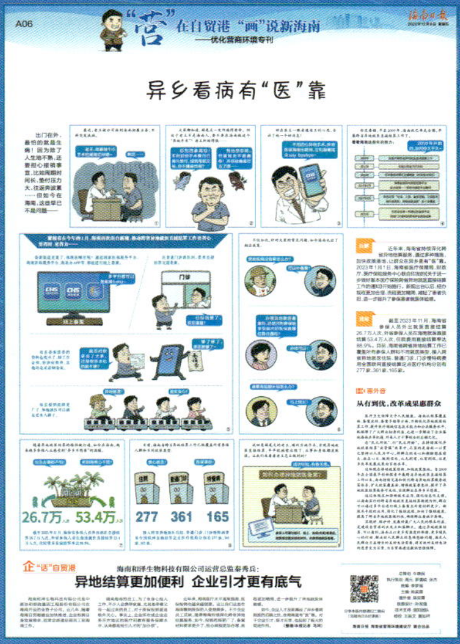

老王，需要做个小手术把阑尾切掉哦。
Mr. Wang, we're going to have to take your appendix out.
啊这……
Oh, no...
①

忍到回家再切！不然异地手术费自己要先垫付，报销周期又长，你不嫌麻烦吗？
You'll just have to stick it out till we can get home. Otherwise, you'll have to pay for treatment upfront out of your own pocket and wait ages for reimbursement. Do you really want that?
我也想忍啊，但阑尾炎不是善茬！再忍就痛晕过去了……
That's good and all, but with appendicitis, you really can't wait. You don't want to pass out from the pain...
②

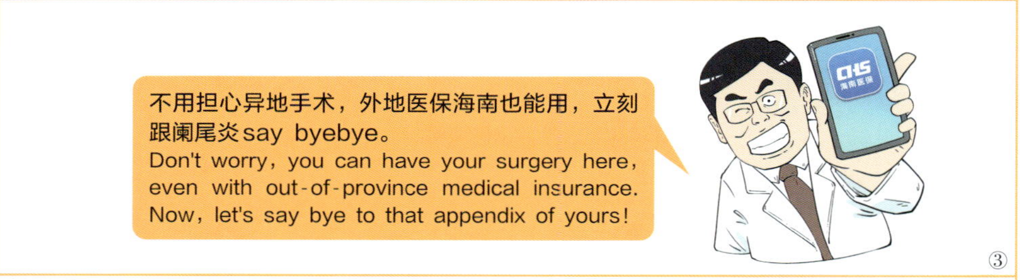
不用担心异地手术，外地医保海南也能用，立刻跟阑尾炎say byebye。
Don't worry, you can have your surgery here, even with out-of-province medical insurance. Now, let's say bye to that appendix of yours!
③

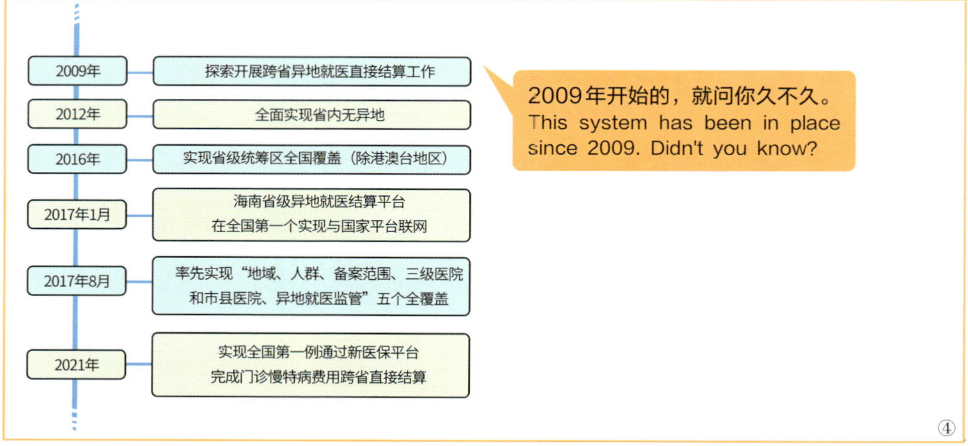
2009年
探索开展跨省异地就医直接结算工作
2012年
全面实现省内无异地
2016年
实现省级统筹区全国覆盖（除港澳台地区）
2017年1月
海南省级异地就医结算平台
在全国第一个实现与国家平台联网
2017年8月
率先实现"地域、人群、备案范围、三级医院和市县医院、异地就医监管"五个全覆盖
2021年
实现全国第一例通过新医保平台
完成门诊慢特病费用跨省直接结算
2009年开始的，就问你久不久。
This system has been in place since 2009. Didn't you know?
④

多平台都可以备案哦。
You can submit an application for inter-provincial settlement on various platforms.
中国医疗保障
海南医保
线上备案
门诊
已经结算了，祝您康复！
Your bill has been settled. Wishing you a speedy recovery!
是否对你承诺了太多，还是我原本给的就不够？
Have I promised you too much or have I given too little?
承诺书
够了够了，承诺就够了。
It's cool. The letter of commitment will do.
异地就医！
Out-of-province medical treatment!
踏实安心！
I'm covered!
异地安置退休人员
异地长期居住人员
常驻异地工作人员
跨省临时外出就医人员
⑤

突发疾病没备案怎么办?
How about if it's an emergency? Can I still submit an application?
可以补备案!
Yes, you can submit it after treatment.
I ♥ HN
办理异地就医备案后，还能回到参保地享受双向的医保直接结算待遇吗?
Once I've applied for inter-provincial settlement, can I still enjoy direct settlement if I return to where I pay my insurance contributions?
必须可以!
Of course you can!
备案有效期太短，怎么办?
What if the registration period is about to expire?
马上延长!
Just extend it!
⑥

出岛去哪都不怕！
Whether you're leaving or coming to Hainan...
来到海南，心不慌！
...you can still enjoy medical insurance coverage!
海南
26.7万人次
53.4万人次
⑦

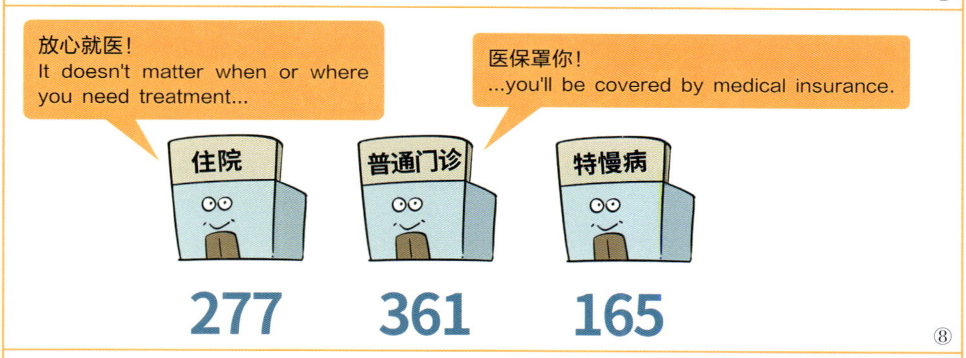
放心就医！
It doesn't matter when or where you need treatment...
医保罩你！
...you'll be covered by medical insurance.
住院
普通门诊
特慢病
277
361
165
⑧

成功经验，有备无患。
Just register for inter-provincial settlement and you're all set.
如何办理异地就医备案?
参保人可通过窗口、线上、电话(传真)等渠道，按照规定提交相关材料，办理异地就医备案。
⑨

案例注解 CASE NOTES

近年来，海南省持续深化跨省异地结算服务，通过多种措施，加快政策落地，让群众在异乡更有“医”靠。2023年1月1日，海南省医疗保障局、财政厅、医疗保险服务中心联合印发的《关于进一步做好基本医疗保险跨省异地就医直接结算工作的通知》开始施行。新规出台以后，经办规程更加合理、流程更加精简，减轻了患者负担，进一步提升了参保患者就医体验感。

In recent years, Hainan Province has continued to intensify inter-provincial settlement services for medical insurance. Through a variety of measures and the accelerated implementation of policies, people are now able to get coverage on medical care received outside their home territory. On January 1, 2023, the Hainan Provincial Healthcare Security Administration, the Department of Finance, and the Medical Insurance Service Center jointly issued the *Notice on Further Improving the Inter-Provincial Direct Settlement of Basic Medical Insurance*. After the new regulations were introduced, handling procedures became more reasonable and the process more streamlined, reducing the burden on insured patients and improving their treatment experience.

案例进展 CURRENT STATUS

截至2025年2月，海南省参保人员外出就医直接结算118.46万人次，外省参保人员在海南就医直接结算295.30万人次，住院费用直接结算率达93.3%。目前，海南省跨省异地结算工作已覆盖所有参保人群和不同就医类型，接入跨省异地就医住院、普通门诊、门诊慢特病费用全国联网直接结算定点医疗机构分别有367家、729家、334家。

As of February 2025, Hainan has facilitated direct settlement for 1.1846 million instances of insured individuals seeking medical treatment outside the province, while enabling direct settlement for 2.953 million instances of insured individuals from other provinces receiving medical treatment in Hainan. The direct settlement rate for hospitalization expenses has reached 93.3%. Currently, Hainan's inter-provincial medical expense settlement system has achieved full coverage of all insured populations and various types of medical services. The province has connected 367 medical institutions for nationwide direct settlement of inter-provincial hospitalization expenses, 729 for general outpatient services, and 334 for outpatient chronic and special disease expenses.

融资有新招

Financing with “Bacon Bonds”

画外音：因融资难、融资贵导致的资金流困境，对于很多经营主体，尤其是中小微企业来说，是能左右其生死存亡的关键因素。如何让企业在关键时刻获得生存下去的机会？以金融“活水”“精准滴灌”，是最有针对性的办法之一。通过生猪活体抵押贷款的创新探索，我们不仅看到了广大农业经营主体的融资渠道正在逐渐铺开，也看到了多元化融资服务模式的更多可能。

Introduction: The cash flow dilemma caused by the difficulty and high cost of financing is a key factor in the demise of many business entities, especially small and medium-sized enterprises. So, how can we help these enterprises stay afloat at critical moments? "Efficient precision financing" is the most targeted approach. The innovative exploration of using live pigs as loan collateral demonstrates that financing channels for the majority of agricultural business entities are gradually being rolled out and hints at the possibility of more diverse financing service models.

A07 “营”在自贸港 “画”说新海南 ——优化营商环境专刊 海南日报

融资有新招

开门做生意，难免碰到资金周转不畅时。想找银行融资，又缺少房子、车子等抵（质）押物？别着急，如今在海南，用这些“宝贝”也能贷到款——

注解 不久前，人民银行三亚市中心支行指导三亚农商银行依托动产融资统一登记公示系统，成功办理海南省首笔生物活体抵押融资登记，为拓宽农业经营主体融资渠道，助力乡村振兴作出新的探索。

企“话”自贸港

OSIM傲胜北亚区品牌管理营销副总经理林晓慧：

把握发展机遇 深耕海南市场

海南日报 海南省营商环境建设厅 联合出品

铲屎官，再不开饭，我们拆家了！
Hey, human! If you don't feed us right now, we're gonna cause a scene!
老王猪场
知道你们很饿，但你们先别饿。
I know you guys are hungry. Have patience!
①
选哪个好呢？银行能看中吗？
Which assets will the bank go for?
②
啥情况？俺要去搞金融了？
Huh? You're gonna put us down as collateral?
老王猪场
就它们了！
These will do!
③

咋定价?
How do we determine their value?
参照省内生猪市场平均售价进行价值评估。
The value is calculated according to the average sale price of live pigs in the province.
都是活物，万一闹个灾咋办?
They're living creatures. What happens if they get sick or die?
没事儿，有保险兜底呢!
No need to worry. They'll be covered by insurance.
再安个监控，随时能线上查看。
We'll also install a camera so we can monitor them in real-time.
④

俺老猪也是凭自己的实力吃上饭呢!
Give a man a pig, and he'll eat for a day. Let us pigs do it for ourselves, and we'll eat forever!
老王猪场
开饭啦!
Dinner is served!
⑤

铲屎官拿我们作抵押，然后贷款给我们买装备，是这么个逻辑吧？
So, the human used us as collateral to get a loan to buy equipment and feed for us. Is that right?
还是牛大哥脑子灵光。
You've got it, Oxxie!
那贷到款了，能给咱分点不？
Can't he give us a bit of it?
有你啥事……
Whatever would you need money for?
⑥

拿到钱可以再发展一波。
With this cash, I can develop the farm some more!
还有这等好事？你最好不要骗我！
Really?! You wouldn't lie to me, would you?
⑦

还是你们有眼光！
You guys know a good thing when you see it.
专利权
知识也能贷款，我看行！
Take my knowledge, just give me the cash!
××工厂
商标权
这些可都是压箱底的宝贝。
I'm glad I had these put aside for a rainy day.
××植物
新品种权
研发经费不愁了，创新动力更足了！
Using IP rights as collateral means there's no need to worry about R&D costs. Just keep on innovating!

⑧

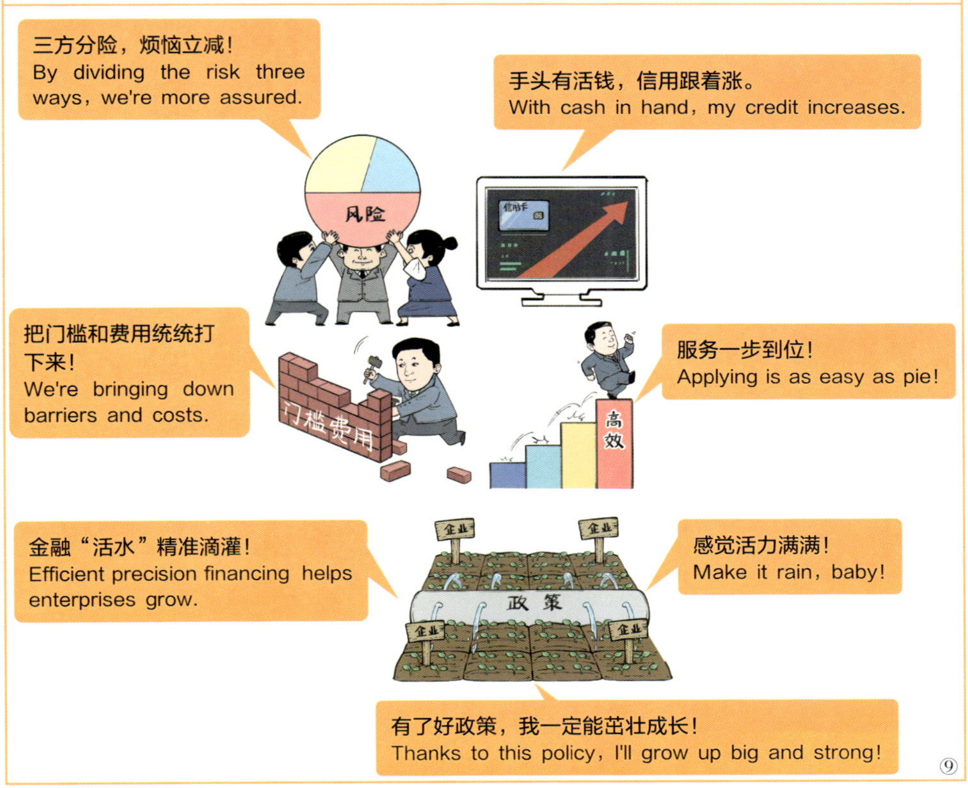
三方分险，烦恼立减！
By dividing the risk three ways, we're more assured.
风险
手头有活钱，信用跟着涨。
With cash in hand, my credit increases.
信用卡
把门槛和费用统统打下来！
We're bringing down barriers and costs.
门槛费用
服务一步到位！
Applying is as easy as pie!
高效
金融“活水”精准滴灌！
Efficient precision financing helps enterprises grow.
企业
政策
感觉活力满满！
Make it rain, baby!
有了好政策，我一定能茁壮成长！
Thanks to this policy, I'll grow up big and strong!

⑨

案例注解 CASE NOTES

2023年，中国人民银行三亚市中心支行指导三亚农商银行依托动产融资统一登记公示系统，成功办理海南省首笔生物活体抵押融资登记，为拓宽农业经营主体融资渠道，助力乡村振兴作出了新的探索。

In 2023, after the Sanya branch of the People's Bank of China guided the Sanya Rural Commercial Bank towards relying on a unified registration and publicity system for the financing of movable assets, said bank successfully handled the first registration in Hainan Province of financing using livestock as collateral, broadened financing channels for agricultural operators, and helped make new explorations in rural revitalization.

案例进展 CURRENT STATUS

为提升金融服务实体经济质效，近年来，海南积极解决中小企业融资难、融资贵问题，不断加大对全省重点产业、脱贫攻坚与乡村振兴等领域的信贷投放力度，有效拓宽了经营主体融资渠道。

To improve the quality and efficiency of financial services for the real economy, Hainan has actively worked in recent years to solve the difficulties and high costs of financing for small-and medium-sized enterprises, effectively broadened financing channels for business entities and continuously increased credit investment in key industries as well as in poverty alleviation and rural revitalization across the whole province.

一纸信用报告　助企“诚”风破浪

Combined Credit Reports Aid Enterprise Development

画外音：一纸报告，其本质是“一纸”服务，切实减轻了企业的“一摞”负担。一纸“服务”，其核心是一种思维，即始终从企业的需求出发优化营商环境。这是海南在提高政府治理能力、提升政务服务水平方面的积极探索，从中可见政府服务意识的强化，充分体现了海南不断优化营商环境的坚定决心。“一纸”替代“一摞”，减去的不仅是企业提供证明材料上的负担，更是阻碍经济发展的行政壁垒和低效环节，进一步为企业发展提供了有力支持。

Introduction: At the heart of the comprehensive public credit report system is the approach of consolidating various reports and certificates of compliance into a single report, thereby reducing the burden placed on enterprises and improving Hainan's business environment. This active exploration by Hainan in improving its governance capabilities and the level of government services demonstrates both heightened awareness and the province's firm determination to optimize its business environment. By replacing several reports and certificates with a single, comprehensive report, enterprises' material burdens have been reduced, and administrative barriers that impact economic development have been removed, providing solid support for enterprise growth.

A08
“营”在自贸港 “画”说新海南
——优化营商环境专刊
一纸信用报告 助企“诚”风破浪
一纸服务减轻一摞负担
企“话”自贸港
企业点单 政府跑腿

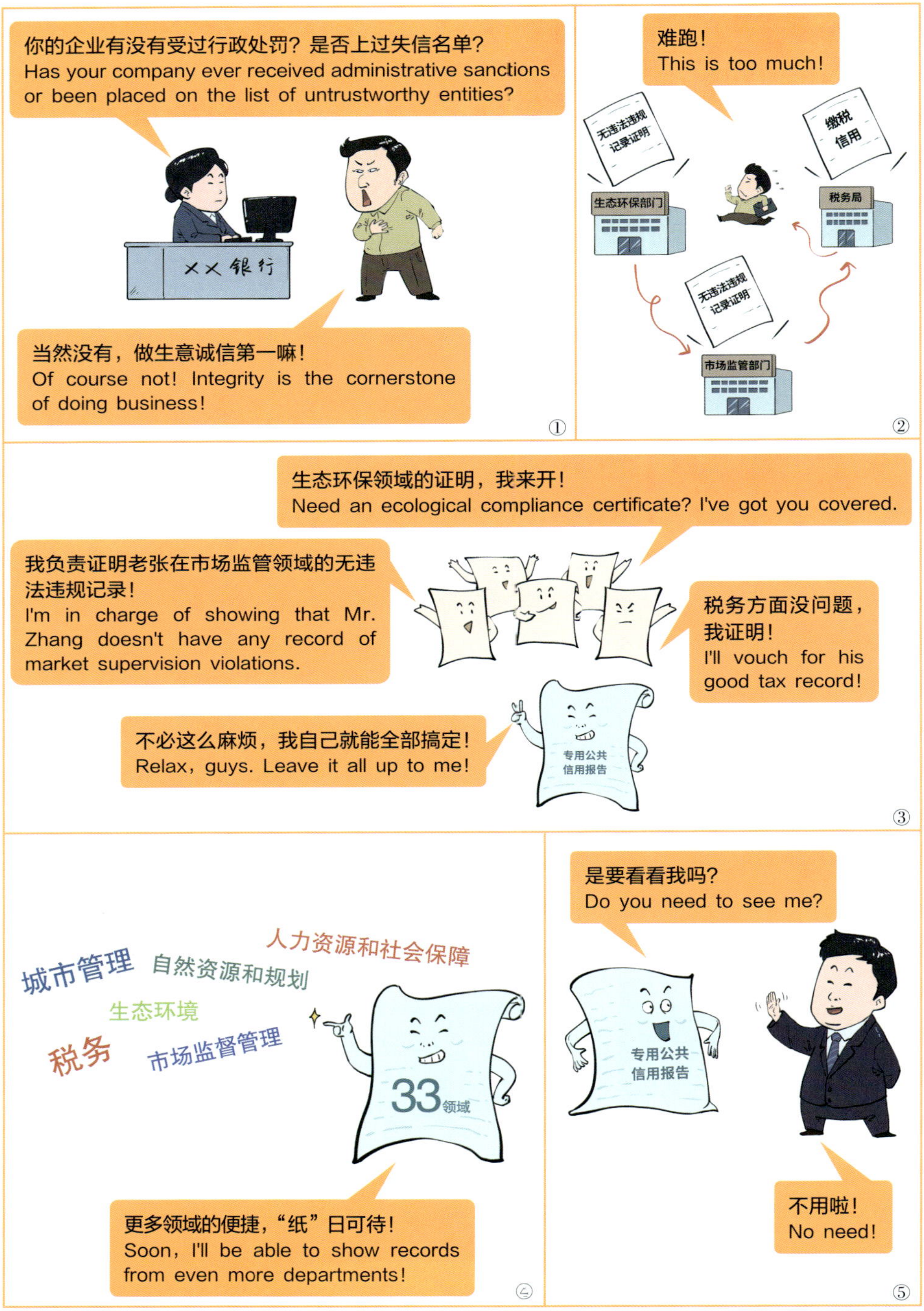
你的企业有没有受过行政处罚？是否上过失信名单？
Has your company ever received administrative sanctions or been placed on the list of untrustworthy entities?
××银行
当然没有，做生意诚信第一嘛！
Of course not! Integrity is the cornerstone of doing business!
①
难跑！
This is too much!
无违法违规记录证明
缴税信用
生态环保部门
税务局
无违法违规记录证明
市场监管部门
②
生态环保领域的证明，我来开！
Need an ecological compliance certificate? I've got you covered.
我负责证明老张在市场监管领域的无违法违规记录！
I'm in charge of showing that Mr. Zhang doesn't have any record of market supervision violations.
税务方面没问题，我证明！
I'll vouch for his good tax record!
不必这么麻烦，我自己就能全部搞定！
Relax, guys. Leave it all up to me!
专用公共信用报告
③
城市管理
自然资源和规划
人力资源和社会保障
生态环境
税务
市场监督管理
33领域
更多领域的便捷，"纸"日可待！
Soon, I'll be able to show records from even more departments!
④
是要看看我吗？
Do you need to see me?
专用公共信用报告
不用啦！
No need!
⑤

信用中国（海南）
XYHN.HAINAN.GOV.CN
海南省政务服务网
海易办
店小二
免费办理，一站搞定！
Get your comprehensive public credit report for free on these platforms.
⑥
报告在手，一路畅行！
One single report opens so many doors!
“滴！快速通过~”
专用信用报告
上市
融资
评优评先……
已经出具和提供的无违法违规记录证明，还是具备同等效力哦！
All previously issued and submitted certificates of compliance are still valid!
店小二
⑦
政务大厅
新老交替，应替尽替！
But you should swap out the old certificates for the new comprehensive public credit report as needed.
交给你咯！
Time to hand over the reins.
专用公共信用报告
大家放心！
Don't worry. Enjoy retirement!
⑧
信任更多了，风险更小了。
The more trustworthy I am, the less risk I present.
全省通办
看完报告，合作更有信心啦！
After reading your report, we're happy to work with you!
⑨
高效智办，“诚”风破浪！
Efficient, intelligent, comprehensive: good credit can take you far!
诚信号
⑩

案例注解 CASE NOTES

2024年，省政府办公厅印发《海南省推行经营主体以专用公共信用报告替代无违法违规记录证明实施方案》，明确今后在全省行政区划内，经营主体可以专用公共信用报告替代46个领域无违法违规记录证明和3类高频管理信息核查，破解经营主体在开具无违法违规记录证明中的“繁、难、久”等问题。

In 2024, The General Office of the People's Government of Hainan Province recently promulgated the *Implementation Plan for Hainan Province to Promote Business Entities to Replace Proof of No Illegal or Irregular Records with Public Credit Reports*, so that in the future, business entities within the province's administrative divisions can use public credit reports for verification checks to replace three types of high-frequency management inspections and the "proof of no illegal or irregular records" required in 46 fidds, thus solving the problem of issuing certificates of "no illegal or irregular records" being "complicated, difficult and time-consuming".

案例进展 CURRENT STATUS

自2024年12月1日起，我省将按照公益免费、便捷高效的原则，采取线上、线下两种方式提供7×24小时不打烊“随时办”专用信用报告服务，供经营主体自主选择。除法律法规另有规定外，我省将在行政审批领域，全面推行专用信用报告替代无违法违规记录证明，实现“应替尽替”。目前累计为367家经营主体出具1193份专用信用报告。

Since December 1, 2024—in accordance with the principles of free, convenient and efficient public welfare—Hainan has provided a dedicated credit report service that is available to business entities 24/7 both online and at government service centers. Unless otherwise provided by laws and regulations, the province will comprehensively implement special credit reports to replace proof of no illegal or irregular records in the field of administrative approval. So far, a total of 1, 193 special credit reports have been issued for 367 business entities.

多年旧账追回记

Placing Arrears in the Rearview Mirror

画外音：政府与企业打交道，对签订的合约置之不顾，企业追问了依旧拖而不决，这种慢作为、不作为现象，是对营商环境的极大伤害。政府公信经不住“欠”。该案例中，当地市政府的积极应对，为解决历史遗留问题提供了借鉴。如今，问题虽然解决，但仍需深思的是，如何以此为戒，摒弃思想上的“优越感”，破除作风上的“庸懒散”，真正当好服务企业的“店小二”，在每项工作中都做到“言必信，行必果”，唯有如此才能朝着一流营商环境不断迈进。

Introduction: Slow and inactive behavior by local governments, such as disregarding contracts it has signed with enterprises and ignoring or fobbing off enterprises that are chasing up payments, causes great harm to the business environment. To maintain public credibility, governments should not owe money to their contractors. The case shown here demonstrates the positive response of the local municipal government and provides a reference for solving historical debt issues. While the problem was solved, the case offers a lesson for other local governments in how to abandon a sense of superiority, shrug off laziness, truly act in service to the public, and maintain integrity in action. Only by learning these lessons can we continue to move towards a first-class business environment.

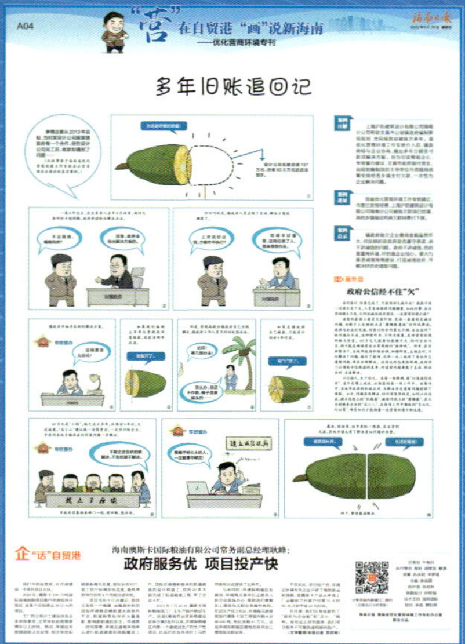
A04

“营”在自贸港 “画”说新海南

——优化营商环境专刊

海南日报

多年旧账追回记

企“话”自贸港

海南澳斯卡国际粮油有限公司常务副总经理耿峰：

政府服务优 项目投产快

为啥剥夺我的甜蜜！
Eh? Where's the rest?
①
别急，政府会给出解决方案的。
Don't worry. The government will come up with a solution.
不还我钱，喝椰风咩？
How am I going to survive if you don't pay me?
XX镇政府
②
哎呀，不好意思，这岗位换了人，我来想想办法。
Oh, sorry. We've had a personnel change. Let me come up with a solution.
上次说好还钱，方案咋不执行？
You said you'd make me whole. Why haven't you followed through?
XX镇政府
③
这钱要怎么还呢？
How exactly are we going to pay him?
XX镇政府
我裂开了。
Slashed again!
④

不行！自己想办法！
Enough! Cough up the money already!
怎么办，说话不作数，椰子是要砸头的……
What am I to do? I can't make good on our promise. Now it's just a case of waiting for the other coconut to drop...
⑤
我无语了。
Slashed...again?!
⑥
不能企业告状的就解决，不告状就不解决。
We can't just keep on greasing the squeaky wheels and forget about enterprises that don't complain.
想点子座谈
⑦
建立诚信政府
爬椰子树长大的人，一定要遵守"椰定"！
Where there's a will, there's a way!
⑧
拨款能补齐。
Funds can be made up through appropriations...
生活甜蜜蜜！
...to ensure that everyone is whole again!
⑨

案例注解 CASE NOTES

上海沪防建筑设计有限公司海南分公司帮助文昌市公坡镇政府编制多项规划，合同尾款却被拖欠多年。省优化营商环境工作专班介入后，镇政府经与企业协商，提出多年分期支付款项解决方案。但为切实帮助企业，专班督办建议，文昌市政府拨付资金，由规划编制项目主导单位市资规局统筹安排给各乡镇支付欠款，一次性为企业解决问题。

Hainan Branch of Shanghai Hufang Construction Design Co., Ltd. helped the Wenchang City Gongpo Town Government to prepare a number of plans. The contract's final payment had been delayed for many years. After the Hainan Provincial Business Environment Optimization Working Group intervened and consulted with the enterprise and the town government, a multi-year installment payment solution was proposed. However, in order to effectively help enterprises, the special task force suggested that the Wenchang Municipal Government allocate funds to pay the debt. The Municipal Bureau of Resources and Planning then coordinated a one-time payment of all of the monies owed.

案例进展 CURRENT STATUS

按省优化营商环境工作专班建议，文昌市已安排经费，上海沪防建筑设计有限公司海南分公司被拖欠款项已结清，其他乡镇偿还同类欠款经费已下拨。

In accordance with recommendations from the Hainan Provincial Business Environment Optimization Working Group, Wenchang City has allocated funds to repay debts owed to the Hainan Branch of Shanghai Hufang Construction Design Co., Ltd., while other townships have also arranged funding to settle similar outstanding obligations.

检查先“亮码” 执法更透明

Staying Transparent and Up to Code with QR Codes

画外音：助力企业发展，不仅要把事办在企业心坎上，还要让企业把心放在肚子里。海南全面推行“亮码检查”，进一步规范涉企行政检查，彰显了海南政府部门依法行政的坚定决心。当然，涉企行政检查，“规范”只是基本要求。期待海南在涉企监管领域不断探索创新，妥善把握精度，着力提升效能，努力做到既不缺位，也不越位。

Introduction: To help enterprises develop, we must not only make things easier for them but also put them at ease. Demonstrating the firm determination of Hainan's government departments to administer according to the law, the province has fully implemented inspection supervision QR codes to further standardize administrative inspections involving enterprises. Of course, for administrative inspections involving enterprises, "standardization" is an essential requirement. We expect government agencies in Hainan to continue to explore and innovate in the field of enterprise-related supervision, be prudent and accurate, focus on improving efficiency, and strive to neither be absent nor to overstep their authority.

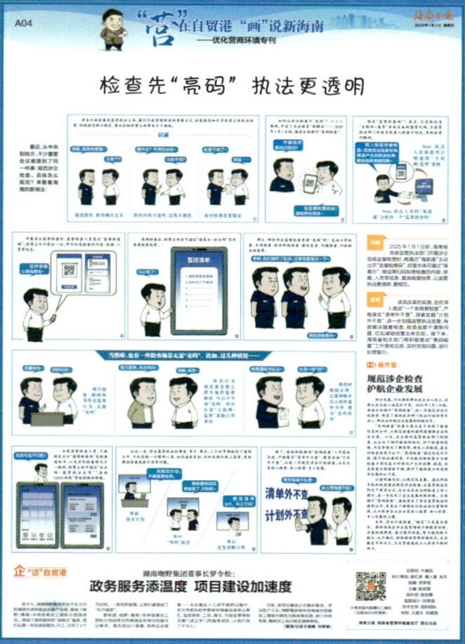
A04

“营”在自贸港 “画”说新海南

——优化营商环境专刊

检查先“亮码” 执法更透明

清单外不查

计划外不查

企“话”自贸港

湖南咖野集团董事长罗令松：

政务服务添温度 项目建设加速度

老板，我来检查了。
Hello, sir. I'm here to perform an administrative inspection.
又来?!
Again?!
查什么不用告诉你。
As for what I'm here to check, I don't have to tell you.
为啥不用?
Why not?
处置下来了。
Here's what you need to fix.
这?
What?
①

是监督检查码啦！要检查，先亮码。
This is an inspection supervision QR code. If you want to perform an inspection, you'd better show it.
干吗突然拿出付款码?
Why are you showing me a payment QR code?
②

网上投诉举报核查或因违法线索在线移送产生的执法检查，都会由系统赋码。
Inspection supervision QR codes are generated by the system every time there are complaints or reports online or digital evidence of illegal behavior exists.
互联网+监管
③

这样我就心里有数啦。
This way, I know what's going on.
检查信息
开始办理
④

学到了！
OK, now I know what needs fixing!
整改清单
1.消防通道要通畅
2.安全出口不堆放
3.
4.
5.
6.
⑤

老板，我们接到了投诉，过来核查一下情况。
Hello, sir. We've received a complaint. We're here to perform an inspection.
亮码，我看看先。
Please show me your inspection supervision QR code.
⑥

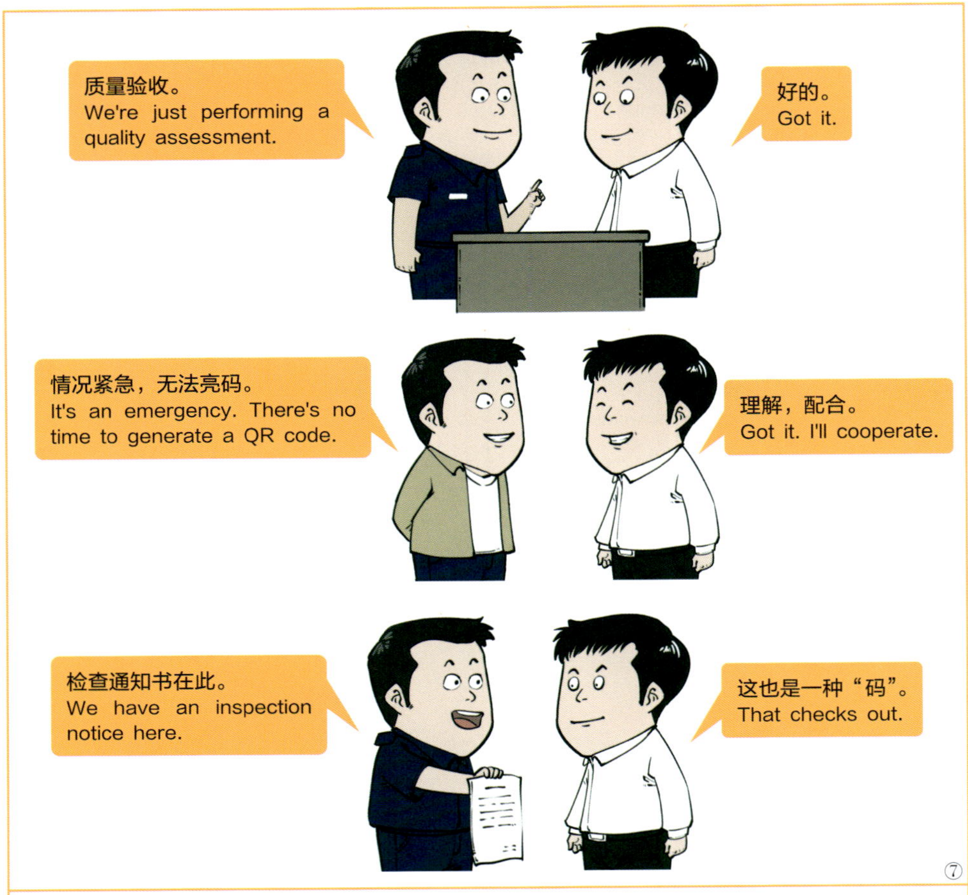
质量验收。
We're just performing a quality assessment.
好的。
Got it.
情况紧急，无法亮码。
It's an emergency. There's no time to generate a QR code.
理解，配合。
Got it. I'll cooperate.
检查通知书在此。
We have an inspection notice here.
这也是一种"码"。
That checks out.
⑦

无码可是不行的！
No code? No way!
我的提醒
我的记录
我的任务
我的权利
陈述申辩
申请听证
一键投诉
评价反馈
对XXXXXXXXXXX的行政检查
行政主体：XXXXXXXXXX
首次告知时间 XXXX-XX-XX
检查时间 XXXX-XX-XX
检查结果 作出行政指导
评价
对XXXXXXXXXXX的行政检查
行政主体：XXXXXXXXXX
首次告知时间 XXXX-XX-XX
检查时间 XXXX-XX-XX
检查结果 作出行政指导
⑧

检查计划书
先制订计划，不能再随意检查了。
Now, we have to come up with an inspection plan.
We can't just drop by.
监督检查码
要检查的项目都清楚了，开始吧。
I know exactly what you're here to inspect.
Please go ahead.
“海易办-企业码”
了解了整改清单，马上行动！
I know exactly what I need to fix.
Let's get on with it!
⑨

“营”在海南不乱查，
No unauthorized or unplanned inspections in Hainan...
清单外不查
计划外不查
安心营商真不错！
...means no unexpected
surprises.
⑩

案例注解 CASE NOTES

2025年1月1日起，海南省各级监管执法部门开展涉企现场监督检查时，可通过"海政通"主动出示"监督检查码"，经营主体可通过"海易办""微信"等扫码知悉检查的内容、依据、人员等信息以及查询检查结果。这让监管执法更透明、更规范。该项改革的实施，旨在深入推进"一个系统管检查"，严格落实"清单外不查"，探索实施"计划外不查"，进一步加强监管执法监督，有效解决随意检查、检查底数不清等问题，切实减轻经营主体负担。

To make regulatory enforcement more transparent and standardized, starting from January 1,2025,whenever any of Hainan Province's regulatory or law enforcement departments conduct on-site supervision and inspection of enterprises, an "Inspection Supervision QR code" will be presented through the Hainan Government affairs collaborative office platform Haizhengtong. Afterwards, business entities can use the government's service platform Haiyiban or WeChat to scan this QR code and either get information (such as content, reason, and personnel involved) related to the inspection or query the inspection results. The implementation of this reform aims to not only promote a "single system for inspection", but also to strictly implement a policy of "no unlisted inspections", ensure that all inspections are done according to plan, further strengthen regulatory enforcement and supervision, effectively solve problems such as arbitrary inspections, inspections with unclear file numbers, and reduce the burden on business entities.

案例进展 CURRENT STATUS

接下来，海南省相关部门将积极推动"亮码检查"工作落地见效，及时发现问题，并处理督办。

For the next step, the province's relevant departments will actively push all inspectors to "show their code" before proceeding with inspections, seek out and find problems in a timely fashion, and carry out processing supervision.

综合查一次　一次就搞定

One Check and You're Done

画外音：多头监管、重复检查，曾经让许多经营主体不堪其扰、疲于应付。瞄准这些痛点，海南推行“综合查一次”改革，将以往“各查各的”变为“联合执法”，实现“进一次门、查多项事”，充分体现了海南从企业获得感和感受度出发，想方设法着力打造“有求必应、无事不扰”服务体系的诚意和决心。随着海南进一步推动监管事项的有效统筹与综合，并依托科技赋能最大化解决执法扰企问题，这些举措必将助力广大经营主体实现更大发展。

Introduction: Multiple repeated inspections by various departments were once the bane of many enterprises, impacting their business and wasting their time. To reduce the burden on businesses, Hainan has combined separate inspections by multiple departments into single, combined inspections. This development fully reflects Hainan's sincerity and determination to create a "responsive service system without interruption" that brings tangible benefits to enterprises. Relying on the effective coordination and integration of regulatory matters and technology to solve the issue of administrative enforcement hampering enterprises, Hainan is set on helping the majority of business entities achieve greater development.

A05
“营”在自贸港 “画”说新海南
——优化营商环境专刊
海南日报
综合查一次　一次就搞定
企“话”自贸港
海南奕海贸易有限公司东风螺养殖厂厂长刘相孜：
服务送上门　企业拓市场

常规检查。 We're here to perform a routine inspection.
理解理解。 Understood.
老莫超市
莫嫌我烦。 We hope you don't mind.
①
我们也来了！ Now we're here to do the same.
老莫我是有点烦…… "Mind"? How could I possibly "mind"?
老莫超市
外出中
莫嫌我烦。 We hope you don't mind.
②
这啥意思? So, what's this then?
综合查一次
简单来说，就是以前各查各的，现在联合执法，进一次门，查多项事。 Basically, we've consolidated various administrative inspections into a single round of inspections.
③
从日历上看这个时段计划比较集中，定这个时间一起去? We seem to all have time around this date. Shall we arrange to go together?
计划日历
好咯好咯，大家一起去。 Sure, let's do it.
A部门
B部门
C部门
D部门
同意。 Agreed.
同意。 Agreed.
④
2024-11-08
【综合查一次】商超联合行政检查通知
“码”上准备，事半功倍！ You can look up inspection times and review inspection results via the administrative inspection supervision platform.
⑤

一次搞定！不打扰您做生意。
Hello，sir. We're to conduct a combined inspection to minimize the impact on your business.
老莫超市
不到1个小时，就都搞定了？太棒了啊！
It'll take less than an hour? Amazing!
⑥
整改
老莫，这些安全隐患要及时整改哦！
Mr. Mo，these things need to be rectified as soon as possible!
⑦
整改后
老莫超市
不错不错，整改到位了！
He's followed through. Good on him!
⑧
市场监管
商务
教育
应急
消防
15个领域
12 12个“综合查一次”通用场景
79 79个“综合查一次”个性化场景
⑨
联手多合作！
We work together to combine inspections...
综合查一次
监管少打扰！
...and minimize the impact on your business!
⑩

案例注解 CASE NOTES

2024年7月1日起，海南在全省推行场景式清单化"综合查一次"改革，将跨部门、跨领域多个检查主体的相关检查事项进行集成，实现进一次门、查多项事。

Starting from July 1, 2024, Hainan has implemented a scenario-and checklist-based "one-time comprehensive inspection" reform across the province which integrates multiple cross-department, cross-field inspection entities' relevant inspection items to realize the ability to check multiple things in one visit.

案例进展 CURRENT STATUS

目前，根据本地产业特点和工作需求，全省共创建"商业综合体综合监管""对小微型客车租赁经营的监管""乡村民宿跨部门综合监管"等2262个"综合查一次"场景，有效提升监管效能，减轻企业负担。

In accordance with local industry characteristics and work needs, the province has created a total of 2,262 "one-time comprehensive inspection" scenarios, including "supervision of commercial complexes", "supervision of small passenger car rental operations", and "comprehensive cross-departmental supervision of rural homestays". This both improves regulatory efficiency and reduces the burden on enterprises.

第四章

Section 4

改革创新，擦亮“金饭碗”

Reforming and Innovating

政策知多少？一站式全GET!

Perplexed by Policies? Check Out This Platform!

画外音：海南自由贸易港一站式政策查询解读平台的上线，一大亮点在于“一站式”，即在此前的基础上，对各相关部门平台信息进行整合，将政策信息集中、系统地展示出来，为各类主体提供了一个便捷、统一的“一站式”查询渠道。这体现了海南自贸港不断提升的政务服务能力和水平，是对经营主体和群众诉求的积极主动回应，有助于提高自贸港政策的“知晓度”，提升海南自贸港的“能见度”，推动政策服务更加适应自贸港建设需要。

Introduction: The key takeaway of the Hainan FTP One-Stop Policy Enquiry Platform is its "one-stop" nature. It integrates information on policies and processes from across the Hainan Provincial Government and displays it in a centralized and systematic way, providing a convenient and unified "one-stop" query channel. It is a reflection of the Hainan FTP's continuous improvement of government service capabilities and a proactive response to the demands of business entities and the public. Helping to improve the awareness of FTP policies, the platform will enhance the visibility of the Hainan Free Trade Port and promote policy services to better meet the needs of FTP construction.

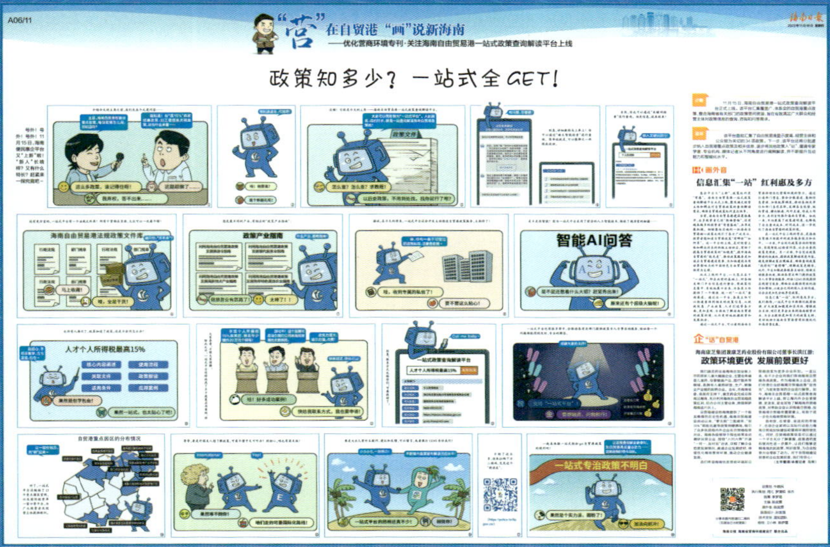

王总，海南自贸港有哪些重点政策，每项政策怎么用，你知道吗？
Mr. Wang. Do you know about the Hainan FTP's core policies and how they are applied?
我知道！有"双15%"税收优惠政策，加工增值免关税政策，还有什么来着……
Yes. Let's see...there's the dual 15% cap on individual and corporate income tax, the value-added processing import exemption policy...erm...
这么多政策，谁记得住呀！
这题超纲了……
我弃权，答不出来……
①

想知道这些，问我呀！
For the answers you seek, look no further. Ask me!
哇！他是谁？
是个新面孔呢！
②

大家可以简称我为"一站式平台"。人如其名，我的特长就是一站式查询解读各种自贸港政策啦！
Just call me the one-stop enquiry platform! As my name suggests, I specialize in providing answers to your questions on Hainan FTP policies.
政策文件
怎么查？怎么查？求教程！
以后查政策，不用到处找，找你就行了吧？
③

有问题，尽管提！
If you have a question, just ask away!
政策查询解读
您把问题提给我，我把政策找给您
我的企业想要落地海南，可以享受哪些优惠
好的，您想了解“我的企业想要落地海南，可以享受什么政策?”的相关政策，小通为您找到匹配的自贸港政策共25条，已在左侧结果页列出。您可以一站式查看政策的解读、案例、使用流程以及配套文件等。您还可以通过“配套文件列表”,查看具体实施文件。
显示检索结果
如以上查询结果不够精确，请进一步描述您的疑问点击“追加提问”，我来为您找到更精确的内容。您也可以在点击“清除提问记录”后，重新对其他政策进行询问。
科技型企业在海南可以享受什么政策?
自贸港政策（25条）
1 实行海南自由贸易港外商投资准入负面清单
2 鼓励类企业实施15%企业所得税
3 企业资本性支出可一次性税前扣除或加速折旧
4 开展合格境外有限合伙人 (QFLP) 试点
5
④

输入关键词就行！
All you need are a few keywords.
一站式政策查询解读平台
个人所得税
发现政策
检索结果
自贸港政策（1条）
人才个人所得税最高15%
2025年前，对在海南自贸港工作的高端人才和紧缺人才，其个人所得税实际税负超过15%的部分，予以免征。2025年后，对一个纳税年度内在海南自贸港累计居住满183天的个人，其取得来源于海南自贸港范围内的综合所得和经营所得，按照3%、10%、15%三档超额累进...
⑤

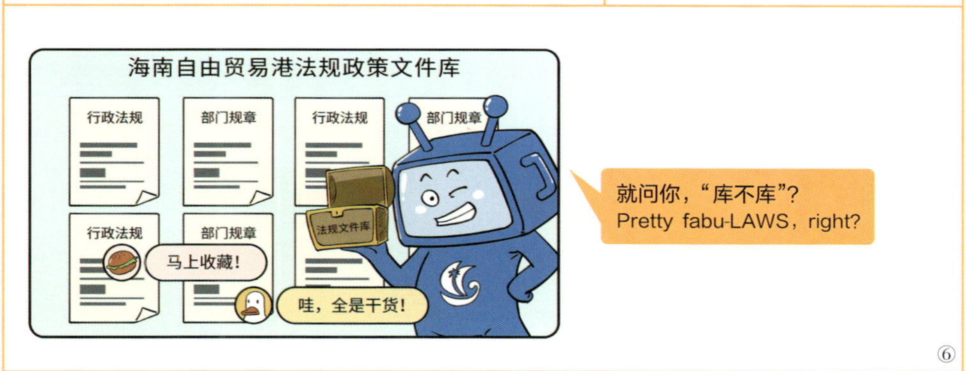
海南自由贸易港法规政策文件库
行政法规
部门规章
行政法规
部门规章
行政法规
部门规章
法规文件库
马上收藏！
哇，全是干货！
就问你，“库不库”?
Pretty fabu-LAWS, right?
⑥

政策产业指南
利用海南自由贸易港政策发展旅游业指南
利用海南自由贸易港政策发展现代服务业指南
利用海南自由贸易港政策发展高新技术产业指南
利用海南自由贸易港政策发展热带特色高效农业指南
做旅游业有思路了！
太棒了！！
什么产业，都有指南。
You've got an industrial dream. I've got the guides!
⑦

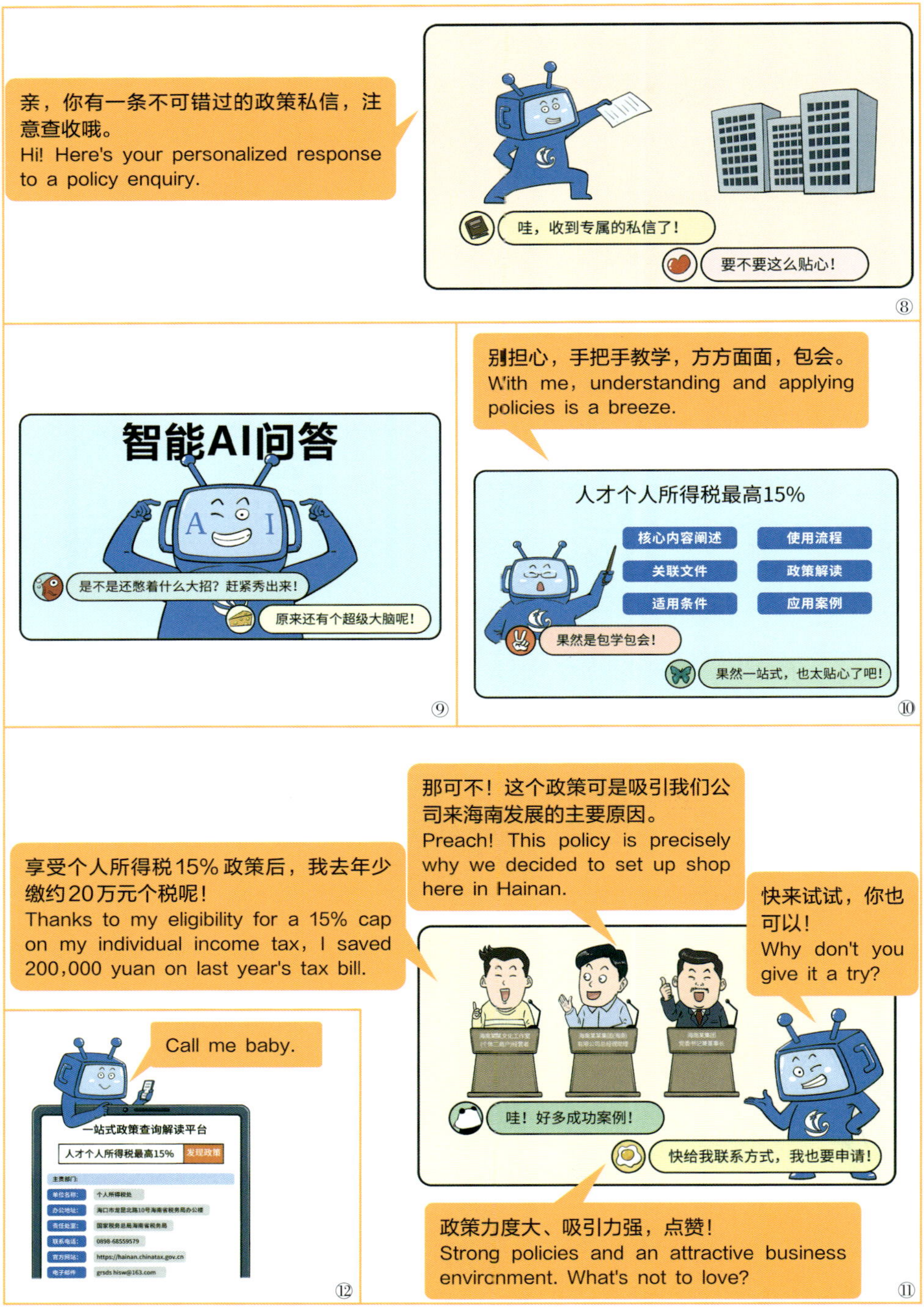
亲，你有一条不可错过的政策私信，注意查收哦。
Hi! Here's your personalized response to a policy enquiry.
哇，收到专属的私信了！
要不要这么贴心！
⑧
智能AI问答
AI
是不是还憋着什么大招？赶紧秀出来！
原来还有个超级大脑呢！
⑨
别担心，手把手教学，方方面面，包会。
With me, understanding and applying policies is a breeze.
人才个人所得税最高15%
核心内容阐述
使用流程
关联文件
政策解读
适用条件
应用案例
果然是包学包会！
果然一站式，也太贴心了吧！
⑩
享受个人所得税15%政策后，我去年少缴约20万元个税呢！
Thanks to my eligibility for a 15% cap on my individual income tax, I saved 200,000 yuan on last year's tax bill.
那可不！这个政策可是吸引我们公司来海南发展的主要原因。
Preach! This policy is precisely why we decided to set up shop here in Hainan.
快来试试，你也可以！
Why don't you give it a try?
哇！好多成功案例！
快给我联系方式，我也要申请！
政策力度大、吸引力强，点赞！
Strong policies and an attractive business envircnment. What's not to love?
⑪
Call me baby.
一站式政策查询解读平台
人才个人所得税最高15%
发现政策
主责部门:
单位名称: 个人所得税处
办公地址: 海口市龙昆北路10号海南省税务局办公楼
责任处室: 国家税务总局海南省税务局
联系电话: 0898-68559579
官方网站: https://hainan.chinatax.gov.cn
电子邮件 grsds hisw@163.com
⑫

感谢大家的支持！
Thanks for all your support!
税 支持“一站式平台”！
金 要想融资，问我就行！
王老板点赞
赵美丽阿姨点赞
厉害集团点赞

⑬

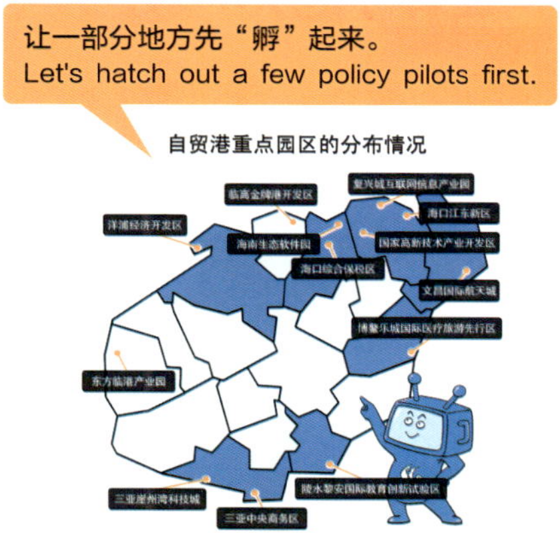
让一部分地方先“孵”起来。
Let's hatch out a few policy pilots first.
自贸港重点园区的分布情况
洋浦经济开发区
临高金牌港开发区
复兴城互联网信息产业园
海口江东新区
海南生态软件园
国家高新技术产业开发区
海口综合保税区
文昌国际航天城
博鳌乐城国际医疗旅游先行区
东方临港产业园
陵水黎安国际教育创新试验区
三亚崖州湾科技城
三亚中央商务区

⑭

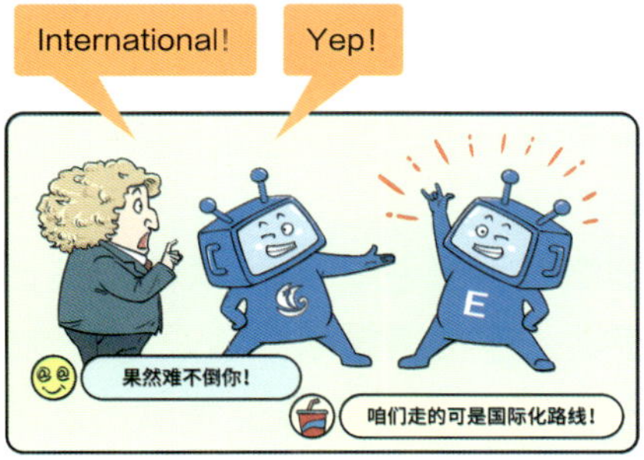
International!
Yep!
E
果然难不倒你！
咱们走的可是国际化路线！

⑮

小5，小5，一起努力！
Hey，12345. Let's work together...
一站式平台的搭档还真不少！
相信你！
不断提升政策发布解读回应水平！
...to constantly improve our response to the release and interpretation of policies.

⑯

⑰

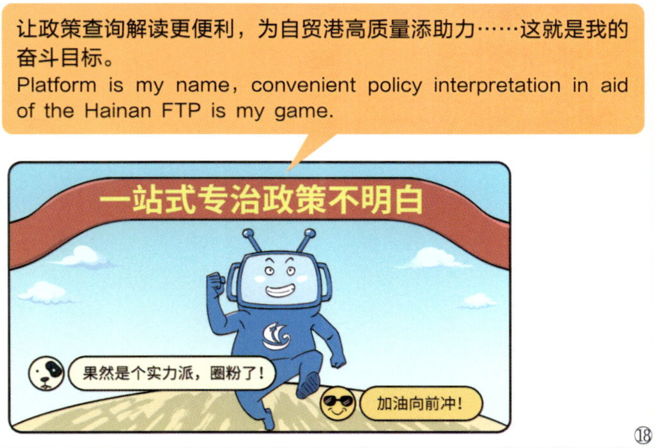
让政策查询解读更便利，为自贸港高质量添助力……这就是我的奋斗目标。
Platform is my name，convenient policy interpretation in aid of the Hainan FTP is my game.
一站式专治政策不明白
果然是个实力派，圈粉了！
加油向前冲！

⑱

案例注解 CASE NOTES

2023年11月15日，海南自由贸易港一站式政策查询解读平台正式上线。该平台汇集覆盖广、体系全的自贸港重点政策，整合海南省有关部门的政策答问资源，旨在有效满足广大群众和经营主体对政策信息的查询、咨询和问答需求。

The Hainan FTP's One-stop Policy Enquiry Platform was officially launched on November 15, 2023. Comprehensively bringing together key policies of the FTP, the platform integrates policy Q&A resources of Hainan's provincial departments and aims to provide the general public and business entities with effective, helpful answers to their queries.

案例进展 CURRENT STATUS

该平台首批汇集了自由贸易港显示度高、经营主体和公众较为关切的39项政策。下一步，该平台还将分批逐步纳入自贸港重点政策及相关信息，逐步将其他政策入“站”，邀请专家学者、专业机构、媒体记者从不同角度进行阐释解读，并不断提升互动能力和智能化水平。

Starting with 39 highly visible FTP policies of concern to business entities and the public, the platform gradually incorporate more key policies and related information. The relevant authorities wil bring additional policies onto the platform, invite experts, scholars, professional institutions, and media to explain and interpret these policies from different angles, and continuously improve the platform's interactivity and intelligence.

惠企政策，找我就“兑”了

Unlocking Policy Benefits, Subsidies, and Incentives the Easy Way

画外音：政策环境，是企业看重的重要因素。但出台了好政策，是否就一定有好效果？显然不是。“海易兑”平台变“企业找政策”为“政策找企业”，在主动服务中充分释放政策红利，展现出服务企业的诚意。这启示我们，唯有多一些“共情”心理、效果导向，既抓政策落实，又抓服务落地，实现政策制定到追踪问效完整闭环，才能把好政策送到企业心坎上，释放出最大效应。

Introduction: The policy environment is an essential factor that enterprises value. But, does the introduction of good policies necessarily lead to good results? Obviously not. The Haiyidui platform has shifted the onus from companies seeking out policies to policies proactively "seeking out" companies, enabling enterprises to take full advantage of government benefits. The success of Haiyidui demonstrates that by focusing on both policy implementation and enterprise-minded service implementation, a complete closed loop from policy formulation to tracking and performance evaluation can be realized, and we can deliver good policies right to enterprises' doorsteps and achieve the best results.

A09

“营”在自贸港 “画”说新海南

——优化营商环境专刊

海南日报

惠企政策，找我就“兑”了

为给市场主体提供成长“沃土”，政府部门常常会出台一些惠企政策。这本是一桩好事，结果有时却不如人愿……就像王总，曾经就有过这样的遭遇：

企“话”自贸港

文昌义方实业有限公司副总经理符策高：

我们的用地缺口终于补齐了

海南日报 海南省营商环境建设厅 联合出品

这补贴政策简直是为我们企业量身定制的啊！马上申请！
This policy is tailor-made for our company. Let's apply!
补贴政策
①
哎呀……
Aiya...
补贴
怎么这么久还下不来呢？
Hello? Are you coming down?
②
都是传说！
That policy is a unicorn.
补贴政策
看不到我吗？
Hasn't it seen us?
就没见过。
Well, I haven't seen it.
③
哦！这就"兑"了！
Oh! Here we are!
④
我想要的，它全都有。
It's got everything I need.
梳理发布
精准推送
解读解答
申报兑现
评价跟踪
《生物医药合同研发和生产服务平台建设专项的通知》
《资金发放实施方案》
海易兑
研发奖励
《专项资金管理暂行办法》
《海南省高新技术企业研发经费增量奖励细则》
这么了解我，是不是暗恋我？
It just gets me, you know?
研发
医疗
匹配指数 95%
药品
⑤

确认过眼神，是我要的券！
Well, look here! Where have you been all my life?
研发券
我“券”你快快行动起来。
Catch me if you can.
⑥
让我看看你走到哪一步啦！
Let me see how far you've got.
研发券
⑦
海南惠企政策助理
有问题，找我就“兑”啦！24小时在线！
If you encounter any issues, just reach out. I'm online 24/7.
⑧
感谢平台！
Thanks a bunch.
研发奖励资金
成“券”我们！
We're a match made in heaven!
⑨
“海易兑”系统入口及操作平台
入口：
操作流程：
⑩
海易兑
海南给的承诺，由我“易”起兑现！
I honor the promises that Hainan makes!
⑪

案例注解 CASE NOTES

海南省工业和信息化厅聚焦惠企政策兑现的痛点、难点、堵点，以企业需求为导向，打造了惠企政策"梳理发布、精准推送、解读解答、申报兑现、评价跟踪"一站式全省惠企政策兑现服务平台"海易兑"。全省惠企政策分散、发布不集中、推送不精准、政策看不懂、资金兑现慢等局面得到较大改观。

Guided by the needs of enterprises, Hainan Provincial Department of Industry and Information Technology focuses on ferreting out and solving the pain points, difficulties, and bottlenecks in the implementation of policies that benefit enterprises. To this end, they have created a one-stop provincial policy implementation service platform Haiyidui so that enterprises can sort through beneficial policies, look for clear implementation guidelines, ask questions, and get explanations. This has greatly improved upon the previous situation in which subsidies were difficult to apply for and the release of information about potentially beneficial policies was haphazard and poorly explained.

案例进展 CURRENT STATUS

截至目前，"海易兑"平台已发布国家级、省级和市县惠企政策3100余个，上线免申即享事项36个，累计办件近20万件，累计注册用户超120余万个。

To date, Haiyidui has listed more than 3,100 national-, provincial-, municipal-, and county-level policies which benefit enterprises, there are 36 categories of information available without registration, nearly 200,000 cases have been handled, and over 1.2 million users have registered.

好信用，享便利！

Good Credit Gets You Places

画外音：海南打造金椰分平台，诚信积分应用场景逐步丰富，越来越多人正切实体验到守信带来的好处。就海南而言，金椰分平台既是强化社会治理的支撑点，也是打造一流营商环境的突破口。同时，该平台广泛运用互联网、大数据、云计算等信息手段，有效整合各类信用数据，对各类主体诚信状况精准画像、精确管理，体现了相关部门善用新技术、善做“精细活”的智慧。

Introduction: With Hainan Golden Coconut Credit Platform, which is being expanded to more scenarios and regions, more and more people are enjoying the benefits of keeping their word. The platform aids in strengthening social governance and is a breakthrough in the work of creating a first-class business environment. Utilizing resources such as the internet, Big Data, and cloud computing, the platform effectively integrates various pieces of credit data to accurately portray and manage the credit status of various entities, reflecting the wisdom of relevant departments in making good use of new technologies and refining their approaches.

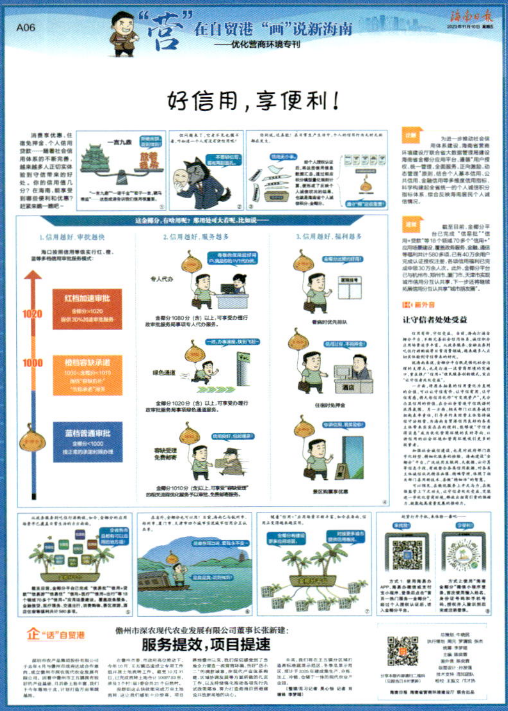
A06

“营”在自贸港 “画”说新海南

——优化营商环境专刊

海南日报

好信用，享便利！

这金椰分，有啥用呢？那用处可大着呢，比如说——

1. 信用越好，审批越快

2. 信用越好，服务越多

3. 信用越好，福利越多

红档加速审批

专人代办

看病时优先排队

画外音

让守信者处处受益

企“话”自贸港

儋州市深农现代农业发展有限公司董事长张新建：

服务提效，项目提速

放着我来
拒绝画饼，说到做到！
I won't make false promises.
①

不要轻信哥，哥有两副面孔。
If you trust in me, I'll gobble you whole.
②

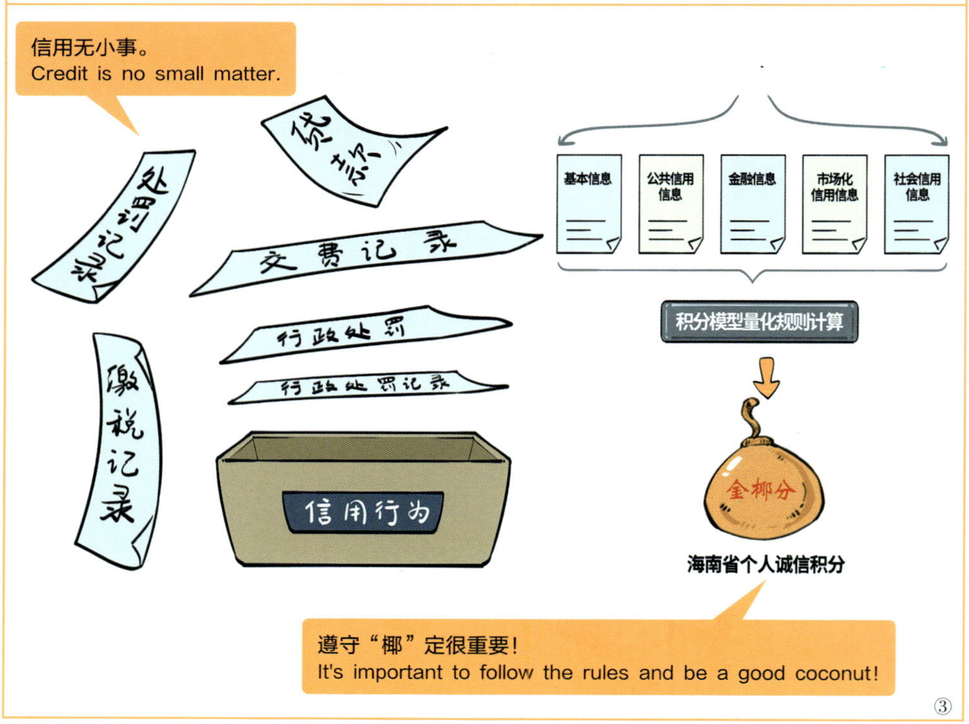
信用无小事。
Credit is no small matter.
处罚记录
贷款
交费记录
行政处罚
行政处罚记录
缴税记录
信用行为
基本信息
公共信用信息
金融信息
市场化信用信息
社会信用信息
积分模型量化规则计算
金椰分
海南省个人诚信积分
遵守"椰"定很重要！
It's important to follow the rules and be a good coconut!
③

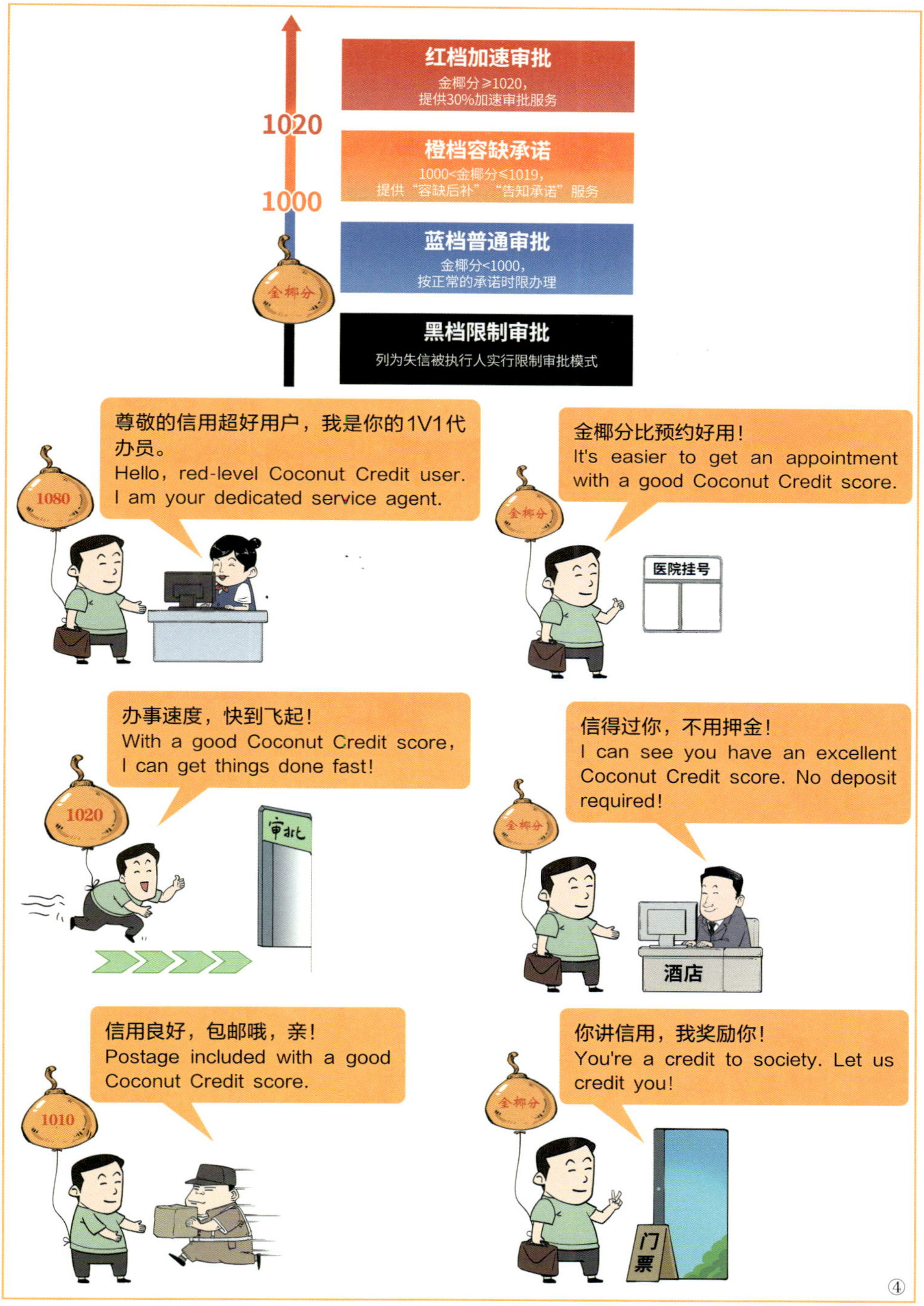
红档加速审批
金椰分≥1020，
提供30%加速审批服务
1020
橙档容缺承诺
1000<金椰分≤1019，
提供“容缺后补”“告知承诺”服务
1000
蓝档普通审批
金椰分<1000，
按正常的承诺时限办理
金椰分
黑档限制审批
列为失信被执行人实行限制审批模式
尊敬的信用超好用户，我是你的1V1代办员。
Hello，red-level Coconut Credit user. I am your dedicated service agent.
1080
金椰分比预约好用！
It's easier to get an appointment with a good Coconut Credit score.
金椰分
医院挂号
办事速度，快到飞起！
With a good Coconut Credit score，I can get things done fast!
1020
审批
信得过你，不用押金！
I can see you have an excellent Coconut Credit score. No deposit required!
金椰分
酒店
信用良好，包邮哦，亲！
Postage included with a good Coconut Credit score.
1010
你讲信用，我奖励你！
You're a credit to society. Let us credit you!
金椰分
门票
④

全省各市县都有可以应用的地方哦！
You can use your Coconut Credit score in cities and counties all across the province!
信易购
信易游
信易批
信易住
信易阅
信用+医疗
信用+农护
信用+贷款
金椰分平台
⑤

是谁在耳边说，爱我永不变……
Who told me that their love was eternal?
1080
是我是我，说到做到！
It was me! I kept my word!
⑥

金椰分将建设更多应用场景。
Coconut Credit is being expanded to more scenarios...
对接更多城市提供信用惠民。
...and more cities, providing credit and benefits to the public.
金椰分平台
⑦

来找我！
Find me here...
享便利！
...and here.
⑧

案例注解 CASE NOTES

为进一步推动社会信用体系建设，海南省营商环境建设厅联合省大数据发展中心建设海南省金椰分应用平台，遵循“用户授权、统一管理、全面服务、正向激励、动态管理”原则，结合个人基本信用、公共信用、金融信用等多维度信用指标，科学构建起全省统一的个人诚信积分指标体系，综合反映海南居民个人诚信情况。

To further promote the construction of a social credit system, the Hainan Provincial Department of Business Environment Development, in conjunction with the Big Data Development Center of Hainan Province, jointly built the Hainan Provincial Golden Coconut Credit Platform. Following the principles of "user authorization, unified management, comprehensive service, positive incentives, and dynamic management," this platform combines multiple credit indicators (such as personal basic credit, public credit, and financial credit) to scientifically build a province-wide unified personal credit score index system that comprehensively reflects Hainan residents' personal credit status.

案例进展 CURRENT STATUS

截至目前，金椰分平台已完成“信易批”“信用+贷款”等23个领域100多个“信用+”应用场景建设，覆盖政务服务、金融、通信等福利共计810多项，已有141万余用户完成认证授权注册，各项信用福利已完成申领341万余人次。此外，金椰分平台已与杭州市、郑州市、厦门市、天津市等6个城市实现信用分互认共享，下一步还将继续拓展信用分互认共享“城市朋友圈”。

The Golden Coconut Credit Platform has completed the creation of more than 100 "credit+" application scenarios in 23 fields (including "Easy Credit Approval" and "Credit+Loan"), covers more than 810 benefits (including government services, finance, and communications), has over 1.41 million users who have completed authentication and authorization, and has been used by more than 3.41 million people applying for various credit benefits. Additionally, now that the platform has achieved mutual recognition and sharing of credit points with six cities (including Hangzhou, Zhengzhou, Xiamen, and Tianjin), the next step will be to continue to expand the number of cities where credit scores are mutually recognized and shared.

企业服务 一站汇聚

Hainan's One-stop Enterprise Service Center

画外音：优化营商环境，提升企业满意度是关键。把事情办到企业心坎上，需要以更优质更高效的服务来打底。海南省企业综合服务平台不断优化功能，不仅让企业办事更方便、更高效，而且实现了集成式服务。这背后离不开多领域、多部门的协同合作，离不开精益求精的服务改进。可以说，企业综合服务平台的升级，让我们看到了海南以企业为先，持续优化营商环境的诚意。

Introduction: One of the keys to the Hainan FTP's success is optimizing the business environment and improving enterprise satisfaction. To achieve this, we need to provide better and more efficient services. With integrated services, the functionality of Hainan's One-stop Enterprise Service Center continues to be optimized, making it more convenient and efficient for enterprises to do business. This breakthrough has been reached thanks to cross-sector, inter-departmental collaboration, and the continuous improvement of services. By upgrading the platform, Hainan demonstrates its sincerity in putting enterprises first and continuously optimizing the business environment.

A04

海南日报

"营"在自贸港 "画"说新海南

——优化营商环境专刊

企业服务 一站汇聚

企"话"自贸港

海南大庄园肉业有限公司负责人刘超：

运营成本降低 发展信心更足

海南日报 海南省营商环境建设厅 联合出品

平台升级2.0，办事更加灵！快来打开"海易办"，在首页就能看到我啦！
The smarter, faster 2.0 version of the platform has been released. You can find it on the homepage of the Haiyiban APP.
欢迎使用海易办！
海南省企业综合服务平台
①
法人库
电子证照库
我可太"库"啦！公司的各种电子证照都在这里了！
You can also access all of your company's various e-licenses and e-permits.
海南省企业综合服务平台
②
太懂我了！正缺资金，补贴政策就来了！
You know me so well! Just as we're running low on funds, here you come with some subsidies.
企业研发补贴政策
海南省企业综合服务平台
③
企业银行一线牵。
The platform also connect enterprises directly with banks.
××银行
④
遇见对的人。
Once you've found what you're looking for...
就"码"上行动！
...just tap to apply.
海南省企业综合服务平台
⑤

测评情况良好，快去认证试试吧。
You seem to meet the conditions. Go ahead and apply!
企业申报条件测评
海南省企业综合服务平台

⑥

来，跟我说说。
You can tell me.
海南省企业综合服务平台
进度我盯着呢。
You can check your application status here.
进展
海南省企业综合服务平台

⑦

线上政策解读
海南省企业综合服务平台
敲黑板，这个政策很重要哦。
Attention, students! This is a key policy.

⑧

“营”在自贸港
海南省企业综合服务平台
有我在，轻松“营”!
With me by your side, you can run your business with confidence!

⑨

案例注解 CASE NOTES

海南搭建海南省企业综合服务平台（企业码），聚焦企业发展中的制度性交易成本高、办事效率低、政策兑现不便利等问题，创新实施企业"一码通全岛"服务机制，为企业提供精准化、个性化服务。

Having already established the Hainan Enterprise Comprehensive Service Platform (Enterprise Code), the province has—in focusing on the problems of high institutional transaction costs, low efficiency, and inconvenient policy implementation in the development of enterprises—innovatively implemented the "One Code for the Whole Island" service mechanism for enterprises to provide precise and personalized services to enterprises.

案例进展 CURRENT STATUS

海南将进一步完善"一码通全岛"服务体系，对接商事登记身份码、企业码、监管码、信用码"多码合一"，扩展更多"一码通全岛"应用场景，继续深化平台功能，扩大服务覆盖面，提升企业满意度和获得感。

Hainan will further enhance the "One Code for the Whole Island" service system, merge business registration identity codes, enterprise codes, supervision codes, and credit codes into a single, unified code, expand the number of scenarios where "One Code for the Whole Island" can be applied, continue to improve platform functionality, and expand service coverage to boost corporate satisfaction and sense of gain.

种子保卫战

Keeping Seeds Secure

画外音：种子虽小，培育难度却很大，不仅要投入大量的真金白银、耗费十年乃至更长的时间，还要承担失败的风险。如果劳动得不到应有的尊重，成果得不到应有的保护，还有多少企业愿意下功夫育良种？护“芯”方能强“芯”。持续优化营商环境，确保发明创造者的权益，才能充分激发人们的想象力和创造力。这是“种子保卫战”带来的启发。

Introduction: Although seeds are small, they are difficult to cultivate. Not only do you have to invest a lot of money, but it can also take a decade or more of sweat, blood, and tears to see results, and the risk of failure is ever-present. If this hard work and its results are not respected as they should be, how many companies would be willing to put in the effort to cultivate good seeds? Only by protecting the "core" can we strengthen the "core". Only by continuously optimizing the business environment and ensuring the rights and interests of inventors and creators can we fully stimulate people's imagination and creativity.

A14
“营”在自贸港 “画”说新海南
——优化营商环境专刊
海南日报

种子保卫战

种子是农业的“芯片”，也是保障国家粮食安全的基石。然而，过去育种专家们历经数年培育出一个新品种，却常常败给“仿种子”“假种子”。这不仅严重干扰种业市场秩序，也挫伤了育种创新积极性……

企“话”自贸港

琼中中域投资有限公司开发部总监陈民：

这群“店小二”办事速度真快

你是谁?
Who are you?
超级稻
我是你!
I'm you!
炒鸡稻
①
辛辛苦苦就种出这玩意儿?
This is all we get after all that hard work?
②
真相只有一个，时间却要三年。
There's only one true seed, but it takes three years to cultivate.
2—3年
种子
幼苗
开花
成熟期
③
有“种”你就来!
Ahem, why not cultivate your seeds here?
海南省崖州湾种子实验室
HAINAN YAZHOU BAY SEED LABORATORY
④
你是谁?
Who are you?
ID:
超级稻
我是谁?
Ehm...
炒鸡稻
⑤
13种作物品种
195份种质资源实体的入库鉴定存证
3198份已授权水稻品种信息
海南省崖州湾种子实验室
HAINAN YAZHOU BAY SEED LABORATORY
⑥

三大护法！
Triple-layer IP protection!
“种”有办法！
There's no fooling us!
⑦
“丹霞红”梨，就是棒！
This Danxia Red Pear is quite great!
⑧
侵害植物新品种权，犯法了！
Infringing new plant variety IP rights, guilty!
⑨
大家要学会用法律保护自己。
You have to learn how to use the law to protect yourself.
科技创新与知识产权保护
⑩
一年任意种，任“种”稻远啊！
When it comes to planting year-round, you can leave it to us!
⑪

案例注解 CASE NOTES

种子被称为农业的"芯片"。但长久以来，种子研发同质化、抄袭现象严重，不少科研人员千辛万苦研发出来的新种子，却轻易败给"仿种子"。为保护种子知识产权，海南在农业农村部科技发展中心指导下建设崖州湾分子检测实验室，作为海南省崖州湾种子实验室的配套项目，建立"种子身份证"信息系统，建立完善种业知识产权一体化服务保障体系，构筑育种科研联合攻关优质生态，有效提升崖州湾科技城种业知识产权保护水平。

Seeds are as critical for agriculture as silicon chips and wafers are to the computer industry. However, the seed industry has long been plagued by parallel research and copying. Many scientific researchers have worked hard to develop new varietals only to have copycats take the market. To protect seed-related intellectual property rights, Hainan—with guidance from the Ministry of Agriculture and Rural Affairs' Science and Technology Development Center—established the Yazhou Bay Seed Analysis Laboratory. As a supporting project of the Yazhou Bay Seed Laboratory, the Analysis Laboratory has set up a so-called "ID card" information system for seeds. This information system creates an integrated service guarantee system for seed industry-related intellectual property rights, constructs a high-quality ecosystem for collaborative seed breeding research, and effectively improves the level of protection for seed industry-related intellectual property rights at Yazhou Bay Science and Technology City.

最新进展 CURRENT STATUS

2023年12月8日，海南省种业实验室揭牌，其前身为海南省崖州湾种子实验室。该实验室以热带水产、热带果蔬等生物为研究对象，利用遗传学、分子生物学、环境生物学、大数据科学、人工智能等多学科交叉手段，开展精准农业技术集成与示范、学术交流和人才培养，承接科技成果就地转化，形成"技术创新—成果转移转化"的创新产业价值链。

Building upon the previously existing Yazhou Bay Seed Laboratory, the Hainan Provincial Seed Industry Laboratory was formally unveiled on December 8, 2023. Using multidisciplinary methods (such as genetics analysis, molecular and environmental biology, big data, and artificial), the lab is to study tropical aquatic products, fruits, and vegetables; carry out academic exchanges, cultivation of talented individuals, and the integration and demonstration of precision agriculture technology; undertake on-site transformation of scientific and technological achievements; and form an innovative industrial value chain from "technological innovation" to "achievement transformation".

多元调解止商事纠纷

There's More than One Way to Resolve Commercial Disputes

画外音：国际商事纠纷一站式解决，归根到底是制度创新效能显现，而机制之新的背后，则是法律服务的观念之变、思路之变、方法之变：主动迎上去，及时发现困扰企业的“堵点”“难点”，而不是坐等问题送上门；拥抱新科技，积极运用新技术、寻找新解法，而不是走老路子、按老办法；靠制度发力，努力建立机制、破解共性问题，而不是追求特事特办、解决个性问题。

Introduction: Hainan's "one-stop" resolution of international commercial disputes is the manifestation of the effectiveness of institutional innovation. Behind the new mechanism are changes in the concept, thinking, and approach of legal services—taking the initiative to identify the obstacles and challenges that plague enterprises in a timely manner rather than waiting for problems to come to the door; embracing new technologies and actively applying them to find new solutions, rather than following the old ways and methods; relying on the system to strive to establish mechanisms and solve common issues, rather than pursuing special cases and solving individual problems.

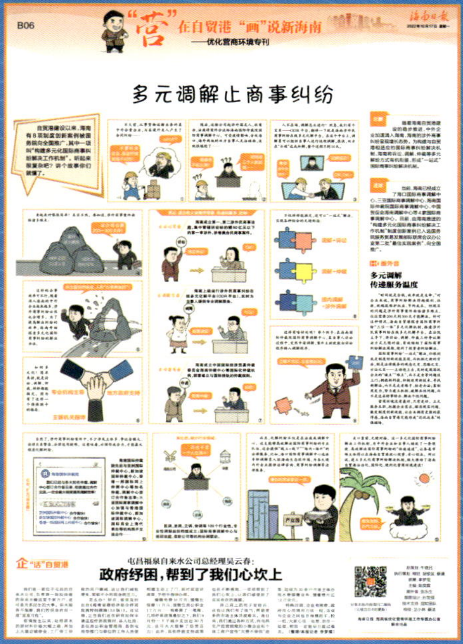
B06

“营”在自贸港 “画”说新海南

——优化营商环境专刊

多元调解止商事纠纷

自贸港建设以来，海南有8项制度创新案例被国务院向全国推广，其中一项叫“构建多元化国际商事纠纷解决工作机制”。听起来很复杂吧？讲个故事你们就懂了。

企“话”自贸港

屯昌福泉自来水公司总经理吴云春：

政府纾困，帮到了我们心坎上

What?!
不要"哇"来"哇"去，你这样做就是不对的！
Don't you "what" me! It's you who's in the wrong!
①
明明是三个人的剧情……
Shouldn't there be three of us?
偏偏他不能出席！
He couldn't make it? How convenient...
②
调解成功！
All's well that ends well!
有空喝茶啊。
Stop by for tea sometimes.
OK，OK.
③

这少说也要200—300天呀！
This'll take almost a year!
案件送达期限
域外证据公证认证
域外法查明……
④
冲出最快的速度，人称“办事苏炳添”！
Nothing can stop me!
⑤
专业机构主导
地方政府支持
主管机关指导
⑥

诉讼
我要诉讼！
I want to sue.
好的！
OK!
调解
我要调解！
I want mediation.
可以！
Sure.
仲裁
我要仲裁！
I want arbitration.
好的！
OK!
⑦

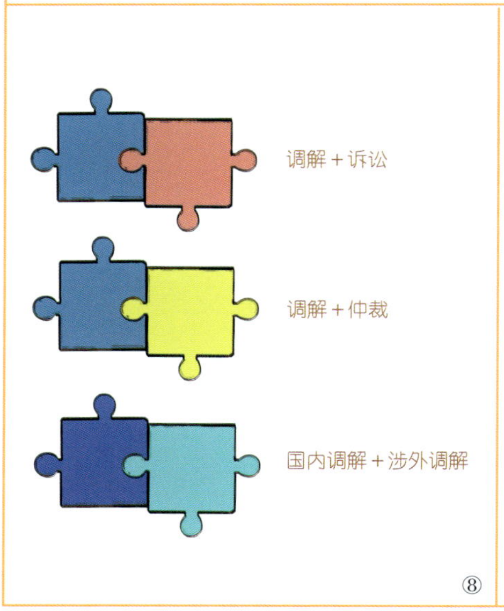
调解＋诉讼
调解＋仲裁
国内调解＋涉外调解
⑧

宜解不宜结，主要省时间。
Save time with mediation. Don't get bogged down in litigation.
调解
诉讼
⑨

海南国际仲裁院
我们已经与各大知名仲裁、调解中心签订合作备忘录，相信通过合作交流，一定会最大程度提高调解效率！
亚洲国际仲裁中心：合作愉快！
新加坡国际仲裁中心：合作愉快！
香港一邦国际网上仲调中心：合作愉快！
⑩
再也不是一个人在战斗！
No one needs to fight alone anymore!
保险公司
法庭
旅调
交调
物调
⑪
产业园
离你的需求更近一步。
Let me come to you.
⑫
椰风海韵，和气生财。
Coconut trees and a breezy shore, harmony and prosperity, who could want more?
⑬

案例注解 CASE NOTES

随着海南自贸港建设的稳步推进，中外企业加速涌入海南，海南的涉外商事纠纷呈现增长态势。为构建与自贸港相适应的国际商事纠纷解决机制，海南将诉讼、调解、仲裁等解纷方式有机衔接，形成一站式国际商事纠纷解决机制。

Alongside the steady construction of the Hainan FTP, the number of domestic and international enterprises pouring into Hainan has been surging. At the same time, the number of foreign-related commercial disputes is also on the rise. In order for the FTP to build a suitable international commercial dispute resolution mechanism, Hainan has formed a "one-stop" international commercial dispute resolution mechanism by organically connecting multiple dispute resolution methods such as litigation, mediation, and arbitration.

案例进展 CURRENT STATUS

当前，海南已经成立了海口国际商事调解中心、三亚国际商事调解中心、海南国际仲裁院国际商事调解中心、中国贸促会海南调解中心等4家国际商事调解中心。目前，由海南推送的"构建多元化国际商事纠纷解决工作机制"制度创新案例已入选国务院服务贸易发展部际联席会议办公室第二批"最佳实践案例"，向全国推广。

For now, measures include the establishment of the Haikou International Commercial Mediation Center, the Sanya International Commercial Mediation Center, the Hainan International Arbitration Court International Commercial Mediation Center, and the China Council for the Promotion of International Trade Hainan Mediation Center. Recently, Hainan's institutional innovation case of "Building a Diversified International Commercial Dispute Resolution Mechanism" was selected by the State Council Office of the Inter-ministerial Joint Conference on Trade in Services Development as one of the second batch of "Best Practice Cases" promoted nationwide.

企业“云”选地　项目快落地

Buying land? Just Head to the Supermarket

画外音：项目与土地，是经济发展的两大要素，可现实中，却常遭遇对接不畅的尴尬。海南创新探索，打破信息壁垒，推出“土地超市”，为破解项目与土地之间的矛盾，提供了行之有效的解题路径。思路变，天地宽。“土地超市”突出了高效便捷，凸显了公平透明，这背后体现的正是制度创新的力量，是海南服务经营主体、优化营商环境的定力。透过“土地超市”可见，只要善于创新、勇于探索，“堵点”同样可变为“亮点”。

Introduction: Projects and land are two major elements of economic development, but in reality, the two are rarely appropriately coordinated. Breaking down information barriers to launch the "Land Supermarket", Hainan has innovated, explored, and provided an effective solution to the common issue of land-project mismatches. The "Land Supermarket" highlights efficiency and convenience, as well as fairness and transparency. Behind this is the power of institutional innovation and Hainan's determination to serve business entities and optimize the business environment. Initiatives like the "Land Supermarket" demonstrate that with innovation and the courage to explore, obstacles can be transformed into opportunities.

A07
“营”在自贸港“画”说新海南
——优化营商环境专刊

企业“云”选地　项目快落地

企“话”自贸港
海南展万投资有限公司项目经理谢志强：
4天拿到“四证”，省时省力

你瞅啥?
What are you looking at?
瞅你是啥地。
Well, I know you're not looking at me!
已拍
农田
①
你究竟有几块好地？为何这些地都闲置在这里?
Everyone around me is being sold off. Why am I being overlooked?
闲置
②
面积
用途
容积率
土地
价格
家大业大啊!
We are family!
③
土地爷开超市了?
Eh? A new supermarket?
特惠
性价比
土地超市
进来看看!
Come on in and browse!
1. 打开“海易办”App或微信小程序
土地超市
2. 进入“土地超市”
3. 根据行政区、用地类型或面积等分类，筛选合适的地块
4. 浏览地块的规划、用途、基准地价、环境分析等信息，可通过三维实景浏览土地现状影像
5. 一键加入购物车，向当地市县招商和资规部门发出购买意向申请
6. 根据市县供地计划和节奏参与公开竞买土地
好地，好地!
I've landed some good land!
④

“小老地”，可找到你了！
Hey there! I've got you.
感谢大数据！
All thanks to big data!
孙总，进度搞快点！
Process that sale ASAP.
宝贝们，上新了！
Ahh, some fresh land on the shelves!
特惠
性价比
性价比
⑤
“前店”
“土地超市”平台
土地超市
“后仓”
“土地仓库”
“中台”
数据平台：海南省项目策划生成平台、土地交易平台、工改平台等
⑥
收！
Come here!
别急，给你找合适的。
Don't panic. We'll find something better for you.
精准配对！
A match made in heaven!
进来看，进来选啊。
Let me know if anything takes your fancy.
土地超市
地就交给你了。
Here we go.
抓紧干活！
Get to work!
⑦
项目多多！
So many projects...
土地多多！
...so much land!
⑧

案例注解 CASE NOTES

随着海南自由贸易港建设的不断推进，资源供给与需求矛盾日益显现，成为影响海南营商环境的一个重要因素。"项目等土地"和"土地晒太阳"等现象并存的用地难问题困扰着企业发展。用地难问题如何破解？海南坚持制度集成创新理念，于2022年6月正式上线运行"土地超市"平台。

Alongside the continuously advancing construction of the Hainan FTP, contradictions between the supply of resources and the demand for those resources are not only becoming increasingly apparent, but they have also become a key factor affecting Hainan's business environment. The coexisting phenomena of "projects waiting for land" and "land lying idle" are plaguing the development of enterprises. How can these land acquisition problems be solved? Adhering to the concept of system integration and innovation, Hainan launched an online "Land supermarket" platform in June 2022.

案例进展 CURRENT STATUS

目前，"土地超市"已上线土地7万亩（约4667公顷），实现土地储备从粗略向精准转变，土地信息从单一封闭向共享对称转变，土地资源利用从粗放浪费向集约高效转变，有效破解"项目等土地"等问题。

As of right now, the "Land supermarket" has posted over 70,000 mu (around 4,667 hectares) of land online. In realizing the transformation from generalized to targeted land reserve allocation, the land information system has transitioned from a single-sided closed model to one that is shared and symmetrical, once-wasteful land resource utilization has become intensive and efficient, and problems of "projects waiting for land" have been effectively solved.

这家超市卖“数据”

The Data Supermarket in the Cloud

画外音：大数据时代，数据资源正成为数据资产。如何培育开发数据要素市场，激活数据要素价值，让海量的公共数据资源更好地服务于经营主体，无疑是一个富有挑战性的新课题。在这样的情况下，海南政府部门携手数据技术企业，探索构建数据产品超市，促进公共数据资源场景化应用和发展。这对优化营商环境、助力企业发展有着格外重要的意义。

Introduction: In the era of Big Data, data resources are valuable assets. Properly cultivating and developing the data element market, realizing the value of data elements, and leveraging the glut of public data resources to better serve business entities is undoubtedly a challenging new topic. Under such circumstances, Hainan's government departments have joined hands with data technology companies to explore the construction of a data product supermarket and promote the scenario-based application and development of public data resources, which is of great significance for optimizing the business environment and boosting enterprise development.

好一个靓仔！
Looking good!
人脸识别
①
不用去排队，坐着慢慢点！
Take a seat and wait. There's no need to wait in line!
②
满腹数据，处处碰壁？
All this data. What am I going to do with it?
确权难
定价难
互信难
入场难
监管难
③
进来看。
Come in...
数据产品超市
进来选。
...and take your pick.
④
发现数据宝贝！
Well, this is data I could work with!
手握数据库，
With data at play...
气预报APP
潮汐数据APP
大气不晚成！
...it's never too late to succeed!
⑤
新品上架！
New items in stock!
进店选购！
Data, data! Get your fresh data here!
New
New
一键加购！
One click and I'm done!
⑥

有个急活儿，有意者来接！
I've got an urgent task here. Anyone interested?
我能！我行！我可以！
Me. I'm interested.
I can take it on!
⑦
几斤几两，心里有数！
Our data can be measured out.
⑧
一条龙服务，稳稳拿捏住！
From input to output, we've got you covered.
货 架
加工
上架
⑨
信息安全，
We keep your data safe...
我们来守护！
...and sound.
网络安全
安全审计
数据溯源
数据脱敏
⑩
数据发展，智慧海南！
Data development for a smart Hainan.
⑪

案例注解 CASE NOTES

自国家数据局挂牌成立以来，国家密集出台了多份政策文件加快数据要素市场化配置。近年来，海南以"海南省数据产品超市"为抓手，率先在公共数据授权运营、标杆数据产品打造、前沿技术及理论研究等方面深化实践，打造数据开发利用与流通交易特色"海南模式"。这一实践入选国家数据局首批数字中国建设典型案例、中国信息协会2024数字政府创新成果与实践案例（数字政府卓越贡献类）。

Since the establishment of the National Data Administration, China has issued a substantial number of policy documents to accelerate the market-oriented allocation of data. In recent years, Hainan has used the creation of a provincial "Data Supermarket" as the starting point for taking the lead in intensifying practices in the fields of public data authorization operations, benchmark data product creation, cutting-edge technology, and theoretical research. Creating a unique "Hainan Model" for the development, utilization, circulation, and trading of data, this "Data Supermarket" was selected by the National Data Administration as one of the first batch of model cases on "Constructing a Digital China", as well as being recognized by the China Information Association's "2024 Digital Government Innovation Achievements and Practice Cases" in the Digital Government Outstanding Contribution Category.

案例进展 CURRENT STATUS

海南省数据产品超市经过三年的建设和发展，充分发挥促进数据要素与实体经济深度融合的重要载体作用，实现为数据要素市场提供一站式基础设施、一体化解决方案、一条龙服务体验、一张网生态资源。目前，其入驻企业1700多家，上架近3000个数据产品、市场交易额超11亿元，持续加快将海南打造成全国数据要素市场化配置改革示范省。

After three years of ongoing construction and development, the provincial "Data Supermarket" gives full play to the important role, which promotes the integration of data elements with the real economy, and provides the data element market with one-stop infrastructure, integrated solutions, a total service experience, and one-network environmental resources. Continuing to accelerate the development of Hainan into a national demonstration province for the reform of market-based allocation of data elements, the Supermarket—with transaction a volume exceeding CNY 1.1 billion—has more than 1, 700 enterprises participating and has launched nearly 3,000 data products.

“碳路”向前

Moving Toward Carbon Neutrality

画外音： 将碳汇“商品化”，既能倒逼排碳方努力节能减排、承担起社会责任，也能让固碳方得到物质补偿，鼓励他们坚持下去，可谓一举多赢。撬动生态资源价值化，把碳汇变为“可量化、可交易、可增值、可持续”的商品，说起来容易，做起来难，探出新路子更难。这就需要各地立足自身优势，勇于创新体制机制，持续探索监测、测算和核算等一系列方法学，为碳汇产品价值实现搭建更多常态化场景，让更多红树林成为“金树林”。

Introduction: The "commodification" of carbon sinks induces carbon emitters to work hard to save energy, reduce emissions, and assume social responsibilities. It also allows carbon capturers to receive material compensation and encourages them to keep at it, bringing mutual benefits to both emitters and capturers. However, leveraging the value of ecological resources and turning carbon sinks into "quantifiable, tradable, value-added, and sustainable" commodities is easier said than done, with innovation in this field being even more of a challenge. Such efforts require each locale to build on its advantages, dare to innovate systems and mechanisms, and continue to explore a set of methodologies encompassing monitoring, measurement, and accounting to create a greater range of scenarios to realize the value of carbon sink products and transform mangroves into "money trees".

A05 “营”在自贸港 “画”说新海南
——优化营商环境专刊

“碳路”向前

画外音

让更多红树林成为“金树林”

企“话”自贸港

海南华德科技有限公司负责人倪夏：

“闲置资产”终于“活”起来了

大家好，我是二氧化碳。
Hello, everyone. I'm carbon dioxide...
也可以叫我的别名，CO_2。
...but you can call me CO_2.
①

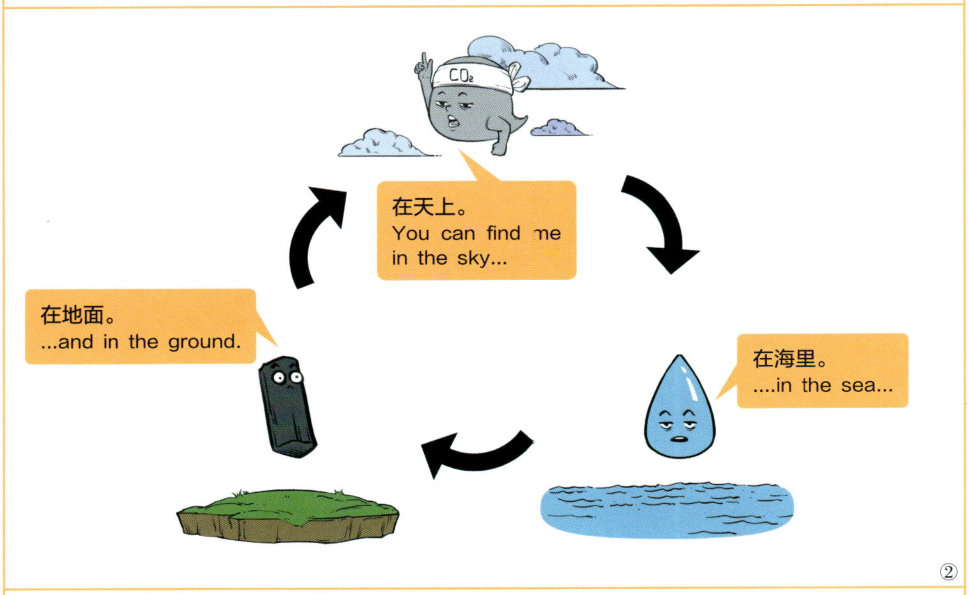
在天上。
You can find me in the sky...
在海里。
....in the sea...
在地面。
...and in the ground.
②

把我捂发烧了，谁都别想好过！
Come on, CO_2, give me a break. I'm sweltering.
③

树大不仅招风，还招二氧化碳！
Big trees not only catch the wind, but also catch carbon dioxide.
碳碳，我叫你一声，敢答应吗?!
Come here, I've got you now!
咋还能卖了我赚钱?
How are you guys selling me for money?
CO2
④

“红”网行动，疏而不漏！
Mangroves at the ready! We can't let carbon get away!
⑤

5年的排量包，不许多排哟。
This is your five years carbon allowance. No going over it!
好的，好的！
Understood.
大排量，努力减。
It's time for us to reduce our carbon emissions!
知道了，但年底了，排量包不够用了！
Fair enough, but it's approaching the end of the year. There's not enough remaining allowance.
憋着点儿排！
Slow your roll!
⑥

“碳”为观止！
Carbon out...
收放自如！
...carbon in.
⑦

碧海蓝天！
Look at the blue sea and sky!
令人“暂碳”！
It's enough to cut carbon for good!
碳达峰
碳中和
⑧

投资自贸港，发展可持续！
For sustainable development, invest in the Hainan FTP!
⑨

案例注解 CASE NOTES

实现绿色发展作为我国新发展理念的重要内容，是需要贯彻到当今一切经济社会活动中的原则要求，这当然也包括营商环境建设。尤其是随着2020年我国提出实现碳达峰、碳中和的“双碳”目标，节能降耗、提高能效已成为推动广大企业实现高质量发展的重要着力点。在这一背景下，海南国际碳排放权交易中心于2022年获批成立。

Achieving sustainable green development is an important part of China's new development concepts and a principle requirement that needs to be implemented in all modern-day economic and social activities. This, of course, also includes the construction of the business environment. Especially with China proposing in 2020 to achieve the dual goals of reaching carbon peak by 2030 and achieving carbon neutrality by 2060, reducing energy consumption and improving energy efficiency have already become an important focal point for most enterprises seeking to achieve high-quality development. Against this backdrop, the Hainan International Carbon Emission Trading Center was approved for establishment in 2022.

案例进展 CURRENT STATUS

2022年5月31日，海南省首个蓝碳生态产品交易完成签约，这是海南省蓝碳资源价值转化的实质性突破，标志海南省在推进海洋生态保护和应对气候变化制度创新方面迈出新步伐，并为国家探索建立健全生态产品价值实现机制提供了海南方案。

On May 31, 2022, Hainan Province's first "blue carbon" ecological product transaction was signed. As a substantial breakthrough in the value transformation of Hainan's blue carbon resources, this step not only marks the province's progress in promoting marine ecological protection and institutional innovation ir addressing climate change, but also provides a "Hainan solution" for China to explore and establish a sound mechanism for realizing the value of ecological products.

创新药械，从乐城“先行”

Piloting Innovative Medical Products in Boao Lecheng

画外音：一个先行区，一片试验田。博鳌乐城国际医疗旅游先行区的突出优势在“先行先试”。透过博鳌乐城，我们看到的、感知的，更多是制度创新的力量，是改革创新的原动力。也正是靠着敢闯敢试的锐意创新，独特的政策优势得以尽快释放，才换来了营商环境的大变样，吸引了国际药械企业的纷纷入驻。锚定“先行区”定位，把“人无我有”的政策用好用足，把政策红利“吃干榨尽”，敢于“吃螃蟹”，勇啃“硬骨头”，必能让博鳌乐城这块金字招牌更加闪亮。

Introduction: Pilot zones like the Boao Lecheng International Medical Tourism Pilot Zone are testing grounds for new ideas and technologies. Through Boao Lecheng, we can truly witness the power of institutional innovation as the driving force of reform. The courage to venture and innovate is precisely why the policies in place here have so rapidly realized their advantages, bringing about a massive change in the business environment and attracting medical product enterprises from around the globe. Centering on its status as a pilot zone, Boao Lecheng strives to fully capitalize on its unique policy advantages and power ahead with innovation to benefit medical consumers in China.

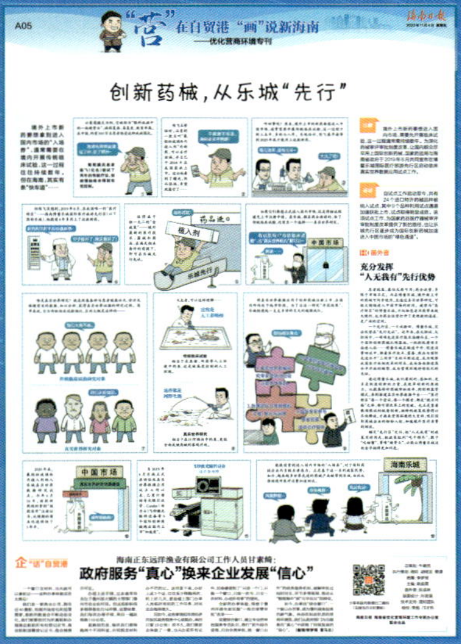
A05

“营”在自贸港 “画”说新海南

——优化营商环境专刊

创新药械，从乐城“先行”

画外音

充分发挥

“人无我有”先行优势

企“话”自贸港

海南正东远洋渔业有限公司工作人员甘素楠：

政府服务“真心”换来企业发展“信心”

是谁在我眼前遮住了帘，忘了掀开？
Aiya, I'm as blind as a mole!
①
不是我不想买，是根本买不到啊！
It's not that I don't want to buy the medicine to treat my condition. It's simply that I can't.
②
等完这年，还有三年。
It's still going to take three more years to develop.
太久了吧！
I can't wait that long!
③
新药剂注射术后检查来啰。
Let's do a post-injection follow-up.
帘子掀开了，我又看见了！
The curtains have parted. I can see again!
④
咱先试试！
Let's pilot them here!
药品进口
植入剂
乐城先行
⑤
有钥匙吗？“传统临床试验”或“真实世界研究”都可以。
Do you have a key? "Traditional clinical trials" or "real-world research" will do.
这……
Erm...
中国市场
外国新药
⑥

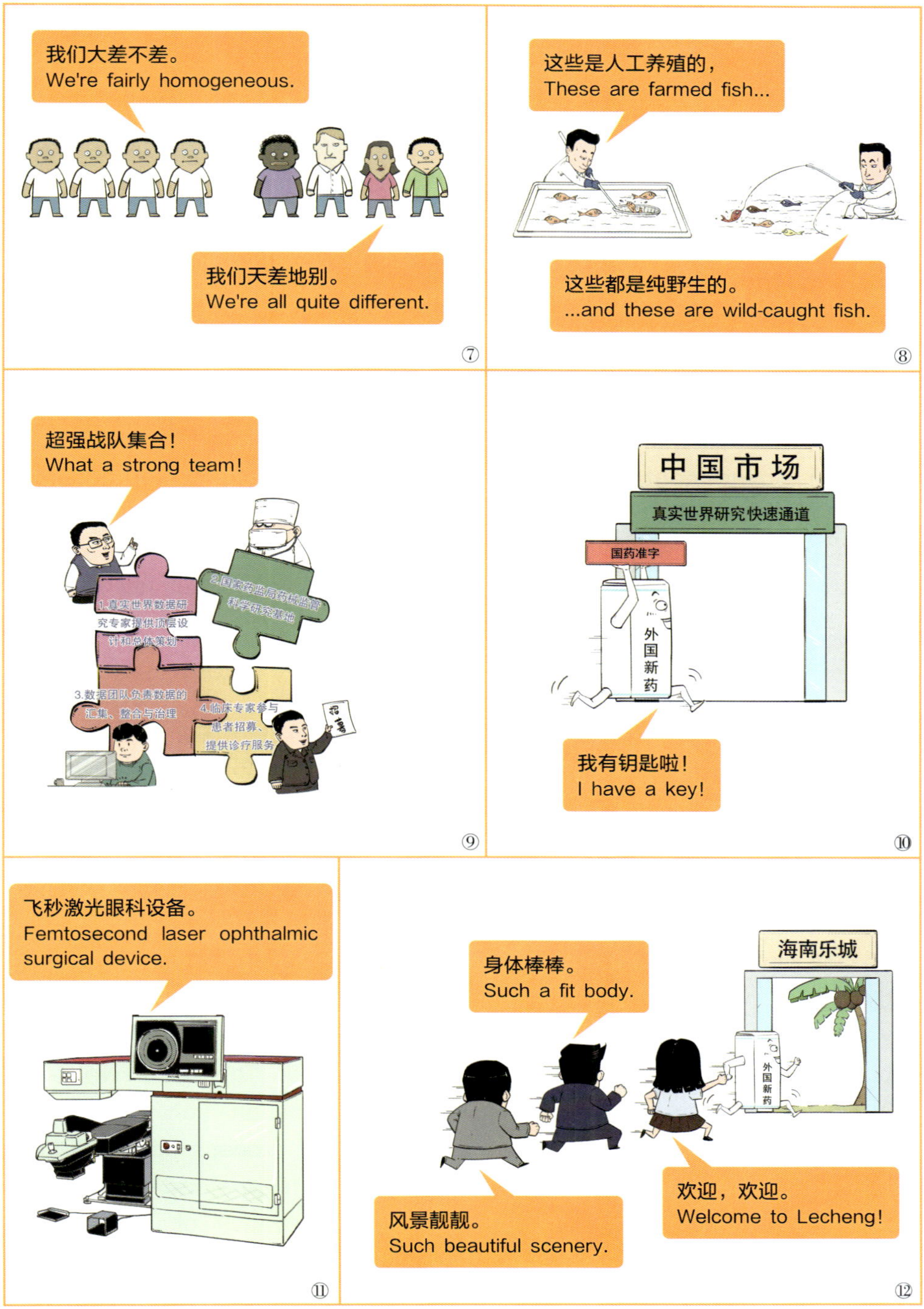
我们大差不差。
We're fairly homogeneous.
我们天差地别。
We're all quite different.
⑦
这些是人工养殖的，
These are farmed fish...
这些都是纯野生的。
...and these are wild-caught fish.
⑧
超强战队集合！
What a strong team!
1.真实世界数据研究专家提供顶层设计和总体策划
2.国家药监局药械监管科学研究基地
3.数据团队负责数据的汇集、整合与治理
4.临床专家参与患者招募、提供诊疗服务
⑨
中国市场
真实世界研究快速通道
国药准字
外国新药
我有钥匙啦！
I have a key!
⑩
飞秒激光眼科设备。
Femtosecond laser ophthalmic surgical device.
⑪
海南乐城
身体棒棒。
Such a fit body.
外国新药
欢迎，欢迎。
Welcome to Lecheng!
风景靓靓。
Such beautiful scenery.
⑫

案例注解 CASE NOTES

境外上市新药要想进入国内市场，需要先开展临床试验。这一过程通常需持续数年。为深化药械审评审批制度改革，让国内群众尽早用上国际创新药械，国家药监局与海南省政府于2019年6月共同宣布在博鳌乐城国际医疗旅游先行区启动临床真实世界数据应用试点工作。

When a manufacturer wishes to sell new pharmaceuticals in the domestic market, China requires a several-year-long series of clinical trials. As part of intensifying the reform of the pharmaceutical and medical device review and approval system and enabling domestic patients to use innovative drugs and medical devices as soon as possible, the National Medical Products Administration and the Hainan Provincial Government jointly announced the Boao Lecheng International Medical Tourism Pilot Zone in June 2019 to pilot the application of clinical real-world evidence for accelerating the approval of medical products that have already received approval in markets outside China.

案例进展 CURRENT STATUS

截至2024年底，累计40款国际创新药械在博鳌乐城国际医疗旅游先行区开展"真研"，累计17个国际创新药械产品利用"真实世界证据"辅助支持在我国加速获批上市。该项试点工作，为国家药品医疗器械审评审批制度改革提供了新的路径，也让博鳌乐城国际医疗旅游先行区逐步成为国际创新药械加速进入中国市场的"绿色通道"。

As of late 2024, Boao Lecheng International Medical Tourism Pilot Zone has developed a total of 40 internationally innovative pharmaceuticals and medical devices, and the domestic approval of 17 internationally innovative pharmaceuticals and medical device products has—with the support of real-world evidence—been accelerated. This pilot work not only provides a new path for the reform of the national pharmaceuticals and medical device products review and approval process, it also allows the Boao Lecheng International Medical Tourism Pilot Zone to gradually become a "green channel" for internationally innovative pharmaceuticals and medical devices to accelerate their entry into the domestic Chinese market.

第五章
Section 5

因地制宜，市县出实招
Local Solutions

海口：投标踏上“筋斗云”

Haikou: Bidding Through the Cloud

画外音：参与投标时，很多企业经营者常常深感“劳神费钱”。开发区块链，保函电子化，信息能共享，流程掌上办，投标更便捷。这里，科技之力当然是一大看点，但更大的看点是政务服务观念之变、思路之变、方法之变。把企业的烦心事当作政府部门的心头事，把“老大难”作为提升服务质量的突破口，探索新办法，建立新机制，方能不断培厚企业成长发展的沃土。

Introduction: Enterprises often balk at the expense and bureaucracy of participating in project bidding. However, thanks to the introduction of blockchain technology, electronic letters of guarantee, information sharing, and smartphone apps, bidding is now much easier. The most prominent change is the technological breakthroughs that have made this possible, but a more significant attraction lies in the breakthroughs made in the concepts and approaches to providing government services. Only by treating the concerns of enterprises as their own, taking "long-standing problems" as starting points for improvement, exploring new methods, and establishing new mechanisms can government departments and agencies continue to cultivate a fertile environment for enterprise growth and development.

A04
“营”在自贸港 “画”说新海南
——优化营商环境专刊

投标踏上“筋斗云”

竞标是企业参与市场竞争的重要手段，但原来的投标过程实在“劳神费钱”，企业有苦说不出……

保证金

企“话”自贸港

保亭七仙温泉康乐旅业有限公司负责人黄彦谋：

税务部门把纳税人需求放在心里

压力山大啊！
The weight of this bid bond is crushing me!
保证金
①
啊啊啊啊……
Aaaaaaah...
头好痛啊！
...such a headache!
②
"猴"辛苦啊！
All this monkeying around for a bid bond.
③
投标速度，腾云驾雾！
Hold it right there! Why not go through the cloud?
④
电子保函
⑤

已发送
电子保函
“猴赛雷”！
Much better!
⑥
“区域链+电子保函”应用系统
北京
广州
珠海
海口
⑦
终于得闲考察一下五指山漂流项目了！
I finally have the time to try out the white-water rafting in Wuzhishan.
⑧
有了云，走好运。
Everything's faster up on the cloud.
⑨
朱总又玩手机呢？
Playing games again，Piggie?
别瞎说，我在给高老庄投标呢。
Actually，I'm bidding on Gao Village.
⑩

案例注解 CASE NOTES

投标成本负担高、跨区域投标难，一直是企业投标工作的痛点。2021年1月18日，海口市公共资源交易中心正式上线运行“区块链+电子保函”应用系统。该系统不仅直接接入金融机构，同时加入由北京、广州、珠海三地共同发起成立的全国首个公共资源交易区块链共享应用平台，运用区块链技术实现“链上”跨区域数据共享互认，通过平台“跑起来”，让投标人“足不出户”即可全程在线办理投标业务。此案例入选海南省优化营商环境工作专班发布的第一批优化营商环境示范案例。

For corporate bidding work, the high-cost burden of bidding and the difficulty of cross-regional bidding have always been the pain points. On January 18, 2021, the Haikou Public Resources Trading Center officially launched a "Blockchain+Electronic Letter of Guarantee" application system that is both directly connected to financial institutions and a member of the national public resource transaction blockchain sharing application platform jointly initiated by Beijing, Guangzhou, and Zhuhai. The platform, which is a first in China, uses blockchain technology to achieve cross-regional data sharing and mutual recognition of items on the "chain". By using this platform, bidders can handle the entire bidding process online without ever leaving home. This case was subsequently selected by the Hainan Provincial Business Environment Optimization Working Group as one of the first batch of demonstration cases to be released.

最新进展 CURRENT STATUS

目前，海口市公共资源交易中心正推动更多招投标事项实现“电子办”“网上办”，进一步为企业“松绑减负”，优化公共资源交易营商环境。

To further "loosen constraints and relax burdens" for enterprises and optimize the business environment for public resource transactions, the Haikou Public Resources Trading Center is currently promoting the electronic and online processing of more bidding and tendering matters.

三亚：三亚营商直通车发车啦！

Sanya: Rapid Access to Government Services in Sanya? Just Board the Bus!

画外音：“直通”意味着堵点疏通、流程连通、渠道贯通。一方面，线下“直通车”积极拓展并向基层延伸就近办、快速办等服务；另一方面，线上“直通车”打通反映问题、了解政策、快速审批等渠道。可以说，高效、优质政务服务背后，体现的是政府部门弄清楚了企业群众的需求是什么，搞明白了办事流程的症结在哪里，推动“人找服务”向“服务找人”转变，及时回应了企业群众所需所盼。

Introduction: "Direct access" means removing bottlenecks, connecting processes, and streamlining channels. On the ground, on-site service teams are actively expanding and extending services like localized assistance and expedited processing to the grassroots level. In the cloud, the online "express service" opens up channels for reporting issues, understanding policies, and obtaining fast approvals. Behind efficient and high-quality government services lies the government's clear understanding of what businesses and the public need, as well as where the bottlenecks in processes lie. This has driven a shift from "people seeking services" to "services seeking people", promptly addressing the needs and expectations of businesses and the public.

A05
“营”在自贸港 “画”说新海南
——优化营商环境专刊

三亚营商直通车发车啦！

大家应该都有体会，出门办事，最怕一个不小心就可能遭遇各种烦心事，比如排队等号、来回奔波、资料遗漏——要咋办呢？且看三亚出招了——

“直通”服务 便企利民

企“话”自贸港

海南万科企业管理有限公司报批报建合伙人郑嘉敏：

“直通车”进项目 企业省时又省力

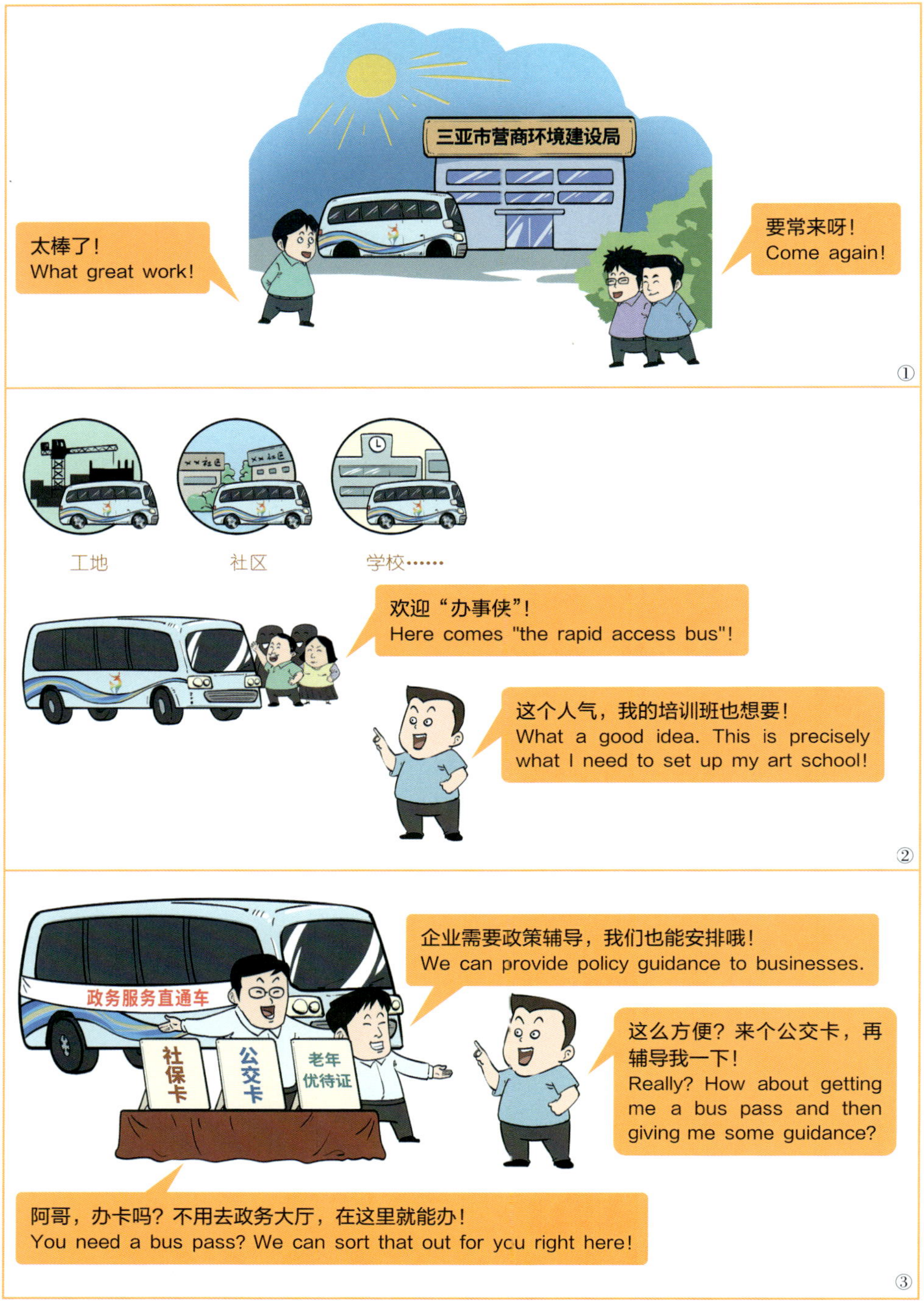
三亚市营商环境建设局
太棒了!
What great work!
要常来呀!
Come again!
①
工地
社区
学校……
欢迎“办事侠”!
Here comes "the rapid access bus"!
这个人气，我的培训班也想要!
What a good idea. This is precisely what I need to set up my art school!
②
政务服务直通车
社保卡
公交卡
老年优待证
企业需要政策辅导，我们也能安排哦!
We can provide policy guidance to businesses.
这么方便? 来个公交卡，再辅导我一下!
Really? How about getting me a bus pass and then giving me some guidance?
阿哥，办卡吗? 不用去政务大厅，在这里就能办!
You need a bus pass? We can sort that out for ycu right here!
③

不用找老默，创业政策咨询，这就送上门！
There's no need to call Mr. Mo. We can provide start-up policy consultation services.
政务服务直通车
告诉老默，我想创业了。
Tell Mr. Mo that I'd like to start a business.
④
还得消防验收。
The venue also needs to pass a fire safety inspection.
想开培训班？得先办证！
Wanna open an extracurricular school? You need a permit!
培训班
市场监管
住建部门
要跑这么多趟才能开起来啊？
How many trips will this take?
公共场所卫生许可证别忘了办哦。
Don't forget to apply for a public places hygiene license.
材料一键上传！
I can upload all the required materials in one go!
90%
材料上传中
培训快速开班！
It's time for class!
培训班
⑤

政企约见平台
想见领导干部？手机下单，有约必见！
Would you like to meet directly with government officials? Just make an appointment on the APP, and we'll make sure they show up!
书记信箱
问题诉求直通车
⑥

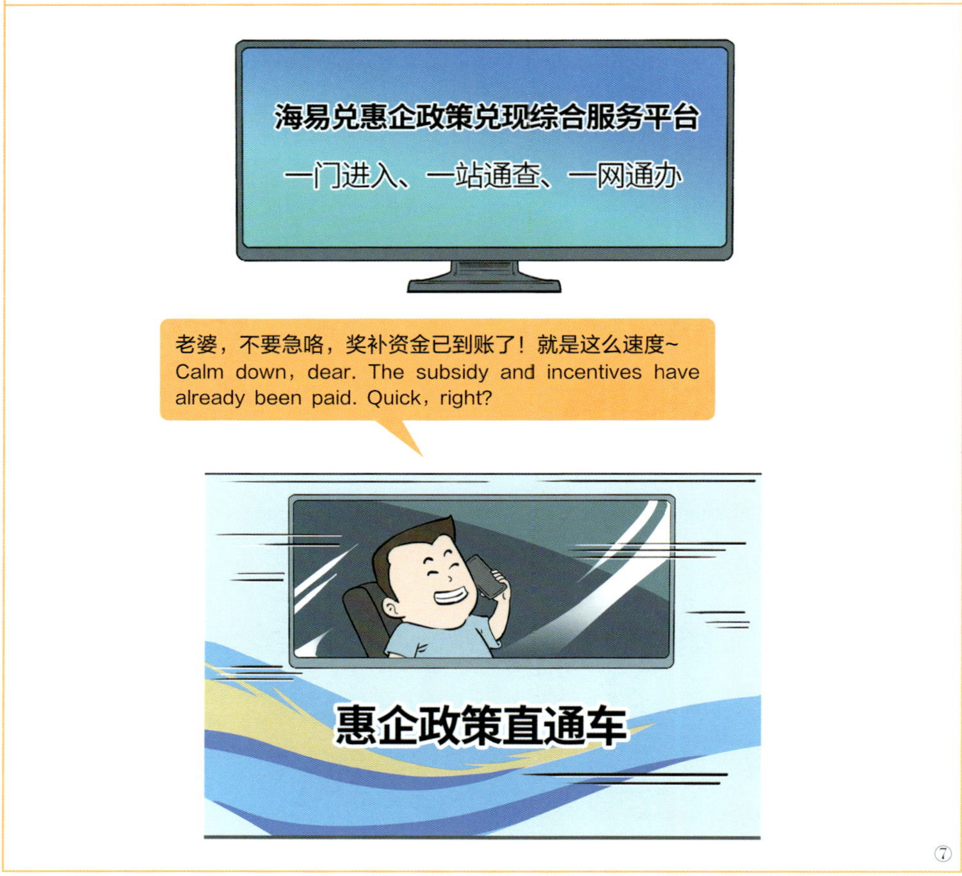
海易兑惠企政策兑现综合服务平台
一门进入、一站通查、一网通办
老婆，不要急咯，奖补资金已到账了！就是这么速度~
Calm down, dear. The subsidy and incentives have already been paid. Quick, right?
惠企政策直通车
⑦

我来协助你！
I'm here to help!
信用修复上门
XX公司
我申请信用修复。
I'd like to apply to repair my company's credit.
⑧

处长办公室
副处长办公室
科长办公室
政务事项
这些事项的盖章审批，以后就交给你啦！
You're now in charge of stamping and approvals!
⑨

三亚市营商环境建设局
政务服务直通车
政府帮咱来想辙~
Whatever issues we need the government's help with...
有问题，就上车！
...just hop on board!
⑩

案例注解 CASE NOTES

为加强政企有效沟通，及时回应经营主体所需所盼，三亚市营商环境建设局通过建立营商"直通车"服务体系，切实践行"企业有事吹哨，政府立即报到"服务理念，全力打造能办事、好办事、办成事的"便利三亚"，助力经营主体发展壮大。

To strengthen effective communication between the government and enterprises, and for the government to respond promptly to the needs and expectations of business entities, the Sanya Business Environment Construction Bureau has established an "express service" for business, has put into practice the service concept of "when enterprises call, the government immediately responds", and—to help business entities grow and develop—is striving to create a "convenient Sanya" where things can be done, done well, and done successfully.

案例进展 CURRENT STATUS

目前，三亚已陆续开设"问题诉求直通车""政务服务直通车""惠企政策直通车""行政审批直通车"。其中，优化营商环境"书记信箱"为一批企业解决问题诉求，兑现政府拖欠账款2400余万元；"政务服务直通车"前往多个村居、学校、项目现场开展服务；"海易兑"三亚平台实现资金兑付超 5.7亿元；推动印发 《三亚市推进市级"一枚印章管审批"改革实施方案》，共完成600个行政审批事项划转。

At present, Sanya has successively opened a "direct line for complaints and appeals" a "direct line for government services" a "direct line for enterprise-friendly policies" and a "direct line for administrative approvals". Of these, the "Secretary's Mailbox" for optimizing the business environment has already solved problems and demands for a number of enterprises, and paid more than CNY 24 million in late funds from government entities. The "Government Service Express" has gone to many villages, schools, and project sites to provide services. The Haiyidui Sanya policy platform has realized more than CNY 570 million in subsidies. The *Sanya City Implementation Plan for Promoting Municipal-level One Seal for Approval Reform* has been promoted, and the transfer of 600 administrative approval matters has been completed.

保亭：咖啡“碰碰杯”问题“消消乐”

Baoting: There's no issue that can't be solved over a coffee and a chat

画外音：对于政府部门来说，推动营商环境优化的决心、诚意，往往体现在为企业解忧排难的一招一式中；而企业评价优化营商环境工作成效的高低，往往就看自己的困难有没有受到足够的关注，反映的问题能不能得到及时解决。政府部门只有将这种认识内化于心，才会主动去想企业之所想乃至想企业之所未想，积极解决企业的急难愁盼问题，从而不仅搭起政企“连心桥”，而且保障其畅通无阻。

Introduction: For government departments, the determination and sincerity to promote the optimization of the business environment are often reflected in the specific measures taken to address and resolve the difficulties faced by enterprises. The effectiveness of these efforts, as evaluated by businesses, often depends on whether their challenges receive sufficient attention and whether the issues they raise are resolved in a timely manner. Only by internalizing this understanding can government departments proactively anticipate the needs of enterprises—even those not yet expressed—and actively address their urgent and pressing concerns. In doing so, they not only build a "bridge of trust" between the government and businesses but also ensure that this bridge remains unobstructed and effective.

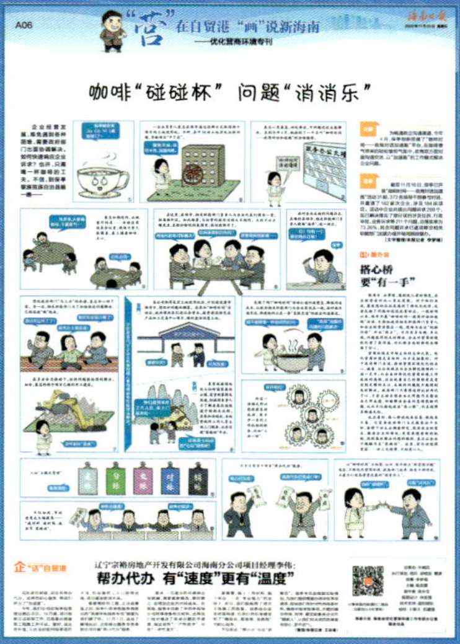
A06

“营”在自贸港 “画”说新海南

——优化营商环境专刊

咖啡“碰碰杯” 问题“消消乐”

企“话”自贸港

辽宁宗裕房地产开发有限公司海南分公司项目经理李伟：

帮办代办 有“速度”更有“温度”

保亭喊你来Jia Go Vi（喝咖啡）了。
You've got a coffee date coming up in Baoting.
①
楼拆不掉，项目卡壳，我脑壳疼。
Without demolishing this building, the project is at a standstill. What to do?
拆
②
政务办公大楼
“咖啡时间”活动邀请
???
③
来来来，大家喝咖啡，不要客气！
Come in, everyone. Grab some coffee!
边吃边说。
Let's have a chat.
④

征拆速度能加快吗？
Can the expropriation and demolition process be accelerated?
用地问题啥时能解决？
When will the issue of land use be solved?
资金周转困难哦……
I'm having cashflow problems...

⑤

叮！你有一个新的待办订单！
Ding! One more thing on my to-do list!
接单！
Keep them coming!

⑥

项目可以开工了！
Hooray! We can start construction!
我去办土地清表！
I'll go sort out the land clearing and leveling!
制定好征拆方案了！
And I'll sort out the expropriation and demolition plan!
这杯咖啡"真香"！
That was one "tasty" cup of coffee!

⑦

农产品交易中心
感谢投资！
Thanks for investing!
共同致富！
Let's get rich together!
我们是资规所工作人员，来上门服务啦！
We're from the Natural Resources and Planning Office. We've come to assist you.
这就是七仙岭的“七仙”服务吧！
This is peak-level service!
⑧

能不能给我一杯咖啡的时间？
Can you spare a few minutes over coffee?
“直直”地跟你沟通把问题解决。
Let's hash this issue out together.
⑨

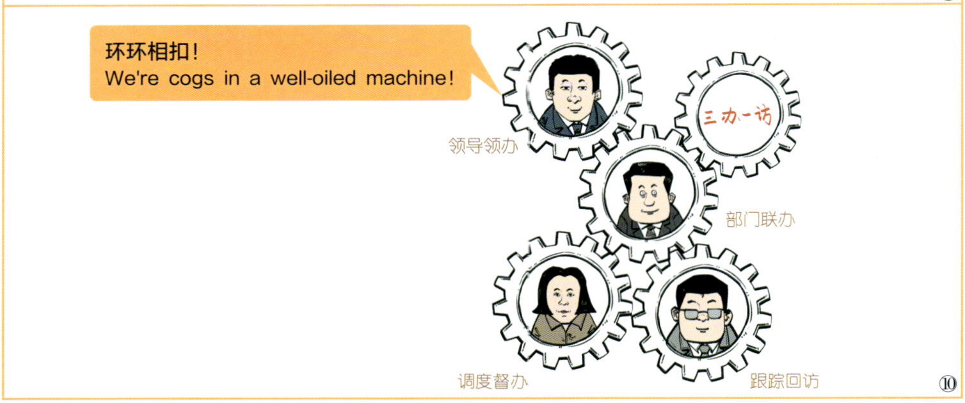
环环相扣！
We're cogs in a well-oiled machine!
领导领办
三办一访
部门联办
调度督办
跟踪回访
⑩

笔笔清楚！
It's all accounted for!
建账
分账
交账
对账
销账
⑪
审核加速度！
An accelerated review process!
是我的脚步。
That's how I like to roll.
⑫
帮办已完成！
They've sorted it out for me!
完成
滴滴代办已完成订单！
Same here!
完成
完成
⑬
咖啡“碰碰杯”
There's no issue that can't be solved...
问题“消消乐”！
...over a coffee and a chat!
⑭

案例注解 CASE NOTES

为畅通政企沟通渠道，2022年4月，保亭创新搭建了"咖啡时间——政商对话加速跑"平台，在咖啡香气带来的轻松愉悦气氛中，政商双方面对面沟通交流，以"加速跑"的工作模式解决企业问题。

To facilitate communication channels between the government and enterprises, in April 2022, Baoting decided to set up the "Coffee Time Dialogues". This platform for the government and businesses provides a relaxed and pleasant atmosphere where government workers and businessmen can solve problems faster by communicating face-to-face.

案例进展 CURRENT STATUS

截至2025年2月11日，保亭已开展"咖啡时间——政商对话加速跑"活动108期，参与企业545家次，活动共收集诉求708个，现已解决落实了部分涉及征拆、行政审批、业务咨询等667个问题，总落实率为94.2%。其余问题诉求已逐项移交相关职能部门加紧办理并每月跟踪督办。

As of February 11, 2025, 545 enterprises have taken part in 108 "Coffee Time Dialogues". A total of 708 complaints have been recorded. Of these, 667 issues (related to land acquisition and demolition, administrative approval, and business consultation) have been resolved, accounting for 94.2% of the total. The remaining issues and complaints have been transferred to the relevant functional departments for expedited handling and monthly follow-up supervision.

琼中：一站办好“万般事”

Qiongzhong: Obtain Documents the Easy Way

画外音： 政府部门多操心，企业、群众就能少烦心；信息数据多跑路，企业、群众就能少跑腿。审批做“减法”，服务做“加法”，说难也难，说容易也容易，关键就在于，政府部门愿不愿增强服务意识，既想企业、群众之所想，又想企业、群众之所未想；能不能“贴着骨头下刀”，将该整合的事项整合，将该压减的流程压减，不拖泥带水；会不会运用信息技术，破除“门户之见”，拆除“信息烟囱”，让信息有序、无碍流动。

Introduction: The more processes local governments take into their own hands, the less the public has to worry about. The more information agencies process and share, the less running around enterprises and the public have to do. Reducing the complexity of approval processes and improving the level of government services is hardly easy, but it's not impossible. It all depends on whether government departments are willing to enhance their service awareness, anticipate the needs of businesses and the public, cut through red tape and consolidate processes that can be consolidated, and use IT and information systems to smash down data barriers between different departments.

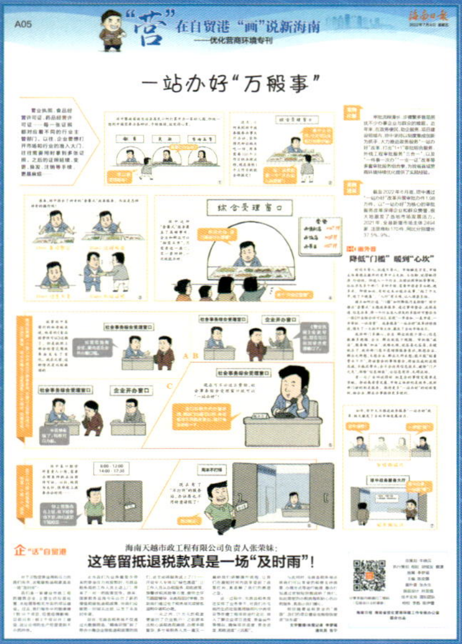
A05

“营”在自贸港 “画”说新海南

——优化营商环境专刊

海南日报

一站办好“万般事”

企“话”自贸港

海南天越市政工程有限公司负责人张荣妹：

这笔留抵退税款真是一场“及时雨”！

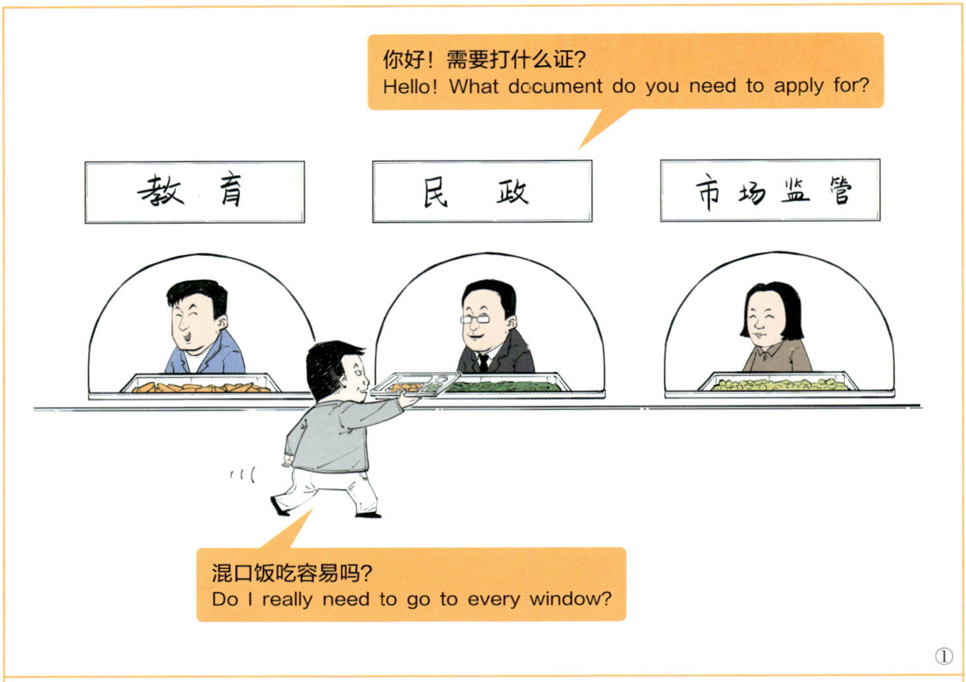
你好！需要打什么证？
Hello! What document do you need to apply for?
教 育
民 政
市 场 监 管
混口饭吃容易吗？
Do I really need to go to every window?
①

综 合 受 理 窗 口
要什么证照，今天可以全部打包带走哦！
We serve whatever document you require here!
麻烦给我一个“开办幼儿园套餐”！
I'd like the "kindergarten opening" meal deal, please!
②

1. 事项整合
2. 流程再造
3. 信息共享
4. 开出证明
③

综合受理窗口
套餐
开便利店 HOT!
开饭店 HOT!
开景区 HOT!
欢迎光临，请问需要什么套餐？
Welcome! Which meal deal would you like?
来个“开饭店套餐”。
I'll have "restaurant opening", please.
④

社会事务综合受理窗口
经营范围有变化，要先去企业开办窗口哦。
Your business scope has changed. I'm afraid you'll need to go to the company registration window first.
⑤

社会事务综合受理窗口
企业开办窗口
营业执照变更好啦，现在可以回到综合受理窗口了。
Your business license has been amended. You can head back to the unified service window.
⑥

社会事务综合受理窗口
企业开办窗口
辛苦林老板了，现在可以办啦。
Sorry to trouble you, Mr. Lin. I can handle your paperwork now.
⑦

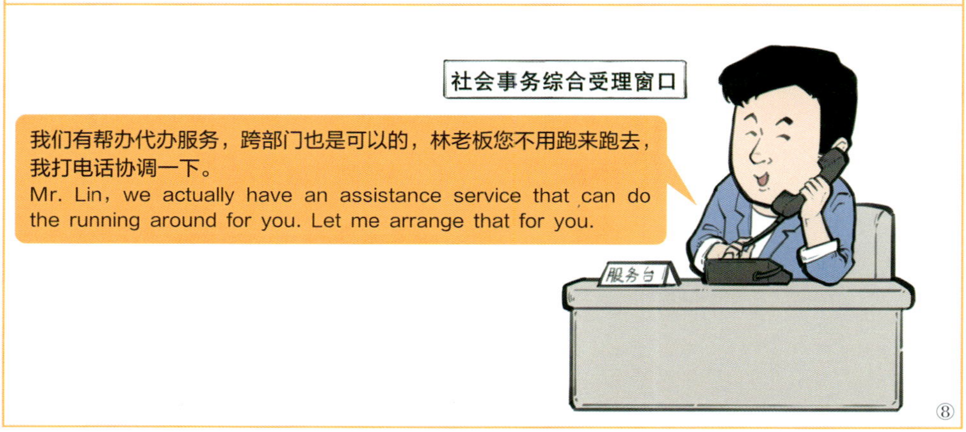
社会事务综合受理窗口
我们有帮办代办服务，跨部门也是可以的，林老板您不用跑来跑去，我打电话协调一下。
Mr. Lin, we actually have an assistance service that can do the running around for you. Let me arrange that for you.
服务台
⑧

8:00—12:00
14:00—17:30
你上班我也在上班，我下班你也下班，咱们注定不能相见！
Seeing as you're only at work when I'm at work, it seems we're destined to never meet!
下班
⑨
周末不打烊
想见就见！
That's better.
24H自助服务区
办公中
⑩
琼中绿橙？
Qiongzhong green oranges?
一律能“橙”！
We've greenlit your export license.
审核做减法
琼中政务服务大厅
24H自助服务区
一站办好、一件事一次办
1+1组合服务、外线工程三合一
琼中办事，一站就“橙”！
In Qiongzhong, we're ready to greenlight all your documents in a single location.
服务做加法
⑪

案例注解 CASE NOTES

审批流程漫长、步骤繁多曾是困扰不少办事企业与群众的难题。近年来，在政务便民、助企服务、项目建设领域内，琼中坚持以制度集成创新为抓手，大力推进政务服务"一站办好"改革，打出"1+1"审批组合服务、"信用+免审"、异地证照单向认可等多套审批服务组合拳，为我省县域营商环境持续优化提供了实践经验。

Long approvals and numerous steps are a problem that has always troubled businesses and members of the public. In recent years, Qiongzhong has—in the fields of government services, business services, and project construction—insisted on taking system integration and innovation as the starting point, has vigorously promoted the reform of "one-stop" government services, has launched a combination of approval services (such as "1+1" approval combination services, "credit+exemption from approval", and one-way recognition of certificates and licenses from different places), and has provided practical experience for the continuous optimization of the whole province's business environment.

案例进展 CURRENT STATUS

截至2024年12月底，琼中通过"一站办好"改革开展审批办件3.87万件。以"一站办好"为核心的审批服务改革深得企业和群众赞誉，极大地激发了当地市场发展活力。

As of late December 2024, Qiongzhong has handled 38,700 approval cases through the "one-stop service" reform. This approval service reform has won high praise from enterprises and the public and greatly stimulated the local market's development vitality.

万宁：好信用换来“金名片”

Wanning: Enjoy the Fruits of Credibility with Coconut Credit

画外音：万宁将信用融入审批，让原本需要10天的服务，10分钟就搞定，如此效率反映出信用所具有的巨大潜在价值。这也启示我们，诚信建设，光靠口头上的呼吁是不够的，还要让诚信由“无形”转为“有形”，成为可感可触的便利。也就是说，必须提升诚信的社会价值，拓宽信用的效用边界，让“守信受益，失信难行”理念融入日常。试想，如果应用场景不够，守信、失信无差异，人们自然就不拿诚信当回事，诚信建设也就无从谈起。

Introduction: Wanning has integrated Hainan's Coconut Credit platform into the administrative approval process, enabling applications that once took 10 days to be processed and approved in as little as 10 minutes. This massive increase in efficiency reflects the huge potential of credit. This case also shows us that it is not enough to simply declare an enterprise or individual as trustworthy. We must also translate good credit into tangible benefits for those who have it. In other words, it is necessary to enhance the social value of integrity, broaden the utility of credit, and integrate the concept of "keeping trust will benefit you, breaking trust will make it difficult to get by" into daily life. Without differentiated treatment for those with better credit, having good credit would be worthless, commitments would not be taken seriously, and there would be no talk of building integrity.

A04

“营”在自贸港 “画”说新海南

——优化营商环境专刊

好信用换来“金名片”

以“信用+”推动“审批-”

海南苏生生物科技有限公司董事长曾胜：

海南自贸港，我们来对了！

步骤也太多了!
That's way too many hoops to jump through!
许可证
①
So easy!
许可证
②
要遵守“椰定”!
Stick to your "cocomitments"!
信用
③
通过审核，是好“椰几”!
We've passed the review stage! "Cocongratulations"!
④
无偿献血+4分
无偿献血+4分
志愿者服务+6
志愿者服务+6
政府表彰+10分
政府表彰+10分
行政处罚-10分
行政处罚-10分
前方有扣分项，请注意躲避!
Ooh, be careful not to get caught out and let your score drop.
⑤
信用
信用+承诺即入
信用+政务服务
审批+监管+执法+信用
⑥

创新前：
“审”啊！救救我吧，一个人审了半天都没审完……
Help! These permits are going to take forever to review...
创新后：
许可证如潮水，一发不可收拾！
Permits! Get your permits here!
⑦

享受专人服务
努力积累“金椰分”，攀登人生新巅峰。
Keep increasing your “coconut credit score” to unlock new items!
加急服务
优先预约
自然人
许可绿色通道
容缺办理
免费邮寄
加急
优先
绿色通道
1080
1050
1030
1020
1010
⑧

流水它带走审核的烦琐，当天就发许可。
This new credit system has made things much more manageable. We can now issue permits on the same day.
一套表单
一次申报
一次核定
审批
许可
许可
⑨

啊哈，坏的都挑出来了，一个都别想浑水摸鱼！
That's all the rotten coconuts picked out. We can't have them going to market!
“审管法信”平台
⑩

讲信用，有甜头！
Savor the sweetness of a good credit score!
⑪

案例注解 CASE NOTES

信用是市场经济的"基石"。万宁市结合"能力提升建设年"活动，创新推行"信用+免审""信用+承诺即入""信用+政务服务""审批+监管+执法+信用"等系列改革，将"社会信用体系建设"一张蓝图绘到底，持续优化营商环境，不断激发经营主体活力。同时，万宁市探索审批、监管、执法、信用4个环节衔接数据化转型，增强联合惩戒力度，确保在管得住的前提下放得更开。

Credit is often referred to as the ccrnerstone of the market economy. In conjunction with activities associated with the "Capacity Building Year", Wanning City has innovatively implemented a series of reforms such as "credit+exemption from review", "credit+commitment to enter", "credit+ government services", and "approval+supervision+law enforcement+credit" to draw a blueprint for the construction of a social credit system, optimize the business environment, and stimulate the vitality of business entities. At the same time, Wanning City is exploring the four links of "approval", "supervision", "law enforcement", and "credit" coordinating their digital transformation, and strengthening joint punishment to ensure the ability to remain in control while also relaxing.

案例进展 CURRENT STATUS

目前，万宁市依托信用监管结果实施多类型的市场准入便利化改革，审批事项平均20分钟可办结1件，经营主体准入时限整体缩减90%以上，办件效率大幅提升；海南省自由贸易港信用信息共享平台归集失信被执行人等不良信用信息1238条，接收到数据中台推送行政许可数据22191条。

To date, Wanning City has implemented various types of market access facilitation reforms based on the results of credit supervision. On average, one approval item can be processed in 20 minutes, the overall time required for business entities to gain access has been reduced by more than 90%, and the efficiency of handling items has been greatly improved. The Hainan FTP Credit Information Platform has collected 1, 238 pieces of bad credit information such as dishonest persons subject to legal penalties, and received 22, 191 pieces of administrative licensing data from the data center.

东方：审批烦冗“合”以解忧

Dongfang: One Less Thing to Worry About with Integrated Approval

画外音：工程建设，最担心的，莫过于审批烦琐。审批，拆分容易合并难。可东方市却大刀阔斧，推出涉及多个部门的系列“多合一”服务，何以力度如此之大？说到底，是观念、理念发生了变化，是把营商环境当成了“金饭碗”，是把企业、项目放在了心头上。如此创新，务实、高效、含金量高，正是制度集成创新的方向所在。各地各部门当以此为借鉴，念好“合”字诀，在大胆创新中实现更多的“多合一”式突破，为项目建设打通“快车道”。

Introduction: In engineering and construction projects, the most concerning issue is often a cumbersome approval process. While it's easy to split approvals into multiple steps, merging them is far more challenging. However, Dongfang City has taken bold and decisive action by introducing a range of integrated approval processes involving multiple departments. Why such a strong push? Ultimately, it comes down to a shift in mindset and philosophy—treating the business environment as a top priority and placing the needs of enterprises and projects at the heart of their efforts. This kind of innovation is practical, efficient, and highly valuable, representing the direction of institutional integration and innovation. Other regions and departments should take this as a model, master the art of streamlining processes, and achieve more integrated service breakthroughs through bold innovation, thereby creating a fast track for project development.

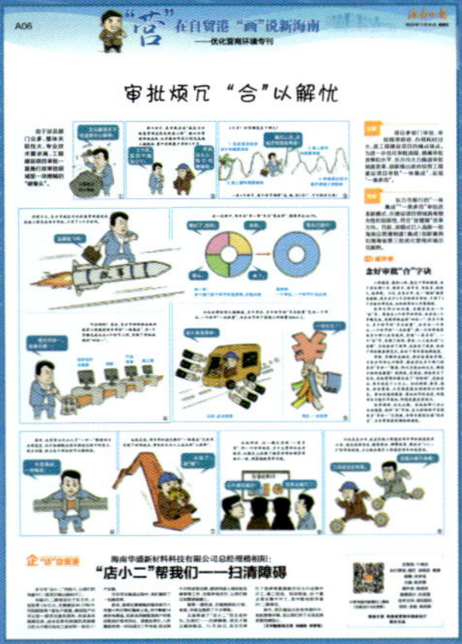
A06
在自贸港“画”说新海南
——优化营商环境专刊

审批烦冗“合”以解忧

“店小二”帮我们一一扫清障碍

怎么就攻不下你这铁石心肠啊！
This is one tough nut to crack!
工程建设 项目审批
①
5个月，真的不能再少了。
It'll take five months at the very least.
审批这么久，我们很难做的！
Such a long time...It really leaves us in a bind!
②
越过山丘，发现还有流程等我？
Climb every mountain, review every project...
③
直接起飞啊！
I'm a rocket man now, baby!
改 革
流程四合一，效率是第一！
Four processes integrated into one, efficiency is number one!
审批通过
④
我好了，到你。
I'm done. It's your turn.
收到。
Got it.
我自己就行！
I can do it all by myself.
拿去。
Onto you.
来了。
Pass it here.
⑤

这么多收费站！
There are fees coming out of my ears!
一站全包了！
You only need to pay a single flat fee here!
⑤
有我跟踪，一路畅通！
I'll keep on top of everything and clear the way.
⑥
太好了！就“降”！
Let the costs keep sliding on down!
⑦
公开透明真好！
It's nice to be so open and transparent.
评审结果公示
结果直接用了！
These are results we can use!
⑧
工程建设在海南，
Building an engineering project in Hainan...
高效办事不再难！
...efficient, quick, according to plan!
⑨

案例注解 CASE NOTES

项目多部门审批、审批程序烦琐、办理耗时过长，是工程建设项目的痛点堵点。为进一步优化审批流程，提高审批效率和水平，东方市大力推进审批制度改革，创新推出政府投资工程建设项目审批“一体集成”，实现“一果多用”。

Many projects require approval from multiple departments leading to cumbersome approval procedures which take too long to complete. In order to further optimize the approval process and improve the approval efficiency and level, Dongfang city has vigorously promoted the reform of the approval system and innovatively launched an "integrated" approval of government-invested engineering construction projects.

案例进展 CURRENT STATUS

东方市推行的“一体集成”“一果多用”审批改革新模式，在建设项目领域具有领先性和创新性，符合“放管服”改革方向。目前，该模式已入选新一批海南自由贸易港制度（集成）创新案例和海南省第三批优化营商环境示范案例。

Dongfang City has implemented an "integrated" model of approval reform which is an innovative leader in the field of construction projects, and in line with the reform direction of "delegating power and improving administration". At present, this model has been selected as one of the newest batches of Hainan FTP Institutional Integration and Innovation Model Cases and as part of the third batch of Hainan Province's demonstration cases for optimizing the business environment.

屯昌：企业按铃，马上响应

Tunchang: Saved by the Bellhop

画外音：“企铃通”在企业和政府服务之间搭建了一个良好的沟通平台。“企业按铃，马上响应”的背后，是强大的数据支持、贴心的政府服务和有力的政策支撑，凸显了当地政府呵护企业利益、呵护营商环境的决心和努力。心交心方能见真心。期待“企业按铃，马上响应”式的助企服务更多一些，让政务“直通车”开到企业的心坎里，跑出营商环境建设“加速度”。

Introduction: Hainan's "Enterprise Bellhop Service" has established an effective communication platform between businesses and government services. Behind the "bellhop" concept lies robust data support, thoughtful government services, and strong policy backing that highlights the local government's determination and efforts to protect business interests and foster a favorable business environment. Genuine care is shown through heartfelt communication. We look forward to seeing this approach to business support expand further, allowing the government's "express service" to truly resonate with enterprises and accelerate the improvement of the business environment.

A08 “营”在自贸港 “画”说新海南

——优化营商环境专刊

企业按铃，马上响应

开办一家公司需要办理哪些手续？经营发展过程中，遇到困难该怎么办？新出台的惠企政策，自己到底能不能享受？……企业经营过程中，经常碰到“不知晓”“不理解”“不会办”的难题。别担心！如今在屯昌，找它就行——

企“话”自贸港

安永大中华区战略与发展主管合伙人谢佳扬：

继续加大在琼投入 助力自贸港再开放

欲练此功，必先……干啥来着？
In order to become a great leader, you must...must...what was it again?
怎样才能当老板
①
王老板，您直接在“海南e登记”上注册就好啦！
Mr. Wang, just register on the Hainan e-Registration platform.
秘籍
原来，就这么简单？
It's really that simple?
②
我怀疑你要搞大事！
I think you're about to make a big move!
这意思是开挂的人生不需要解释？
Are you saying I don't need to explain how I hacked the issue?
③

公司法人咋变更?
How do I amend the company's legal representative?
经营范围咋变更?
How do I amend the company's business scope?
屯昌首富咋变成?
How did the richest man in Tunchang get so rich?
④

来来来，这是你擅长的领域。
Here we go. This query was made for you!
关于咨询xx问题
这个同样可以在“海南e登记”上操作，具体操作流程给您发过去了，记得查收哦!
This is something you can do on the Hainan e-Registration platform. I've sent you specific instructions. Check your inbox!
⑤

这块地我想临时用用，咋申请啊？
I'd like to use this land temporarily. How do I apply for it?
待租
⑥

这个呀，您直接在海南政务服务网上就可以申报哦。
Oh, you can apply directly on the Hainan Government Services Portal.
哇，原来这么简单！
Wow, so it's that easy.
一次就可以搞定哦！
And you only need to submit a single application.
⑦

是时候展现真正的技术了。
It's time to show off our tech smarts.
从来就没有什么奇迹，都是服务企业的诚意。
There's nothing miraculous to it, just a genuine desire to serve enterprises.
⑧

啥不懂，就问我！
If there's something you don't understand, just come to me!
人送外号“企事通”！
That's why people call me "Master of Enterprise Solutions"!
政策问题来找我，更加专业更加酷。
We answer your policy questions with professionalism and pizzazz.
12345热线
我会全程监督的哦！
And I'm here to make sure everyone follows through.
加急件，赶紧送！
Make way! Express delivery coming through!
⑨
风里雨里，这里等您哦！
We're here for you come rain or shine!
海南12345热线
HAINAN HOTLINE 12345
⑩
有我们守护，老板放心冲！
You work hard for your business, we'll work hard for you!
⑪

案例注解 CASE NOTES

屯昌坚持把打造优质营商环境作为促进经济高质量发展的重要载体和有效抓手，创新"企业按铃，政府直通"的服务模式，在全省首推"企铃通"企业服务专席建设工作，推动营商环境持续提优。

Tunchang has come up with an innovative service model where the government responds promptly and directly to calls from enterprises. As the first in the province to launch the construction of the "Enterprise Bellhop Service" to promote the continucus improvement of the business environment, Tunchang is committed tc the idea that creating a high-quality business environment is an important carrier and effective means to promote high-quality economic development.

案例进展 CURRENT STATUS

自2023年4月21日正式运行以来，屯昌"企铃通"企业服务专席快速响应企业需求，积极解决企业难题，加大服务企业力度，提升政府治理效能，实现企业诉求"一号响应"。目前，已办理多件企业咨询类事项，迅速、细致、周到的服务模式得到企业称赞。

Since it officially began operations on April 21, 2023, Tunchang's "Enterprise Bellhop Service" service desk has quickly responded to enterprise needs, actively solved their problems, increased service, improved government governance efficiency, and achieved "fast response" for complaints. At present, it has not only consulted on many matters, but its rapid, meticulous and thoughtful service model has also been praised by enterprises.

澄迈：在海南，7.5小时能办多大的事？

Chengmai: What Can You Achieve with 7.5 Hours in Hainan?

画外音：纵观海南“项目直通车”改革首单的实践，有两个关键点：一个是“快”，快人一步上线“产业地图”，提高企业选址效率；快马加鞭，预制审批，快速响应，帮办代办；另一个是“全”，多部门联动发力，全流程跟踪服务，全周期配合，全力打通各个环节，这才让“项目直通车”驶出了令人惊叹的速度。如今，首单已成功“打样”，接下来就是要将其中的好经验好做法转化为常态化长效机制，让更多的项目坐上直通车。

Introduction: Looking at the first case of Hainan's "Project Express Train" reform, two key points stand out. The first is speed: launching an "industry map" ahead of others to improve site selection efficiency for businesses and moving swiftly with pre-approval rapid responses, and assistance services. The second is comprehensiveness: multiple departments working together to provide end-to-end tracking services, full-cycle coordination, and fully streamlining every step of the process. Together, these elements enable the "Project Express Train" to achieve such an impressive pace. Using the first case as a template, the next step is to turn these effective practices and experiences into a long-term, standardized mechanism, allowing more projects to board the "Project Express Train".

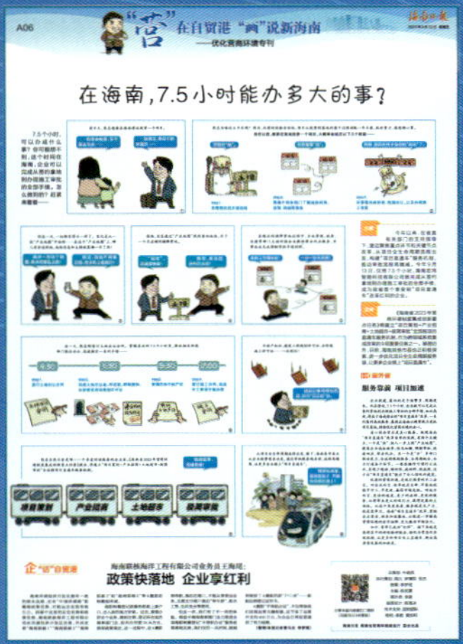
A06

“营”在自贸港 “画”说新海南

——优化营商环境专刊

在海南，7.5小时能办多大的事？

政策快落地 企业享红利

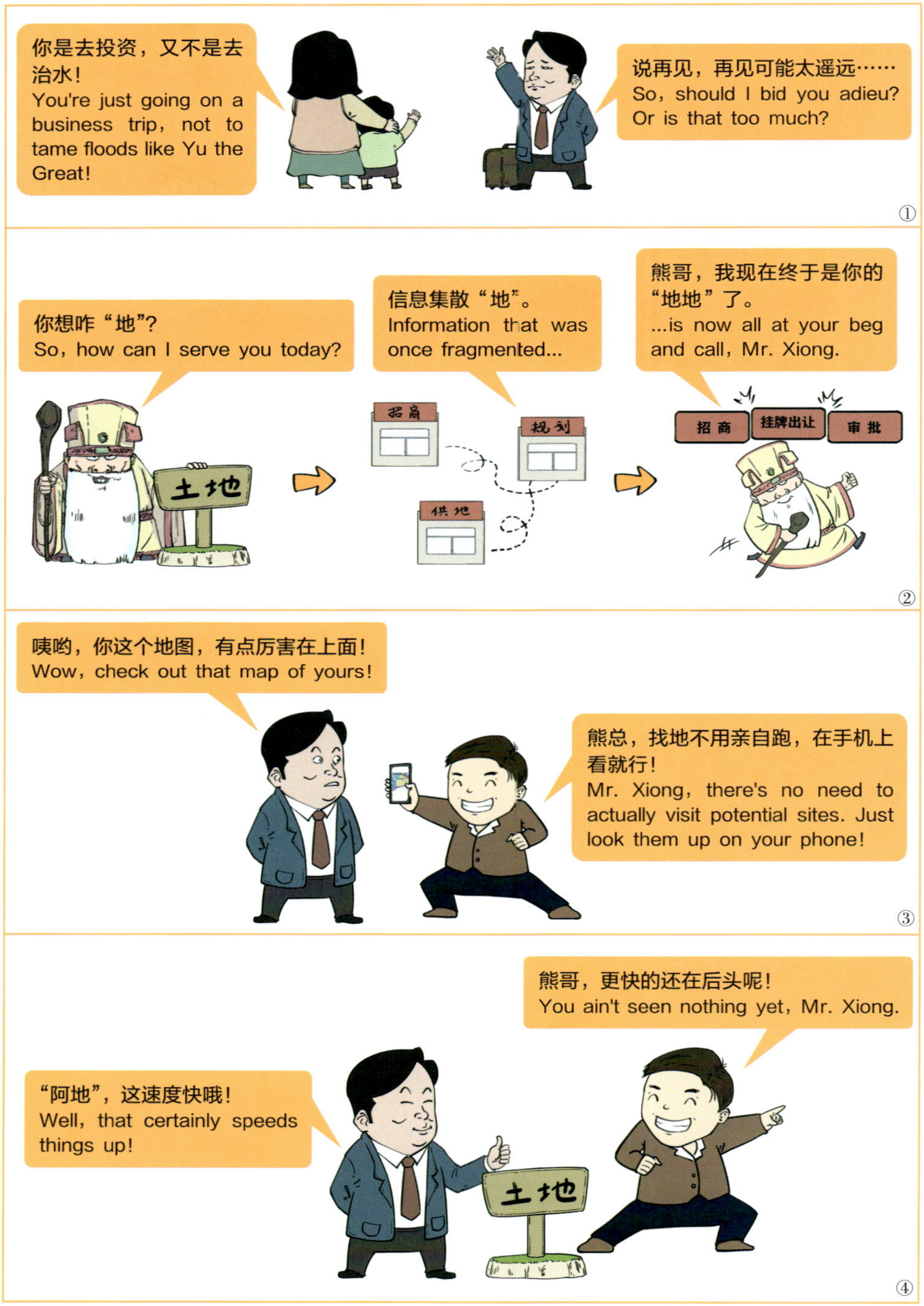
你是去投资，又不是去治水！
You're just going on a business trip, not to tame floods like Yu the Great!
说再见，再见可能太遥远……
So, should I bid you adieu? Or is that too much?
①
你想咋"地"?
So, how can I serve you today?
土地
信息集散"地"。
Information that was once fragmented...
招商
规划
供地
熊哥，我现在终于是你的"地地"了。
...is now all at your beg and call, Mr. Xiong.
招商
挂牌出让
审批
②
咦哟，你这个地图，有点厉害在上面！
Wow, check out that map of yours!
熊总，找地不用亲自跑，在手机上看就行！
Mr. Xiong, there's no need to actually visit potential sites. Just look them up on your phone!
③
熊哥，更快的还在后头呢！
You ain't seen nothing yet, Mr. Xiong.
"阿地"，这速度快哦！
Well, that certainly speeds things up!
土地
④

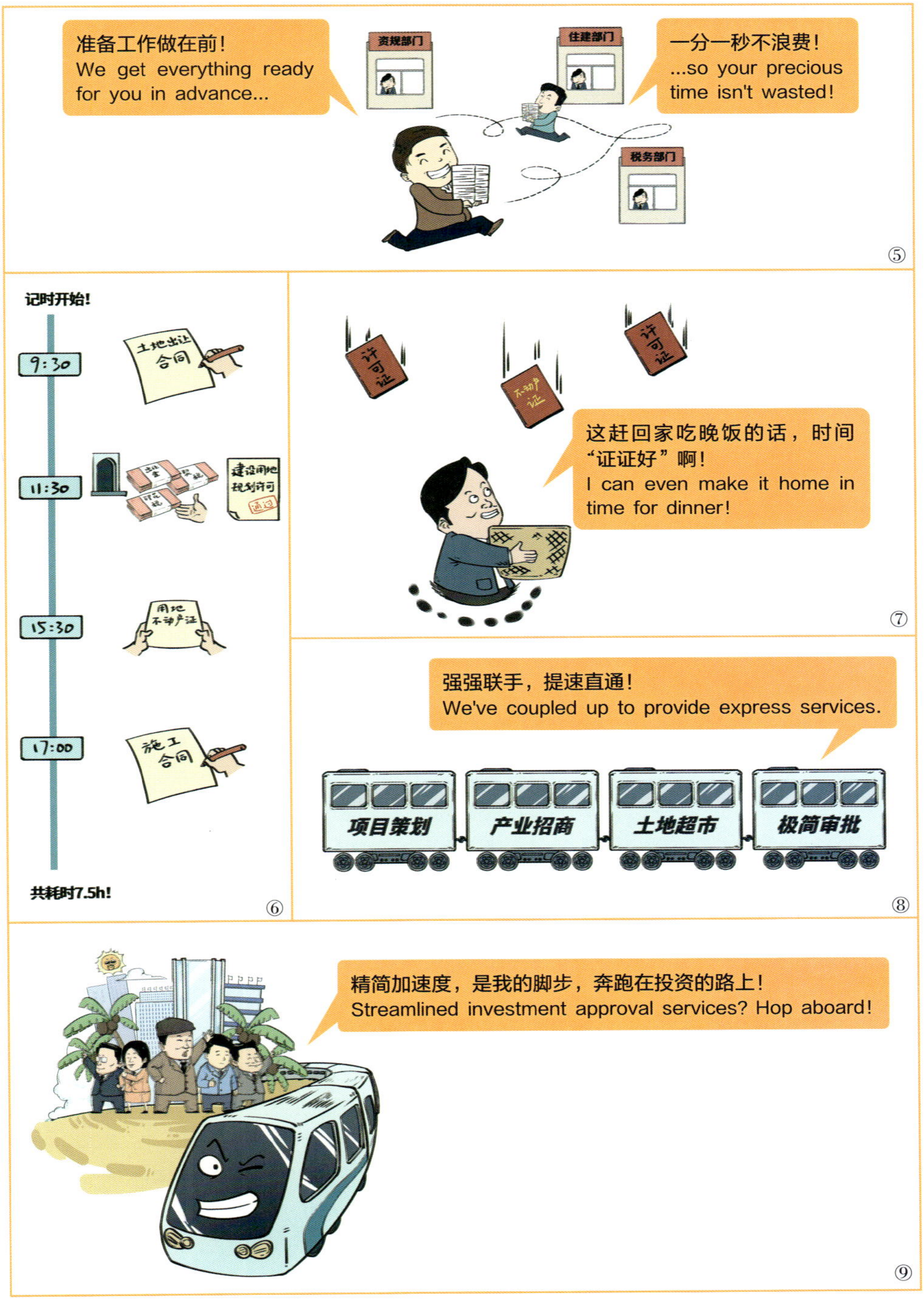
准备工作做在前！
We get everything ready for you in advance...
资规部门
住建部门
税务部门
一分一秒不浪费！
...so your precious time isn't wasted!
⑤
记时开始！
9:30
土地出让合同
11:30
建设用地规划许可
通过
15:30
用地不动产证
17:00
施工合同
共耗时7.5h!
⑥
许可证
不动产证
许可证
这赶回家吃晚饭的话，时间“证证好”啊！
I can even make it home in time for dinner!
⑦
强强联手，提速直通！
We've coupled up to provide express services.
项目策划
产业招商
土地超市
极简审批
⑧
精简加速度，是我的脚步，奔跑在投资的路上！
Streamlined investment approval services? Hop aboard!
⑨

案例注解 CASE NOTES

2023年以来，在省直有关部门的支持指导下，澄迈聚焦重点环节和关键节点改革，从项目全生命周期流程出发，构建"项目直通车"服务机制，推动审批流程再精减。2023年9月13日，仅用7.5个小时，海南宏玮智能科技有限公司就完成从签约拿地到办理施工审批的全部手续，成为我省首个享受到"项目直通车"改革红利的企业。

Since the beginning of this year, with the support and guidance of relevant provincial departments, Chengmai has—starting from a holistic view of project's entire life cycle—been focusing on the reform of key links and key nodes, on building the "Project Express Train" service mechanism, and promoting the further streamlining of the approval process. On September 13, 2023, Hainan Hongwei Intelligent Technology Co., Ltd. completed all procedures from signing contracts to obtaining land to handling construction approval in just 7.5 hours, becoming the first company in our province to enjoy the benefits of "Project Express Train" streamlining.

案例进展 CURRENT STATUS

《海南省2023年营商环境制度集成创新重点任务》将建立"项目策划+产业招商+土地超市+极简审批"全流程项目直通车服务机制，作为跨领域系统集成改革的9项重要任务之一。自2023年9月以来，澄迈县通过"项目直通车"机制推进5个项目"拿地即开工"，实现精准供地约460.62亩，企业预估投资额达到约11亿元。除澄迈外，目前，海南其他市县也正积极探索，进一步优化项目全生命周期服务链，让更多企业搭上"项目直通车"。

The *2023 Key Tasks for Integrated Innovation of Hainan Province's Business Environment System* established a full-process "Project Express Train" service mechanism of "project planning+industrial investment promotion+land supermarket+simplified approval" as one of the 9 important tasks of cross-domain system integration reform. Ever since September 2023, Chengmai County has used the "Project Express Train" mechanism to promote the "start of construction as soon as the land is acquired" on five projects. This has achieved precise land supply of about 30 hectares, and estimated enterprise investment of around CNY 1.1 billion. In addition to Chengmai, other cities and counties in Hainan are also actively exploring full project lifecycle service chain optimization.

乐东：海上“盖房”也能拿证！

Ledong: Deeding Offshore Structures

画外音：海上养殖平台无法登记确权，资产登记、抵押贷款、购买保险也就缺乏依据。伴随海南自贸港建设深入推进，需要面对并解决的问题必然越来越多样、越来越复杂。从深远海养殖平台登记确权问题的解决中，我们可以得到启示：发展带来新问题，把问题作为创新的起点、当作发展的动力，在解决企业、群众急难愁盼问题中，形成更多制度集成创新成果，必定能把堵点、难点转化为推动高质量发展的优势点、加快自贸港建设的支撑点。

Introduction: The inability to register or confirm the ownership rights of offshore aquaculture platforms means asset registration, secured loans, and insurance purchases for such platforms lack a legal basis. As the construction of the Hainan FTP continues to advance, the issues that need to be addressed will inevitably become more diverse and complex. From the resolution of the registration and ownership rights confirmation issues for deep-sea aquaculture platforms, we can draw an important lesson: development brings new challenges, and by treating these challenges as starting points for innovation and drivers of progress, we can address the urgent and pressing concerns of businesses and the public. In doing so, we can achieve more institutional integration and innovation, transforming bottlenecks and difficulties into advantages that drive high-quality development and accelerate the construction of the Hainan FTP.

A05

“营”在自贸港 “画”说新海南

——优化营商环境专刊

海上“盖房”也能拿证！

企“话”自贸港

辉致医药有限公司大中华区总裁倪向阳：

海南拥有一流的政策环境、管理体系和服务理念

海水淡化
污水处理
仓储空间
观光旅游
对啊！
Yes!
老龙你养鱼呢？
Are you planning to farm fish, Mr. Long?
海上龙宫
①
龙哥啊，我们这里之前没办过这类事嘞！只能给你办个海域使用权登记先哦。
Mr. Long, I'm afraid we've never encountered such a situation. All we can do for now is help you register sea area use rights.
我不听，我“龙”了！
I can't hear you! La la la!
海域使用权
资规部门
②
龙哥，拿照片是不能贷款的哦，要开证明的哟！
Mr. Long, a photo of your facilities is not sufficient evidence for a loan. You need to provide proof of ownership.
产权证
银行
这又不是照“骗”！
But the camera never lies!
③
养殖周期长，我很费钱的！
Farming fish takes a lot of time and money!
不能拿我去抵押贷款，老龙好难。
Mr. Long is having a tough time attempting to use us as collateral.
建在海上的工厂，只能听海哭的声音。
I think we're going to have to let this dream sink to the bottom of the sea.
④
龙哥龙哥，我们来帮你！
Mr. Long, we're here to help!
⑤

这些坑，都给填上！
We've smoothed over all of these pitfalls!
登记系统平台板块缺失
申请材料不齐
登记范围难以确定
测绘标准缺乏依据
面积描述难度大
⑥

“海”有什么问题？
Do you "sea" anything else that needs sorting?
“域”到难题就解决！
Solving these issues is our "domain".
海域使用权及建(构)筑物所有权不动产登记平台板块
⑦

不动产权证书
我的海上龙宫，终于名正言顺了！
Finally, Long's Sea Palace has been classed as real estate.
⑧

咱们现在这身份，肯定能贷个好价钱！
As bona fide real estate, we're sure to fetch favorable loan terms.
建在海上，咱也一样能拿证！
Even though we're not built on land, we're still property!
龙哥再也不怕资金周转了！
Mr. Long's cashflow woes are a thing of the past!
⑨

海上粮仓！
Mankind's granaries of the ocean...
乘风破浪！
...boldly braving the wind and waves!
⑩

案例注解 CASE NOTES

长期以来，因缺乏成熟完备的登记系统、登记办法、操作流程，海南海上建设项目只办理海域使用权登记，海上建（构）筑物所有权一直没有被纳入登记，导致企业不动产权属不明，发展受到限制。在多方合力攻关下，海南首本海域使用权及建（构）筑物所有权不动产证书于2023年6月在乐东颁发，制约深远海养殖产业可持续发展的企业平台产权问题基本得到解决。

For a long time, due to the lack of a mature and complete registration system, registration methods, and operating procedures, Hainan's offshore construction projects only handled sea area use rights registration, and the ownership of offshore structures was not included in their registration. This resulted in unclear ownership of corporate real estate restricted development. With the joint efforts of multiple parties, Hainan's first real estate certificate for sea area use rights and structure ownership was issued in Ledong County in June 2023, and the property rights issue that restricted the sustainable development of the deep-sea aquaculture industry has been basically resolved.

案例进展 CURRENT STATUS

下一步，海南将"以点带面"整合借鉴"乐东经验"，在全省范围全面实施海域与建（构）筑物所有权一体登记。

Next, the rest of the province will integrate and learn from the "Ledong experience" to fully implement the integrated registration of the ownership of offshore structures throughout the province.

文昌：“无感”审批“可感”服务

Wenchang：Invisible Approval，Visible Services

画外音：透过“无感”审批，我们看到了职能部门的“有感”努力。从“被动”提供服务，到主动靠前服务，变的不只是工作方式，更是服务理念的升华。优质高效的政务服务，带来的往往是润物细无声的效果。进一步推广像文昌这样兼具创新与用心的务实之举，不仅要推广那些让人称道的实招、硬招，还要推广“更主动、更精准、更贴心”的服务意识，才能让办事创业更高效，让人民群众更满意。

Introduction：Through "invisible" approvals，we can see the "visible" efforts of functional departments. The shift from passively providing services to proactively offering them reflects not just a change in working methods but also an elevation in service philosophy. High-quality and efficient government services often bring about subtle yet profound effects，like gentle rain nourishing the earth. To further promote practical initiatives like those in Wenchang，which combine innovation and thoughtfulness，we must not only advocate for much-welcomed practical and robust measures but also encourage a service mindset that is more proactive，more precise，and more considerate. Only then can we make business and entrepreneurship more efficient and leave the people more satisfied.

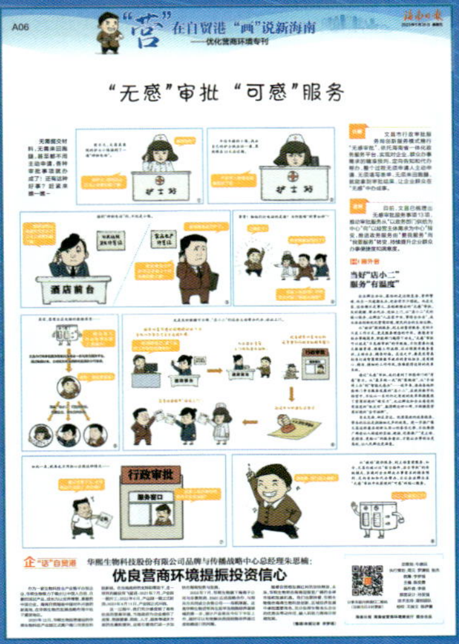

陈护士，您的执业证马上就要到期了哦！
Nurse Chen, your nursing license is about to expire!
真的假的？
Seriously?
护士站
①
不会有人偷偷在这装监控了吧？
I'm not being secretly surveilled, am I?
护士证
护士站
②
您的食品生产许可证还有2个月就要到期了哦！
Your food production permit is set to expire in two months' time!
您酒店的公共场所卫生许可证马上就要到期了哦！
Your hotel's public places hygiene license will expire soon.
公共场所卫生许可证
食品生产许可证
酒店前台
差点就无证生产了，谢谢告知我。
Oops, I totally forgot! Thanks for telling me.
③
正是在下！
That's me!
你在我家装监控了？
Are you the one secretly monitoring me?
你未卜先知吗？不然怎么对我了解得这么清楚？
Are you an oracle? How else would you know so much about my situation?
④

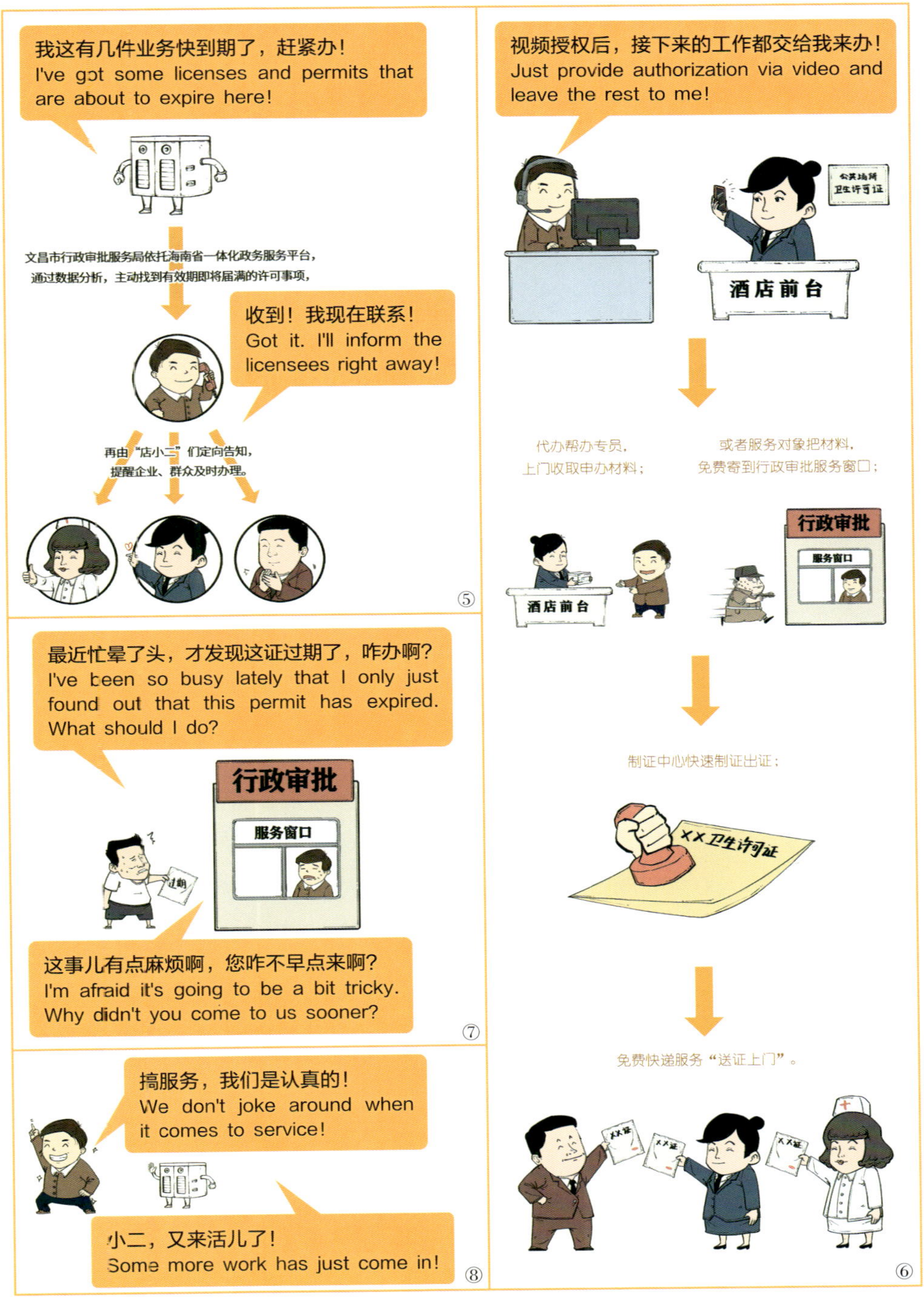
我这有几件业务快到期了，赶紧办！
I've got some licenses and permits that are about to expire here!
文昌市行政审批服务局依托海南省一体化政务服务平台，
通过数据分析，主动找到有效期即将届满的许可事项，
收到！我现在联系！
Got it. I'll inform the licensees right away!
再由“店小二”们定向告知，
提醒企业、群众及时办理。
⑤
视频授权后，接下来的工作都交给我来办！
Just provide authorization via video and leave the rest to me!
酒店前台
代办帮办专员，
上门收取申办材料；
或者服务对象把材料，
免费寄到行政审批服务窗口；
酒店前台
行政审批
服务窗口
制证中心快速制证出证；
XX卫生许可证
免费快递服务“送证上门”。
⑥
最近忙晕了头，才发现这证过期了，咋办啊？
I've been so busy lately that I only just found out that this permit has expired. What should I do?
行政审批
服务窗口
过期
这事儿有点麻烦啊，您咋不早点来啊？
I'm afraid it's going to be a bit tricky. Why didn't you come to us sooner?
⑦
搞服务，我们是认真的！
We don't joke around when it comes to service!
小二，又来活儿了！
Some more work has just come in!
⑧

案例注解 CASE NOTES

文昌市行政审批服务局创新服务模式推行"无感审批"，依托海南省一体化政务服务平台，实现对企业、群众办事需求的精准预判、定向告知和代办帮办，整个过程无须申请人主动申请、填写表单、来回跑腿，就能拿到审批结果，让企业群众在"无感"中办成事。

Wenchang City Municipal Administrative Approval Service Bureau has innovated its service model and implemented "seamless approval". Relying on Hainan Province's integrated government service platform, it has achieved accurate prediction, targeted notification and agency assistance for the needs of businesses and the general public. The process no longer requires applicants to actively fill out numerous forms, or run back and forth to get approval results. Thus, businesses and the public can now get things done seamlessly.

案例进展 CURRENT STATUS

目前，文昌市已梳理出无感审批服务事项13项，推动审批服务从"以政务部门供给为中心"向"以经营主体需求为中心"转变，推进政务服务由"要我服务"向"我要服务"转变，持续提升企业群众办事便捷度和满意度。

At present, Wenchang City has impemented 13 "seamless approval" processes, promoted the transformation of approval services from "government department supply-centered" to "business entity demand-centered", promoted the transformation of government services from "I have to serve" to "I want to serve", as well as continuously improving the convenience and satisfaction of enterprises and the public in doing business.